LUCKY
666

THE IMPOSSIBLE MISSION THAT
CHANGED THE WAR IN THE PACIFIC

BOB DRURY AND
TOM CLAVIN

SIMON & SCHUSTER PAPERBACKS

NEW YORK   LONDON   TORONTO   SYDNEY   NEW DELHI

Simon & Schuster Paperbacks
An Imprint of Simon & Schuster, Inc.
1230 Avenue of the Americas
New York, NY 10020

First Simon & Schuster trade paperback edition October 2017

SIMON & SCHUSTER PAPERBACKS and colophon are
registered trademarks of Simon & Schuster, Inc.

For information about special discounts for bulk purchases,
please contact Simon & Schuster Paperbacks Special Sales at
1-866-506-1949 or business@simonandschuster.com.

The Simon & Schuster Speakers Bureau can bring authors to your live event.
For more information or to book an event contact the Simon & Schuster Speakers
Bureau at 1-866-248-3049 or visit our website at www.simonspeakers.com.

Interior design by Ruth Lee-Mui
Maps by Jeffrey L. Ward

Manufactured in the United States of America

10 9 8 7 6 5 4 3 2 1

Library of Congress has cataloged the hardcover edition as follows:

Names: Drury, Bob, author. | Clavin, Thomas, author.
Title: Lucky 666 : the impossible mission / by Bob Drury and Tom Clavin.
Description: New York : Simon & Schuster, [2016] | Includes bibliographical
    references and index.
Identifiers: LCCN 2016017924| ISBN 9781476774855 (hardcover) |
    ISBN 9781476774862 (trade pbk.)
Subjects: LCSH: Zeamer, Jay, Jr., 1918–2007. | United States. Army Air
    Forces. Bombardment Group, 22nd—Biography. | Bomber pilots—United
    States—Biography. | B-17 bomber. | World War, 1939–1945—Aerial
    operations, American. | World War, 1939–1945—Campaigns—Pacific Area. |
    World War, 1939–1945—Regimental histories—United States.
Classification: LCC D790.253 22nd .D78 2016 | DDC 940.54/4973092 [B]—dc23 LC
record available at https://lccn.loc.gov/2016017924

ISBN 978-1-4767-7485-5
ISBN 978-1-4767-7486-2 (pbk)
ISBN 978-1-4767-7487-9 (ebook)

Previously published as *Lucky 666: The Impossible Mission*

For Susan Margaret Drury
B.D.

To the memory of
Nancy Clavin Bartolotta and
Jacquelyn Dayle Reingold
T.C.

CONTENTS

Prologue   1

PART I

1. Wanderlust   9
2. The Wild Blue Yonder   17
3. Jay & Joe   26
4. "The Sacred Duty of the Leading Race"   35
5. The Fortress   44
6. The Winds of War   52
7. The Japanese Citadel   64
8. Into the Fight   76

PART II

9. Breaking the Code   91
10. The Renegade Pilot   104
11. The Bulldog   113
12. A Microscopic Metropolis   122

CONTENTS

13. Ken's Men   134

14. A Place Where Trouble Started   145

15. "Clear as a Bell"   152

16. The Missing General   159

17. Pushing North   165

18. A Fine Reunion   176

PART III

19. "A Motley Collection of Outcasts"   185

20. Blood on the Bismarck Sea   195

21. The Flight of the Geishas   201

22. Old 666   210

23. The Outlaws   219

24. No Position Is Safe   229

25. New Additions   238

26. "Hell, No!"   248

27. Buka   255

28. "Give 'Em Hell!"   263

29. The Desperate Dive   269

30. Get It Home   274

31. "He's All Right"   280

32. Dobodura   285

    Epilogue   289

    Afterword   305

    Acknowledgments   309

    Notes on Sources   313

    Notes   315

    Bibliography   333

    Index   343

PROLOGUE

THEY WERE CLOSE NOW, THE ZEROS. RUNNING HIM DOWN FROM BEHIND.

Thirty minutes ago his belly gunner had counted over 20 on the Buka airstrip, close to a dozen kicking up dust as they taxied for takeoff. They would be on him soon; they should have been on him by now.

"Give me forty-five more seconds."

It was Kendrick, over the interphone. The waist gunner and Photo Joe. Asking, begging, for just a little more time to get his pictures. The photographs, they'd said back at the base, that could change the course of the war. Almost four hours in the air and this is what it had come to. Forty-five seconds.

Below him the low sun caused the stunted eucalyptus trees to cast dappled shadows on the flowering frangipani of Japanese-held Bougainville Island. Far to the east the active volcano, Mount Bagana, spewed

1

slender flutes of black smoke into the cloudless sky, like veins in blue granite. But it was neither the island's flora nor its topography that interested Captain Jay Zeamer and the anxious crew of his B-17 Flying Fortress this morning. It was the hidden reefs of Empress Augusta Bay. The reefs that lay submerged just beneath the breaking waves where the Marine landings would take place. The reefs waiting like bear traps to snag their LSTs.

The reefs, the airfields, the enemy defenses: these were the reasons why Jay and his men were here. A lonely B-17 600 miles from home. Soon to face the might of the Japanese Imperial Navy's most elite fighter pilots, a desperate enemy determined to prevent the Americans from returning with their photos. The impossible mission, someone had called it. Now Jay Zeamer knew why.

Not that every recon flight wasn't a deadly gamble. No fighter escort. Not even a friendly formation to help ward off the swarms of bogeys. Jay knew too many recon crews who had never returned. That was the rub. Scouting enemy positions was only half the job. Getting the information back would be the "impossible" part. The Zero pilots knew it as well.

Jay scanned the bay again. Visibility was clear. Just a scrim of ground haze over the shore, which the infrared camera filters would cut through with ease.

Now the tail gunner's voice crackling over the interphone. Another fighter squadron lifting off, this time from Bougainville. A dozen at least.

Jay thought about cutting and running. No one would blame him. No one could. He had volunteered for this job with the clear understanding that he'd run the operation his way. His way meant any way—*any way*—he wanted. They had already reconnoitered Buka Island. The flight wouldn't be a total waste. Hell, Buka was where the wolves behind him had picked up his scent.

Why hadn't he trusted his gut, gone with his initial response? At first he'd said no when they'd tacked on the Buka run at the last minute. Just Bougainville, he'd told them. Forget Buka; Buka was suicide. He should have held firm. What could they have done? Grounded him? He'd been disciplined before, too many times to count. Washed out of one Bomb Group for being too flaky, nearly court-martialed by another for that stunt over Rabaul. A lot of people didn't like Jay. Aloof, they called him. A screwoff. No respect for authority.

And this was where it had gotten him.

When they wouldn't give him a plane he'd foraged one, plucked from the boneyard at the rump end of the runway, and rebuilt it from the wheels up. When they wouldn't give him a crew he'd recruited one, men like himself; misfits they called them at first, but each now an Airman with whom he'd entrust his life. And when they wouldn't give him assignments he'd volunteered for them, recon missions no one else wanted, missions they all had to be a little crazy to take on. Missions like this one, which right now his every good sense was screaming at him to abort.

But then Jay envisioned the Marines. It was the middle of June 1943, and the war in the Pacific hung by a thread. In the 18 months since Pearl Harbor the Japanese had controlled the game, spreading like algae across the vast, watery theater, securing far-flung bases with impunity. Yet now the tide just might be turning. First at Midway, then on Guadalcanal. Small steps. But steps. And the island below him—Bougainville—was next. The key to unlocking the stranglehold of the Empire of the Rising Sun.

After Bougainville there would be New Guinea, and from New Guinea a return to the Philippines, until finally the ships of the U.S. Navy would be lapping at Japanese shores. Forget the great and grand strategies transmitted from Washington, pushpins on a map. The turnaround in this war would begin with boots on the ground at Bougainville. Marines depending on his photos in order to reach that beachhead. If he didn't do the job, if he throttled and fled, someone else would have to come back and do it all over again. He could not live with that.

Then another thought, creeping into his mind on cat's paws. *A man's character is his fate.* He hadn't been much for philosophy back at M.I.T. He was an engineer, a maker, a builder, with little use for pious pronouncements. But he never forgot that line. A man's character is his fate. One of the Greeks. Heraclitus? He considered himself a man of character, a pilot of character. He was the captain of a United States Army Air Force bomber crew, a leader of men. Well, he'd soon find out his fate. Their fate.

The first wave of Zeros hit them from the front. Through his port window he caught the bright yellow strobes of the twin 7.7-millimeter machine guns winking from the Zeke's nose. Then the larger red flare from one of its two 20-millimeter cannons flashed from the wing. The sound of the shells like shotgun blasts fired into a bucket of sand as they smashed into his plane.

They were going for the bomber's front bubble, blasting it with cannon fire. But the bombardier Joe Sarnoski down in the Greenhouse was giving as good as he got, the red tracers from his twin .50-cals cutting bright curving arcs through the azure sky. Joe nailed the lead Zero, sending it into a spin, and now the entire crew opened up, even Kendrick at the waist windows, finished with his photos. Seventeen machine guns streaking the sky with evanescent streams of gray-black smoke. The old Fortress juddered and wheezed from their recoil.

The rumble reached the cockpit first from the nose and then converged on him from behind, up from the belly gun and down from the top turret. Finally it growled through the fuselage from the tail gunner's blister all the way to the flight deck. It was the kind of noise you never forget, accompanied by the familiar odor, the *smell* of the fight, the grease and powder.

From the corner of his eye he saw Joe Sarnoski blast a second bogey, raking the Zeke from the engine cowling to the wing tanks, the enemy fighter's aviation fuel erupting into orange flames that streaked to its tail. It was as if the bombardier were plowing a highway. The irony was not lost on Jay—Joe was his best friend and had insisted on coming along on this one last mission before cashing his golden ticket back to the States, his kit already packed back in his quarters.

Jay silently thanked God that he had just as another Zero hove into view in front of him. He pressed the trigger button on his wheel that fired the special nose gun he'd installed just for this purpose. The bullets punctured the Zeke's fuselage, and he watched the aircraft flame out, making certain that it spiraled into the Solomon Sea.

He was still craning his neck when the flash erupted in the cockpit. There was the briefest effusion of colors.

And then everything went dark.

PART

I

On my honor, I will do my best
To do my duty to God and my country and to obey the Scout Law;
To help other people at all times;
To keep myself physically strong, mentally awake, and morally straight.
—Boy Scout Oath

1

WANDERLUST

JAY ZEAMER JR.'S PARENTS SUSPECTED EARLY ON THAT THEIR OLDEST child was a born renegade. The boy was not long out of cloth diapers, no older than four, when he began disappearing from the Zeamer household in the verdant suburb of Orange, New Jersey. Sometimes his mother, Marjorie, would find him sitting on the roof of the porch jutting from their clapboard Victorian home, having crawled out of an upstairs window to study the stars in the night sky. At other times he went missing for hours, before a frantic Jay Sr. would receive a call from a local policeman informing him that his son had been discovered wandering among the breweries and hatmakers that dominated the city's downtown streets.

Jay's wanderlust should not have come as a surprise to his parents, particularly Jay Sr. The branches of the Zeamer family tree were thick with wayfarers and adventurers, including at least fifteen of Jay's German-born forebears who had fought for the Colonies during America's Revolution. Continuing the custom, Jay Jr.'s great-great-grandfather John had become a teamster by the age of fourteen, hauling lumber and whiskey across hundreds of miles of Pennsylvania backcountry over bone-jarring tracks. And his grandfather Jeremiah had traced the Oregon Trail to California by covered wagon and sidewheeler steamer at the conclusion of the Civil War. Then he had sailed home to Philadelphia via the Cape Horn passage to edit and publish a weekly newspaper.

After Jay Sr. had served a short apprenticeship on his father's newspaper, he too took to the road, wrangling an appointment through a family friend to Puerto Rico's Department of Education. "The job involved bookkeeping," he wrote back to his family, "of which I had no practical knowledge." His government employer apparently agreed, and dismissed him after seven months.

But Jay Sr. had made use of his short stint in San Juan to become fluent in Spanish, an achievement that he parlayed into a job as a stenographic interpreter on various Spanish-speaking Caribbean islands and, later, for the Mexican Railway in Veracruz. Sensing that revolution was imminent, he left Mexico in 1911, and spent his next 42 years, he wrote, as a globe-hopping "traveling man," selling leather belting for machinery "the world over covering all industrial countries except Australia, New Zealand, and South Africa."

Jay Sr. made his home base in the southeastern Pennsylvania town of Carlisle, not far from where his great-great-grandfather had purchased a 218-acre homestead in 1765 from the family of William Penn himself. And it was into this cosmopolitan family that Jay Jr., the first of four Zeamer children, arrived on July 25, 1918.

World War I was well into its fourth grinding year when Jay Jr. was born. Since America's entry into the conflict a little over a year earlier, newspapers had covered the war like no other before. That July was no different, and as the Zeamers welcomed their first child into the world the front pages of newspapers and radio broadcasts were replete with reports

from the Western Front chronicling the latest bloodletting at the Second
Battle of the Marne, Germany's last great offensive. Like hundreds of
small towns across the country, Carlisle, with close to 11,000 residents,
did its patriotic part, and had also mourned its fallen sons, including the
privates Doyle Ashburn and Harvey Kelley, who were killed that week on
the banks of that faraway French river.

Jay Sr. had enlisted in the Army infantry at the war's outset and
earned his "doughboy" credentials in boot camp, although the lingering
effects of a childhood bout with tuberculosis had kept him stateside. Still,
if the appellation of the "War to End All Wars" was to be believed, he
and Marjorie hoped and prayed that babies born in 1918, including their
older son, would never have to fight in another global conflict.

Jay was only two when his father pulled up stakes in Pennsylvania and
moved the family to New Jersey in order to be nearer to the major trans-
portation hubs of Newark and New York City, a mere 15 miles away from
Orange. It was around this time that Marjorie, a striking, dark-eyed bru-
nette whose cheekbones could cut falling silk, realized that if she didn't
keep a constant eye on her oldest boy she often would have no idea where
he'd vanished to.

Despite its proximity to New York, Orange in the 1920s had only
recently shed its pastoral roots. And though its main streets were by then
crowded with breweries and thriving boot- and shoemaking factories taking advantage of the tannic acid produced by the town's thousands of
hemlock trees, spinneys of thick oak enclosing small farmsteads were only
a short distance away. These rural areas virtually called out to be explored
by a boy who was, as Marjorie wrote of Jay Jr., "brimming with an almost
unrestrained energy, a curious spirit of investigation and adventure."

At the same time Jay also exhibited a natural mechanical bent. His
parents marveled over the toy trains and automobiles he built in his father's workshop, mobile facsimiles propelled by springs or elaborate
elastic-band motors that the boy concocted from scratch. Foremost in the
Zeamer family's memory, however, was Jay's fascination with airplanes;

his brother Jere, three years younger, described the model planes Jay constructed as "impressive for both their complexity and quality."

In 1926, when Jay was eight, his father's successful career had allowed the family to put away enough money to purchase a clapboard vacation cottage in the bucolic seaside hamlet of Boothbay Harbor, Maine. By this time the Zeamer family had expanded to six with the arrivals of Jere and two sisters: Isabel and Anne. The first summer that the family packed into their station wagon and headed north, it was as if an entire new world opened up to their eldest child. In fact, Boothbay Harbor would have a hold on Jay for the rest of his life.

The Zeamer cottage was hard by the seashore and surrounded by a seemingly unending forest that made the outlands of Orange seem sparse. This heightened young Jay's innate curiosity. It was as if the little New England hamlet had sprung from the ground solely for his amusement, and he would disappear for hours on end exploring the ancient Abenaki Indian trails that crosshatched the thick north woods. There was also a timeless aspect to the harbor itself, and the buzzing hive of fisherman and shipbuilders made it seem to Jay like the busiest place on earth.

On summer afternoons, when the prevailing southwest breezes strengthened to form thunderheads to the north, Jay imagined being transported back in time. One day he fancied himself fighting in the Revolutionary War, perhaps as the captain of the ship of the line in the Continental Navy which had traded shot with a British antagonist right outside the cove; the next, he was a mate aboard the Confederate schooner that sneaked into Portland Harbor a few miles down the coast at the height of the Civil War and made off onto the high seas with a captured Union revenue cutter.

Jay's love of the water came to fruition with the rowboat that he built from scratch, like his toy cars, trains, and airplanes, shortly after his tenth birthday. He had nailed it together from cadged planks and stray building material he found lying about the village—even its oars had been fashioned from hardwood scavenged from behind an abandoned sawmill—

and it was the joy he took in sailing this flat-bottomed dory that sealed his parents' suspicion that he was a different kind of boy.

Though Jay Sr. took his older son's adventurous nature in the spirit of a proud father, Marjorie hated it when Jay rowed off alone during the predawn hours in what she referred to as "the tub," sculling across the placid cove, dipping out of sight into the harbor's every rocky nook. She would watch nervously from her front porch as he weaved among the rows of tall-masted schooners, survivors of the Great War's Merchant Marine fleet, lying at anchor far off in the Gulf of Maine. Jay's little rowboat, she remembered, "was no masterpiece, to be sure," but it was watertight and shipshape, and Jay never seemed to tire of tying onto those old schooners and clambering up through their rigging, staring out to sea. It was if something was beckoning him to make a mark in the wide world.

Soon Jay became a regular sight prowling the fishing wharves down at the harbor. His mother was taken aback one afternoon when, as she walked into the village center with her son, several fishermen and lobstermen waved and paused to chat with her boy about everything from the tide tables to the day's catch. On special occasions, such as a birthday or holiday, Jay would even be invited to accompany these hard, leather-skinned men out on their day trips. Later, when the Zeamer family sat down to dinner, Jay regaled them with fishing lore and the rudiments of navigation he had soaked up like a sponge. He made certain, of course, to leave out the salty phrases his new friends were teaching him. Jay's parents sensed that it was on these day trips that their son was discovering what it was like to be part of a crew working together toward a shared goal.

Sometimes in the early evenings Jay rowed out to the harbor mouth to await the return of the village's small commercial fleet, his dory nearly obscured by the flocks of complaining seagulls swooping for scraps. This was when Marjorie fretted the most. It was not unusual for sudden squalls to blow in at that time of day, scouring rocky Popham Beach with pelting sheets of vertical rain that turned the bay into a roiled cauldron. But fishermen rushing home would spy Jay in his little eggshell craft, throw him a rope to tie on, lift him aboard, and then proceed while his rowboat bounced along in the wake of their vessels.

Jay was also known about the village as the boy to see for any odd job that needed doing and doing well, and by his early teens he had saved up enough money to buy a small, used daysailer. From then on, his excursions became even more daring. Once he'd been far out in the bay with his two best friends, Norton Joerg and Russell Thompson, when a late-afternoon thundergust capsized the boat and left the three boys clinging to the upturned keel. A passing lobsterman helped them right the craft and towed them back to port. Jay was as humiliated as he was thankful. But that was far from the worst of it.

His mother was fond of telling the story about the first time her son and his two friends tacked out beyond the last lookout station on distant Squirrel Island. The morning had begun as a fine summer's day to be out on the water, and for once Marjorie felt no trepidation as she packed lunches for Jay, Norton, and Russell. She did not even notice when an eerie summer calm settled over the sea, although her son and his friends certainly did. The boys were stranded miles from shore, and forced to take turns paddling toward land with the little boat's single oar. Dusk came and went, and then darkness fell, and search parties in motor craft crisscrossed the sea-lanes beyond the harbor's opening to no avail. At last, near midnight, the exhausted and famished threesome splashed onto the beach and nearly collapsed.

Jay was grounded from sailing for two weeks, a punishment somewhat mitigated by the second passion of his young life, the Boy Scouts of America. The Maine forests were God's gift to a curious young man who reveled in the Scout ethos of individuality and responsibility. In 1930, as the United States plunged deeper into the Great Depression, most 12-year-old boys were happy just to have Scouting as a relief from the frightening economic times. The nation was still predominantly rural, and Scouting offered a chance to master skills they could very well use when they became men. Jay appreciated that, but there was something more to the organization for him. He wanted to be the best Boy Scout who ever lived.

He so took to the Scout essentials of swimming, camping, Morse Code, mapmaking, first aid, knot-tying, canoeing, and all the rest—neighbors would listen and smile as he practiced his campfire songs in the backyard—that in time there was hardly room left on his uniform's sash for the scores of merit badges he earned. On family blueberrying hikes up nearby Mount Pisgah he assumed the role of field guide, pointing out the different types of trees, animals, birds, and even insects. And on clear nights he would gaze at the sky and mentally sketch the constellations while memorizing the origins of their ancient names. Within a year he had risen from Tenderfoot to the highest rank, Eagle Scout; and back home in New Jersey he became the youngest patrol leader in the history of Orange's local Troop 5.

This presented a problem. Despite Jay's Eagle Scout rank, his scoutmaster recognized that placing a 13-year-old in charge of older boys was bound to create tensions. So instead of assigning Jay his rightful place in the troop, the Scoutmaster culled a group of 10-, 11-, and 12-year-olds for Jay to mentor and train. Soon Jay's charges were not only holding their own against the older Scouts in local and regional competitions, but besting them outright at informal jamborees.

This was all well and good until Jay Sr. and Marjorie noticed a steady decline in Jay's test scores during his freshman year at Orange Public High School. Despite his obvious intelligence, Jay found his schoolbooks virtual chloroform in print and preferred instead to devote most of his energy to honing his Scouting skills. His father was befuddled. Jay Sr. considered the Boy Scouts a worthy venture, but not at the expense of his son's studies. After several warnings that Jay seemed to ignore, at the conclusion of the school year his parents pulled him from Orange High School and enrolled him in Indiana's Culver Military Academy. It was his father's hope that the boarding school's reputation for academic rigor would, as Jay put it later in life, "knock some schooling into me."

So it was that in late August 1933, as the last days of summer shortened and the fishing boats of Boothbay Harbor were refitted for the coming cod season, Jay left behind his beloved sea. He was, for the first time, bound without surrounding family to make his own way in the world. For his parents, it was a prescient decision.

2

THE WILD BLUE YONDER

JAY TOOK TO CULVER'S MILITARY ATMOSPHERE LIKE A HOUND TO THE FOX. The institution, existing today as the collected schools of the coed Culver Academies, was an all-boys boarding school when Jay made his way to northern Indiana in the autumn of 1933. The academy had been founded in 1894 by the magnate and philanthropist Henry Harrison Culver, whose oven business had earned him the name "Cooking Range King." Culver's mission statement for the school was succinct: "For the purpose of thoroughly preparing young men for the best colleges, scientific schools and businesses of America." In Jay's case, Culver's promise held true.

Jay's grades improved immediately and dramatically, and by the midpoint of his first year at Culver he had also established himself as a better rifle shot than most of the older students, earning a spot on the school's intercollegiate rifle team as well as membership in the Culver

Rifles Honor Guard. He soon held the school record of better than 100 shots without missing the bull's-eye, a distinction he would maintain until his graduation and beyond.

Yet even the strict discipline maintained by the Culver staff could not manage to knock all the insouciance out of the Eagle Scout with the eagle eye, who still managed to find time to flout school regulations. His greatest transgression was purchasing and refurbishing a dilapidated Overland Whippet, the precursor to the Jeep and at the time America's smallest car. The Whippet, manufactured by the legendary Willys-Overland motor company, was on the market for only five years before being replaced by a larger coupé, and the model Jay picked up had been discontinued two years before his arrival at Culver. It was, in the vernacular, a jalopy with more than 100,000 miles on it. But when Jay inspected its engine he determined that he could rebuild the thing, and that is exactly what he did after school and on weekends, testing and refining the vehicle on the long, lonely roads abutting nearby Lake Michigan. There was only one problem: Culver had a regulation against students owning automobiles.

Jay surreptitiously stored the Whippet in the academy's community garage, more or less hidden in plain sight among the school and faculty vehicles. But one day the unaccounted-for car with the unaccountable owner was discovered, and Jay was summoned by the academy's dean of discipline. Jay strode into his disciplinary hearing on the offensive, arguing that since he was already enrolled in the school's engineering program, working on the automobile constituted an unaccredited extracurricular activity. He even demonstrated how, in his spare time, he had completely dismantled and rebuilt the vehicle's engine.

To Jay's surprise, the dean demanded a trial run in which the car performed so admirably that the Whippet was designated a school project. Incredibly, instead of being punished for his infraction, Jay not only was allowed to keep the car but was given extra credit for his work on it. At the conclusion of his junior year he even drove the rebuilt roadster home to New Jersey. With his startling blue eyes and thick auburn hair combed into a Woody Woodpecker swoop, he must have seemed every bit the young bon vivant motoring through the cornfields of the Midwest that spring. He subsequently put another 50,000 miles on the Whippet. It was an indication of things to come.

JAY GRADUATED FROM CULVER ACADEMY IN 1936 AND APPLIED TO THE Massachusetts Institute of Technology, already a venerable university. As at Culver, Jay's ambition at M.I.T. was to study civil engineering. He envisioned himself, he once put it, scampering over half-built bridges spanning high above great rivers. But first he had to talk his way into the school because the university initially rejected his application.

Despite his academic turnaround at Culver, Jay's poor grades from his freshman year at Orange High had dragged down his overall grade-point average, and in a polite but firm form letter the school informed him that he was free to reapply after spending a year at another college or university. Refusing to take no for an answer, Jay drove to Cambridge and camped outside the office of the director of admissions until he was granted an audience. The director was so impressed with the young man's persistence that he made an offer—if Jay attended M.I.T.'s summer school courses in physics and science and maintained an A average, the school would review his application. Jay did just that and was accepted into the university's engineering school that fall.

At M.I.T. Jay enrolled in the ROTC program of the Army Corps of Engineers, and one day after drills a fellow junior officer suggested that he tag along with a group heading to Boston's Logan Airport. There was a long tradition of "flying students" at M.I.T.—the U.S. Navy had established its first ground school for pilot training in 1917 on the school's campus, where selected candidates underwent training in navigation, gunnery, electrical engineering, aeronautical instruments, photography, and signals. And though the Navy's flight school had been closed at the end of World War I, the popular student Flying Club still maintained the tradition.

Jay's fellow ROTC junior officer was a member of the club, and that afternoon he took Jay up in its lone aircraft, a sturdy little 40-horsepower, tandem-seat Piper Cub, one of the most popular airplanes of the era. Awed by his first experience in what the British called the "Flitfire," Jay enrolled in the Flying Club the moment his feet hit the ground.

Like Saint-Exupéry, Jay discovered that flight released his mind "from the tyranny of petty things," and within a year he had obtained his pilot's license, accumulated more than 100 hours of solo flying time in his logbook, and been elected the club's manager. Now, instead of running his old jalopy up and down the East Coast during school vacations, he often borrowed the Piper Cub to fly home to New Jersey. It was during one these breaks that he took his father and then his teeth-gritting mother aloft on their first flights.

In the meanwhile, it had been nearly a year since Hitler's Third Reich had completed its Anschluss with Austria and seized the Sudetenland, and young men of Jay's generation recognized that it was only a matter of time before the European conflict expanded. Though as late as 1938 political isolationists in the United States still held sway—that year a mere 2,021 Americans enlisted in the armed services—Jay sensed that world war loomed. The following summer, between his sophomore and junior years at M.I.T., he enlisted in the Army Infantry Reserves on his twenty-first birthday—July 25, 1939, less than six weeks before Nazi Germany would invade Poland.

Although his father had not been deployed overseas during the Great War, volunteering to serve his country was for Jay a continuance of a long Zeamer tradition; it also harked back to those elements of Scouting that so enthralled him, particularly the Boy Scout credo with its emphasis on the Bill of Rights and the Constitution. Those tenets had drilled into Jay the idea that such freedoms were worth not only fighting for but, if need be, dying for. And though it was a natural tendency to follow in his father's footsteps, Jay still wanted, awfully badly, to be a flier. To that end, barely a month after being sworn into the Army Infantry Reserves as a second lieutenant, he applied to Navy Flight School to be trained as a pilot. His application was rejected. Since childhood he had been plagued by poor eyesight, a type of nearsightedness that ran in the family and also affected his younger brother, Jere. The two boys refused to wear eyeglasses, considering their use "the height of laziness," and instead consumed carrots "by the bushel" on the theory that the vitamin A produced by the beta-carotene-rich root vegetable was a cure for bad eyes. It did not help.

Jay's suspicion that he had inherited his bad eyes from his father was correct, but not for the reasons he believed. When Jay Sr. was a newborn he had shared a bedroom with a tubercular cousin and had contracted what was then known as scrofula infantum, a childhood tubercular infection also called the king's evil. The infection attacked the lymph glands in his throat, and for the first eight years of his life, Jay's father had suffered from such a serious speech impediment that only his family could understand him. He had also been the victim of periodic bouts of "tubercular blindness." As Jay Sr. noted in an account of the family's history, "Growing to manhood the vocal deficiencies were overcome—but not the eyesight."

When Jay researched the symptoms of his father's childhood condition he discovered that scrofula infantum could not be passed down through family genes but that general nearsightedness, which also affected his father, could. As angry as he remained at the Navy's rejection, he was also relieved that his father's illness had not been the reason for it. Still, whatever the cause of his bad eyesight, he vowed that this obstacle would not end his dream of going to war in the air. Rummaging through the M.I.T. library he found a book describing an alternative therapy for improving one's eyesight, called the Bates Method.

The then-revolutionary Bates Method had been introduced by the eye-care physician William Bates around the turn of the century. Bates held that nearly all eyesight problems were the result of a habitual strain on the eyes, and that eyeglasses only worsened the conditions. Such was his disdain for eyeglasses that he kept an anvil in his office to smash those

worn by new patients. Bates had died in 1931, but one of the major pro-
ponents of his method was the ophthalmologist Dr. Harold Peppard,
whose New York City practice drew patients from around the country. In
due course Jay began taking the train from Boston to visit Peppard.

Following Bates's prescribed treatments, Peppard's controversial
process for improving vision included exposing his patients' eyes to direct sunlight in order, as Bates had written, to change the shape of their
eyeballs and alleviate eyestrain. Even at the time professionals in the field
of established ophthalmology condemned this as outright quackery, and
Bates's theories were subsequently proved a physiological impossibility
in humans. But for Jay these eccentricities were offset by the testimonials
of enthusiastic followers of the Bates Method, who included the health
and fitness guru Bernarr Macfadden and the noted British writer Aldous
Huxley, whose corneas had been scarred in a fire during his childhood
and who claimed that the Bates Method had improved his damaged eyesight significantly.

Moreover, Jay had come of age in an era of modern scientific mar-
vels that only a generation earlier would have been considered miracu-
lous. These inventions and discoveries were rapidly transforming a world
mechanized and electrified by combustion engines, instant transoceanic
communications, power grids, and even the first small steps toward
unlocking the secrets of the atom. For many, particularly the American
doughboys and the shattered European soldiers and civilians who had
survived the horrors of the mechanized killing of the Great War, the inter-
war period was a time of introspection, of searching for the means to cope
with this frightening new world.

To Jay's generation, on the other hand, infinities were being over-
taken in rapid order and they embraced these changes as the harbingers
of everything good that could be accomplished through science and engineering. After all, many of these astounding technological advances had
come in the field of medicine, and within his lifetime Jay had witnessed
the identification of separate human blood types, the acceptance of phar-

macology as a science, and the discovery of penicillin and the insulin molecule. Amid all this progress anything seemed possible to bright young men like Jay, even if it involved staring at the sun.

In September 1939, following a dozen or so visits to Dr. Peppard, Jay returned to the Navy recruiting station in Boston to retake his eye test on the same day that Britain declared war on Germany. This time, he passed. But the United States was not yet in the European fight, and the peacetime U.S. Navy had a policy of rejecting reapplicants who had originally failed their physicals. To Jay it must have seemed a godsend when, only two days later, a flight surgeon from the Army Air Corps arrived on the M.I.T. campus to administer physicals to any students interested in that branch's flight school. Jay joined twenty-one other applicants in undergoing the physical, and was one of only four to tentatively qualify for postgraduate flight training. He was told he would be notified if the Army's aviation branch needed him.

By the time of his graduation in June 1940, Jay had heard nothing from the Army's flying arm and, honoring his infantry commitment, he said good-bye to his brother, by then also an engineering undergraduate at M.I.T., and flew home to Orange to bid farewell to his parents. The slow train that transported Jay to boot camp at southern New Jersey's Fort Dix was in direct contradiction to the seeming suddenness with which his younger sisters felt that their big brother had been transformed from an aspiring civilian engineer to an Army second lieutenant. Jay and his family were further taken aback when less than a month after his arrival at Fort Dix a telegram came, notifying him that he had been accepted into the Army Air Corps Flight School.

Though he felt that his perseverance—all those visits to Dr. Peppard's Manhattan ophthalmology center; all those days and nights training his eye muscles—had finally paid off, his ecstasy turned to anger when he learned that he would not be allowed to carry the seniority for the time he had accrued since his enlistment in the Infantry Reserves. In fact, in order to resign from the infantry and reenlist in the Army Air Corps, he would

lose his two years of time "in grade" as a second lieutenant. But his desire
to fly overcame any doubts, and within days Jay reported to the Army's
Primary Flying School in Glenview, Illinois, for three months of initial
training. Glenview was a weeding-out process, with Jay and the other flying cadets spending dawn to dusk either at calisthenics or at "ground
school"—classroom lessons in the various skills needed to fly an aircraft.
If you showed an aptitude for these requirements you moved on to pilot
training. If not, you were returned to a general army assignment.

Despite his Piper Cub experience, Jay was far from the best potential pilot at Glenview. But the leadership skills he had forged in the Boy
Scouts caught the attention of his superiors, who appointed him captain
of cadets. At the conclusion of the 12-week course only 15 of the 47 candidates who had reported to the Primary Flying School that summer were
deemed Airmen material, Jay among them. From Illinois he was sent to
Alabama's Maxwell Field for another six months of training at the Army's
Advanced Flight School, where he finally was allowed to step into a military aircraft.

His mornings at Maxwell were stacked with classes in communications, technical supply, radar operations, weather forecasting, armament
identification, and radio operation. He proved a natural at distinguish-
ing the silhouettes of German and Japanese aircraft from British and U.S.
planes as they flashed in rapid succession across a projector screen. And
while the other students complained during Morse Code classes that trying to decipher the clicks and clacks was like listening to Rice Krispies
being poured into a bowl, Jay enjoyed showing off the *dit-dah* proficiency
he had honed in the Scouts. Each cadet was also expected to be fluent in
close order drill and the handling of small arms, from pistols to rifles to
riot guns. Again, Jay's experience with the Culver Rifles put him on a par
even with pilots from rural backgrounds who had been raised to hunt for
their dinners.

Afternoons at Maxwell were reserved for actual flights with an instructor, usually in a two-seat trainer. It was here that Jay was introduced

to aviation maneuvers—loops and chandelles, spins and touch-and-gos—that he had only read about. He spent hours practicing takeoffs and landings, go-arounds, instrument flying, cross-country navigation, and night-formation flying. He'd often exit the cockpit dripping sweat, his flight suit soaked to its logbook pockets.

When the trainees were finally allowed to solo, the instructors at Maxwell expected them to abide by several hard-and-fast rules. One maxim involved takeoffs: the student pilots were taught to take a hard right turn as soon as they gained altitude. On one of his first solo flights Jay was so excited that he forgot his "starboard procedure," and as punishment he was forced to wear his parachute strapped tight around his chest and legs that night at chow. He never forgot again.

But aside from that rare miscue, Jay was a model cadet behind the yoke of both single-engine and twin-engine trainers, and in March 1941 he graduated from Maxwell and received his coveted wings. He was again commissioned a second lieutenant, this time in the United States Army Air Corps.

3

JAY & JOE

TO THE ADVENTUROUS YOUNG FLIERS OF JAY'S GENERATION, NOTHING was more captivating than the martial images of World War I's dashing "Knights of the Sky." Jay was enthralled by the romance of these early fighter pilots, particularly the several Americans who had dominated wartime headlines while succeeding one another to claim the coveted title "Ace of Aces." Two decades later their names still resonated—Raoul Lufbery, Frank Luke, Frank Bayliss, David Putnam. But Jay identified most closely with the greatest of them all, Eddie Rickenbacker. It was the tales of Rickenbacker's derring-do that he had pored over as boy, and it was not hard to recognize the similarities between the two Airmen.

Like Jay, Rickenbacker was an automobile buff. In his youth he had competed in the first Indianapolis 500 and set land speed records at the Daytona Raceway. Rickenbacker enlisted when America entered the Great

War and, given his background, he was assigned a position as a driver on the staff of Gen. John J. "Black Jack" Pershing, the commander of the American Expeditionary Force in Europe. But Rickenbacker chafed at his role as a glorified chauffeur and within months he fast-talked his way into the recently established U.S. Army Air Service as a pilot in training. Much as Jay would not allow his rejection from the Navy's flight program to stand in his way of becoming a flier, nothing could stop Rickenbacker from climbing into a cockpit.

Once aloft, Rickenbacker took his cue from his mentor, the Franco-American ace Lufbery, and honed his reputation as a lone-wolf fighter pilot. It was a habit that served him well as he patrolled the skies deep inside Germany by himself. And though aerial tactics and fighter-plane design had naturally advanced by leaps in the decades between the two world wars, Jay never forgot the solitary aspect of the Rickenbacker legend, and imagined himself following the same flight patterns over the same French and German terrain.

The comparisons between the two men, however, went only so far. Rickenbacker had been born into poverty, and after his father died in a construction accident he was forced to drop out of elementary school and work at two jobs in order to help support his mother and six brothers and sisters. Jay had been fortunate enough to attend a prestigious university while Rickenbacker had settled for a mail-order diploma from the International Correspondence School based in Scranton, Pennsylvania. But like Jay, at heart Rickenbacker was a consummate if amateur engineer who lived by the code "A machine has to have a purpose."

There was one other major difference between Jay and Rickenbacker. Though Jay carried a relatively scant 155 pounds on his six-foot frame, the configuration of the instrument panels common to the Army's attack and pursuit aircraft in the early 1940s led the service to prefer shorter men in the cockpits of its fighter planes. So Jay was rejected yet again, this time by the Air Corps' fighter branch, and instead assigned to bomb-

ers. This time he could not concoct any clever arguments to reverse the
Army's decision, and with his ambitions of honing his dogfighting skills
in preparation for duels against Germany's new Red Barons dashed, he
was assigned to the 43rd Bomb Group based at Langley Field near New-
port News, Virginia.

The 43rd had recently been carved from the Army Air Corps' venerable 2nd Bomb Group, and it consisted of four squadrons readying to fly
the new B-17 Flying Fortresses. The bombers were only just trickling off
the Boeing Airplane Company's assembly lines, and initially Jay and his
fellow rookies had to content themselves with flight simulation drills and
hours upon hours of classwork. This did not mean Jay could not admire
the Flying Fortress from afar, and a few days after his arrival at Langley
he attended an aerial exhibition put on by the 43rd for what Airmen
called the "brass hats" from Washington. The politicians who attended
these mock combat demonstrations controlled the purse strings for the
nascent USAAF, and in order to leave the best impression, the Group's
commanding officers chose only the unit's most accomplished Airmen
to take part.

That day Jay watched in amazement as the bombardier in the lead
B-17 planted several 500-pound dummy bombs within 75 feet of his target at altitudes ranging from 5,000 to 8,000 feet. Afterward, Jay sought
out the Airman whose uncanny accuracy had piqued his curiosity. Most
bombardiers were not hard to find. A B-17 bombsight's eyepiece was
rimmed with a black rubber ring, and as the bombardier sighted his
targets the rubber would mix with sweat and rub off, inevitably giving
the "rock dropper" what looked like a permanent shiner. That night Jay
combed the barracks and mess halls at Langley, stopping to chat with any
man who looked as if he had just been in a bar fight. Though he never did
find his man, he did learn his name—Joseph Sarnoski. Sarnoski, he was
told, was considered the most skilled bombardier on the base, if not in the
entire U.S. Army Air Force.

The next morning Jay reported to his first Bombing and Gunnery class. He nearly fell out of his chair when the lithe, open-faced instructor with the faint black outline rimming his left eye introduced himself as Staff Sgt. Joe Sarnoski. After class Jay offered to buy him a beer. He needed to know, he said, how Sarnoski got those bombs so close.

Joe wasn't certain what to make of this. He was well aware that every bomber pilot in the service was expected to be able to perform the duties of each member of his crew, whether navigating, flight engineering, or even tail gunning. So it was not completely unheard of for an officer to pick the brains of enlisted Airmen. Still, it wasn't often that a lieutenant approached a sergeant, a complete stranger at that, and offered to stand him a drink. Joe went along, and as the weeks passed and Jay picked Joe's brain about the B-17's idiosyncrasies, the two became fast friends. Joe was only too happy to share his expertise. Joe, who hailed from the hard regions of Pennsylvania coal country, was not only flattered by the attention, but a bit in awe of the college man so eager to befriend him. Conversely, it did not take long for Jay to discover that Joe was one of those special men who wear their grace lightly. As he would one day write to Joe's sister Victoria, "In the end, Joe took me under his wing."

Given Jay's personality and Joe's sly sense of humor, it is very likely that Jay intended the pun.

THREE YEARS JAY'S SENIOR, JOE SARNOSKI WAS THE FIFTH OF 16 CHILdren born to Polish immigrants who had settled in the coal-rich Carbondale area of northeastern Pennsylvania around the turn of the century. His father Johann—later Americanized to "John"—had found work in the mines there, but when his health began to fail in the late 1920s he and his wife Josephine used the little money he'd saved to purchase a ramshackle farmhouse with no indoor plumbing on a small plot of land on the outskirts of town.

His timing could not have been worse. He had barely signed the deed when the Great Depression hit. For the next decade the lean economic times would lie over the Sarnoski farmstead like an illness.

Though Jay and Joe were both Pennsylvanians by birth, the 130 miles that separated Carbondale from Carlisle might as well have been an ocean. Whereas Jay had grown up in the semi-luxury of an upper-middle-class household, Joe and his family had never known anything but hard manual labor. For reasons that baffled even his children, John Sarnoski refused to refer to his two-and-a-half-acre spread as a farm—"our land" was how he always referred to it. Nonetheless the Sarnoski boys and girls were a regular sight by the side of the road selling the tomatoes, beets, beans, and cucumbers their mother cultivated in her small vegetable garden, and the brood also hawked wild blueberries and mulberries they collected from the nearby woods.

As the years passed the Sarnoski children arrived almost annually, with the aid of a midwife; none was born in a hospital. When they were old enough their parents assigned them all specific jobs, whether canning vegetables, tending chickens, washing diapers, putting up jam, or feeding the lone milk cow. Josephine, whose halting English masked her proficiency in four other languages, also taught her daughters how to sew most of the family's clothes.

Like so many emigrants to America, John and Josephine revered the educational opportunities their adopted country offered. But with money tight and the older children needed at home, it was not until Joe's graduation that any of the Sarnoskis earned a high school degree. This accomplishment reflected Joe's personal work ethic as much as his eclectic sense of wonder.

Between school and assisting his older brother Walter with dawn-to-dusk chores—which included near-daily hunting and fishing forays to put food on the table—Joe managed to explore an astonishing range of interests. Though he was slight of stature, his natural athleticism took form in his deftness not only as a skier and ice skater, but also on his high school baseball team, where he was a star infielder. He also taught himself to play a passable accordion and was a gifted and extroverted crooner who would burst into song in either English or Polish at the hint of an audience. When word of his talent spread through Carbondale's large Polish community, he found himself picking up extra cash on weekends singing and playing at weddings and anniversary parties. He also took a part-time job as a chauffeur for a neighbor who owned a car but did not know how to drive. Most of the money Joe earned he turned over to his parents, who allowed him to keep a few dollars for himself. This extra cash was usually deposited into his "Buy a Motorcycle Fund"—a rusty tin box he stored under his bed.

Meanwhile, Joe's schoolteachers were astonished that this son of a dirt farmer had such a wide range of interests, which included not only music but classical poetry. This may have stemmed from Joe's deep spirituality. His family and friends noted that he rarely went anywhere without his hand-carved wooden rosary beads stuffed deep into his pocket. Joe was what his sister Matilda called "fussy" over his younger siblings, particularly the girls, slyly imparting life lessons in the form of stories and yarns.

"When he tried to teach us things, we listened," says Matilda, ten years Joe's junior. "He wanted us to grow up to be good people, and as young as I was, he could tell I wanted to be educated like him." To that end, Joe promised Matilda that if she studied hard enough to become the valedictorian of her high school class, he would buy her a wristwatch.

Finally and perhaps most important—and much like the young Jay— early in his youth Joe developed a passion for airplanes. He plastered the walls of what the Sarnoskis called their farmhouse's "Great Room," where he bunked with his six brothers, with photos and drawings of all manner of aircraft torn from newspapers and magazines, and his bed was strewn with facsimiles of gliders, fighter planes, and bombers he had carved from softwood or fashioned out of metal detritus such as shotgun shells. Despite his longing to save all his cash for a motorcycle, there were times when he could not resist the allure of a new model airplane kit he'd spotted in a downtown store window, and he would dig into his wedding-singer cache and splurge. He would then disappear for hours—or as long as his chores would allow—to assemble his new toy.

Though Joe's strong hands helped make the farm run, John and Josephine recognized that they could not hold their son back forever. In March 1936, two months after Joe's twenty-first birthday, they presented him with a bus ticket to Baltimore. He tried to argue, but his parents convinced him that his younger brothers were now strong enough to assume his workload. When Joe exited the bus depot in downtown Baltimore the next day, he walked straight to a nearby army recruiting station and enlisted in the Air Corps as a cadet.

The Polish immigrants' son proved an adept and eager student, and after completing boot camp he was shipped to Lowry Field in Colorado. There he passed the Corps' Chemical Warfare course, its advanced Aircraft Armorer course, and, finally, the intellectually rugged Bombsight Maintenance course. He was then promoted to sergeant and transferred to the 41st Reconnaissance Squadron of the 2nd Bomb Group, a part of the very unit soon to be spun off into a separate Bomb Group numbered the 43rd.

Through all his travels and despite his workload, Joe wrote home as often as he could—his sister Matilda remembers how the family considered it "a big occasion" whenever a letter arrived. His mother answered his letters just as regularly, dictating her thoughts in Polish to one of her daughters, who would transcribe her words into English. She would also relay any comments from her more reticent yet equally proud husband. On his first Christmas furlough Joe took advantage of his $700 annual base salary to arrive back at the homestead with a new tricycle for his youngest brother, Francis, the baby of the family. It was the first store-bought gift any of the Sarnoski children had ever received, and the entire brood greeted Joe as if he were Santa Claus. It also convinced Matilda that he was not joking about buying her a wristwatch.

After what Matilda remembered as "one of the best Christmases our family ever celebrated," Joe returned to Langley to report to his new Bomb Group. Three months later the first B-17s began to arrive at the airbase for a series of operational flight tests. Joe took one look at the gleaming B-17 Flying Fortresses just assigned to his outfit and—like Jay Zeamer a few years later—fell in love.

THE CLOSER JAY AND JOE GREW, THE MORE JAY CAME TO ADMIRE THE hardy bombardier. Here was someone who had known an economic despair that Jay had never suffered, yet there was always a smile dancing about his pale blue eyes. Both men gradually came to realize that they had more in common than their love of flight, and Jay was delighted to learn that before Joe had enlisted he'd finally saved enough money to purchase a decrepit Indian motorcycle that, like Jay with his boarding school jalopy, Joe had rebuilt nearly from scratch. Joe loved to take his bike out to explore the backcountry dirt trails that crisscrossed the wooded fields surrounding his family's rural property, much as Jay had delighted in leading his Boy Scout excursions into the Maine forests.

More urgently, by the summer of 1941 any Airmen with a modicum of military sense recognized that war with Germany was not far off, and the two often joked about how, if given the opportunity to fly together, they would drop a couple of 500-pounders down the chimney of Hitler's Reichskanslei in Berlin and be home in time to watch Joe's sister Matilda, in high school by this time, graduate as valedictorian.

In mid-1941 Joe was transferred from Langley to serve as a bombing instructor in Bangor, Maine. He was so certain that his next posting would take him across the Atlantic that he and his girlfriend Marie—a Betty Grable look-alike from Richmond, Virginia, whom he had met at a mixer off-base—invited Jay to a small going-away dinner where they announced their engagement. Though Jay also saw his future in the skies somewhere above Europe, both men recognized that this might be the last they ever

saw of each other until the war was over—if they survived it. Despite their
jokes about being home for Matilda's graduation, the increasingly shrill
newspaper headlines left no doubt that the coming conflagration would
be a long and bloody slog against Hitler and his seemingly inexhaustible
supply of men and war machines.

What neither man likely reckoned was that before the year was out
they would indeed be fighting determined enemies, just not the ones they
had envisioned.

4

"THE SACRED DUTY OF
THE LEADING RACE"

WHEN JAY ARRIVED AT LANGLEY AIRBASE AS A GREEN SECOND LIEUTEN-
ant, the U.S. Army Air Corps was, in many respects, still in its infancy.
It had become an official branch of the service only 15 years earlier, and
Army traditionalists, most notably from the Infantry and Artillery Corps,
often derided its pilots as nothing more than glorified mailmen. But as
the United States' entry into the conflict raging across Europe became
increasingly expected, the Air Corps' leadership realized that it had one
major tool it could employ against its service rivals—publicity.

The American public at the moment was riveted by news reports out
of England describing the beleaguered Royal Air Force's last-stand hero-
ics during the Battle of Britain. With German bombs falling literally outside the radio studios from which journalists like the CBS correspondent
Edward R. Murrow and NBC's Fred Bate and John MacVane broadcast,

U.S. Secretary of War Henry Stimson and Army Chief of Staff George Marshall collaborated to use this opportunity to advocate for a stronger role for their own Army's aviation branch. Consequently, at Stimson's and Marshall's decree, in June 1941 the Air Corps was redesignated the United States Army Air Forces. This specification not only provided the air arm of the service with greater autonomy but also was an attempt to curtail the increasingly divisive arguments within the Army over control of aviation doctrine and organization.

Marshall placed the gruff and versatile Gen. Henry H. "Hap" Arnold in command of this new air force. Arnold, the 56-year-old scion of a prominent Pennsylvania family known for its political and military service, proved a natural fit. In his youth Arnold had overcome his initial fear of flying to take to the air under the tutelage of the Wright brothers before becoming a barnstorming stunt pilot. Later, as a protégé of the legendary and controversial Gen. Billy Mitchell during World War I, he had overseen the expansion of what was then called the U.S. Air Service.

Like most seasoned military men of the era, Arnold—known throughout the Army as the "Chief"—had no doubt that the United States would soon be embroiled in a world war. He set his priorities for the USAAF accordingly, particularly emphasizing the rapid expansion of its training and procurement operations. He spent the summer and fall of 1941 overseeing the construction of military airfields across the country while also ensuring that the nation's airplane factories and machine shops were adapted to a war footing. As a member of the Joint Chiefs of Staff, Arnold knew that he would be responsible for attaining a quasi-autonomous status for the USAAF when the United States entered the hostilities. And of course this is exactly what occurred following the attack on Pearl Harbor.

It was amid this operational frenzy that in the spring of 1941 Jay and a number of other young lieutenants from the 43rd Bomb Group received orders to report to Ohio's Wright Airfield to service-test a new twin-engine medium bomber, the B-26 Marauder, just coming on line. Jay was certified as a copilot and engineering officer aboard the

Marauder—nicknamed the "Widow Maker" for its dive speed and 4,000-pound payload—and he spent the next several months in Ohio before deploying back to Langley in September. Much to his chagrin, his old Flying Fortress outfit, the 43rd, was in the process of being transferred to New England, and instead of rejoining it he was folded into a new Bomb Group, the 22nd, scheduled to receive a shipment of B-26 Marauders. Though initially conceived as a heavy bomber unit, the recently activated 22nd—soon to be known as the Red Raiders—had been allotted only one of the four-engine B-17s still only slowly trickling into service. Worse for Jay, that lone Fortress was reserved for use by the Group's colonels and majors, while Jay and his fellow junior officers were relegated to training on the unit's old, undersized, underpowered B-18 Bolos as they awaited the arrival of the Marauders.

In theory, Jay's transfer to the 22nd should have been a seamless fit. He had spent months flying the stubby-winged B-26, and his experience gave him a leg up on his fellow officers in the Group. In fact, Jay was devastated, and viewed the downgrade from heavy bombers to medium bombers as something akin to a demotion. Worse, he was still rated as only an engineering officer and copilot, and seemed destined to remain so. As his superiors made clear in their field-jacket reports, Jay just did not seem to have the *feel* for piloting a B-26. He was not alone.

With its two powerful eighteen-cylinder radial engines, its low-drag fuselage, and the largest propellers and shortest wings of any military aircraft in the world, the Marauder was above all else designed to be flown fast. Yet the plane's colorful nickname, Widow Maker, often cut both ways; as one of the 22nd's more experienced navigators wrote in his diary, "It's a very safe airplane once it gets up in the air because it's so awfully fast and bristling with guns. But the amazing thing is, the damn airplane itself has been our most treacherous enemy."

Takeoffs proved particularly problematic. A Marauder fully loaded with fuel and ammunition needed to attain maximum thrust practically immediately, especially on short runways. And only the smoothest of surfaces could accommodate the odd tricycle configuration of the aircraft's landing gear. Should a B-26's single nose wheel collide with even the smallest object as it sped down a runaway or, more likely, should it descend into an unseen rut or trough, the odds of the plane flipping were great. For that reason Marauder pilots were instructed to always leave their landing gear retracted when making a crash landing on unfamiliar terrain. Referring to the aircraft's developer, the same navigator who had called the plane "our most treacherous enemy" added, "Sometimes I wish they were stuck up Glenn Martin's fanny. He makes them and he ought to have to fly them."

But it was landings that earned the B-26 a second, more pejorative nickname—the Flying Coffin. Most American bombers of the era, including the massive Flying Fortress, were designed to approach an airstrip in a semi-glide pattern. A Marauder, however, had to be brought in hot and fast at 140 miles per hour until, at the last moment, its pilot yoked back hard before touching down. Jay had never completely mastered this skill back in Ohio, and that had prevented him from attaining pilot's status. Now, with the 22nd, this shortcoming was catching up to him.

Whenever an instructor would take Jay aloft to check him out for his pilot's certification at Langley, he repeatedly failed to stick his landings. He would begin his approaches too early or too late. Or he would come in too fast or would be too slow and "washy," threatening to either overspeed his props or stall out his engines. Jay later recalled that his lack of technique on approaches so "terrified" his check-ride trainers that the senior men would invariably seize control of the instruments from him and land the crafts themselves. What made Jay's inability to handle the Widow Maker all the more mystifying was that in every other aspect of flying his competence, if not expertise, shone. Indeed, he was considered one of the most dexterous pilots in the Group behind the wheel of a Bolo bomber.

"For some reason Jay just couldn't hack the [B-26] landing," Jay's close friend and fellow pilot Walt Krell recalled. Krell had been a year behind Jay at both the Glenview and the Maxwell flight schools, and considered him one of the most relaxed pilots he had ever seen. "Nothing ever seemed to bother him," Krell noted. "No emergency could shake him. On the ground, he was the kind of guy that everyone took to."

But once in the air, it was if Jay became another person. "Every one of us tried to check him out," Krell reported. "We figured that someone, somewhere along the line, would find the monkey that was riding Jay's back. But whatever it was we couldn't find it. We kept trying, of course; everyone felt he belonged in the left seat.* But the way he'd come in would turn your hair white."

The fact that Jay was not alone was small consolation. For all the pilots like Walt Krell, "who could just about make the B-26 sit up and sing songs to them," there were an equal number "who dreaded flying in the B-26 under even normal conditions."

Perhaps most frustrating to Jay's superiors was his seeming obliviousness to his shortcomings. After he botched a landing his trainers would quiz him on what he thought he had done wrong. To their astonishment, Jay invariably replied that he felt as if he had made a perfect approach. As time passed he could only watch in frustration as new pilots who had graduated from flight school after him were promoted to the left-hand seat.

Despite these setbacks on the flight deck, Jay considered prewar life at Langley "easy and fun." In addition to training on the Marauders and Bolos, he also learned to pilot (and land with no problems) such disparate aircraft as tandem-seat biplanes and Catalina Flying Boats. And so avid was his curiosity about all things aeronautical that he went out of his way to befriend any Airmen from whom he thought he could pick up an edge. Still, at the end of the day he was left to gaze longingly at the lone B-17 set aside for the Bomb Group's senior officers, a touch of melancholy

* As in an American automobile, the pilot sat on the left-hand side and the copilot on the right.

clouding the corners of his eyes. If war was imminent, he wanted to be a part of it, and this was the plane he wanted to fly into it. He would get half his wish.

BY THE TIME JAY HAD SETTLED BACK IN AT LANGLEY IN SEPTEMBER 1941 most of continental Europe lay prostrate beneath the Nazi blitzkrieg. A year earlier the German-Soviet alliance had collapsed, and as Jay and his fellow Airmen were flying training sorties that month, Kiev was falling to Wehrmacht invaders, the siege of Leningrad had begun, and Operation Typhoon—the German march on Moscow—was just getting under way. It was also during September that CBS's Murrow broke the news from London that in order to curb pockets of resistance against Nazi advances in Yugoslavia, Hitler had decreed that 100 civilians be executed for every German casualty. American newspapers also carried disturbing stories describing how every Jew over the age of six residing in German territories was required to wear a yellow Star of David, but it would be years before it was discovered that the same month was also the occasion for the first experiments with Zyklon-B in the gas chambers of Auschwitz.

As the course of the European war became increasingly obvious it was understood by even the lowliest American buck private that President Franklin Roosevelt would never allow Great Britain to stand alone against the Führer. Even if the Soviet Union held firm—something viewed at the moment as unlikely—there was little the Russians could do to aid the English. But what Jay and Joe and their cohort could never have envisioned was that in the coming weeks they would become embroiled in combat on two fronts. For on the other side of the globe, the isolated and resource-poor nation of Japan had inched closer to its decades-long plan of subjugating its Asian neighbors in preparation for one objective—war with the United States.

Buoyed by their swift conquest of the Chinese province of Manchuria in 1931, the armies of Emperor Hirohito and Gen. Hideki Tojo began rolling into the remainder of China six years later. What Japan lacked in commercial prowess it made up for in military proficiency as well as in a deep-seated national essence often referred to as *kokutai*—a belief similar to the Nazis' concept of their own racial purity. The Japanese routinely referred to themselves as *shido minzoku*, the leading race. Unlike Western white supremacists, however, the Japanese were far more preoccupied with glorifying themselves than belittling others, and as the coming world war progressed, this superiority complex would often be their undoing.

To Japan's war planners, to take one example, it was a given that China's defeat would serve as a springboard to spread the Empire's doctrine of racial preeminence across the Far East. That military resistance from the vast Chinese interior might in fact continue never entered their calculations. In 1940 the influential Japanese politician and industrialist Chikuhei Nakajima declared, "There are superior and inferior races in the world, and it is the sacred duty of the leading race to lead and enlighten the inferior ones." There was little doubt that he included in the latter group the "mongrel" United States.

Nakajima, the founder of an aircraft company, was a vocal proponent of building long-range bombers that could reach the American mainland. But Tokyo's Imperial General Headquarters had other plans: specifically, to lure the U.S. Pacific Fleet westward and ambush it at some unspecified date in the future, in what senior officers predicted would be "a once-and-for-all encounter."

The tentative location of this strategic naval battle with the United States shifted over time as Japan took advantage of advances in military technology. Within the Imperial Navy there was even bitter opposition to Adm. Isoroku Yamamoto's plan to target Pearl Harbor. The pervading school of thought among officers of the Combined Fleet considered it a safer bet to lay a trap for the Americans by attacking Manila Bay in the Philippines and waiting in ambush for U.S. ships to sail to the rescue. But the overall Japanese purpose remained constant—to knock the United States out of the war early and entirely by destroying its ocean power.

Japan's military planners also decided that while simultaneously going to war with the United States somewhere in the Pacific, they would—contra to Nakajima's call to strike fast and hard at the American mainland—first direct their military might to the south in an Asian version of blitzkrieg. To that end, while the main Japanese forces would move to seize territory in a swooping arc from Burma to Thailand to the Dutch East Indies to the Philippines, a smaller military arm dubbed the South Seas Force would capture a series of peripheral island chains, including the Bismarck Archipelago and Guam in the Marianas, to serve as a picket line to protect their larger conquests. From this vantage point the South Seas Force would be situated but a short step from a near-defenseless Australia, which had already sent the bulk of its fighting men to Europe. Finally, with Australia overrun, Tokyo could turn its attention to Hawaii and, ultimately, what its leaders considered the "satanic and diabolical" United States mainland.*

During these campaigns the soldiers, sailors, and Airmen of Nippon would show no mercy; their rules of engagement consisted of not much more than the sharp point of a 15-inch bayonet. The horrific violence Japan inflicted on its conquered enemies was exhibited most explicitly during what came to be known the "Rape of Nanking," in which historians estimate that the Imperial forces murdered between 200,000 and 430,000 Chinese, including 90,000 prisoners of war. One American Army general said that the Japanese soldier was "undoubtedly a low order of humanity" whose sole reason for going to war was to indulge a "liking for looting, arson, massacre, and rape."

Indeed, across Asia the Japanese war machine would subject defeated soldiers and civilians alike to torture, enslavement, and arbitrary

---

* In *War Without Mercy: Race and Power in the Pacific War*, his exhaustive study of Japanese racial attitudes during the conflict, John Dower notes that Imperial propagandists were fond of describing Americans variously as "mercenary, immoral, unscrupulous, vainglorious, arrogant, soft, nauseating, superficial, decadent, intolerant, uncivilized, and barbarous," among other choice pejoratives.

murder, which a Japanese fighter considered merely a means to a divinely mandated end. Yet that American general who saw the Japanese race as a lower order of humanity was mistaken, for there was more to these tactics than the diabolical desire to steal, burn, kill, and molest. From early childhood Japanese boys were bathed in a brainwashing *Bushido* mentality—literally, the Samurai's "Way of the Warrior"—that invoked a ruthless ethos which not only cultivated brutality but celebrated it for its own sake. Conversely, to the Empire's desensitized young men marching, sailing, and flying into combat, the idea of being taken prisoner was considered, as the Australian author Thomas Keneally noted, a chronic psychological disorder.

With few exceptions, the Japanese soldier's goal was combat to the death, either his enemy's or his own. That aim had the ironic effect of making him, in the eyes of his enemies, the very subhuman creature that he considered all non-Nipponese races to be. Consequently, as the war progressed through the Pacific, American GIs and Marines would resort to a kind of racist, anti-Japanese brutality that would appall their right-thinking countrymen.

Americans troops would come to think nothing of sending home severed Japanese ears and fingers as good-luck charms or souvenirs, or plucking gold-filled teeth from dead enemy soldiers. Some even boiled Japanese skulls in 50-gallon drums to use as trading chips with the sailors who transported them from island to island. This attitude was summed up by the war correspondent Ernie Pyle soon after he reached the Pacific Theater from the Western Front: "In Europe we felt that our enemies, horrible and deadly as they were, were still people," wrote Pyle. "But out here I soon gathered that the Japanese were looked upon as something subhuman and repulsive; the way some people feel about cockroaches and mice."

Jay, the frustrated fighter pilot, did not yet realize it, but his assignment to the bomber branch would soon place him in the role of exterminator.

5

THE FORTRESS

THEY PLANNED TO CALL IT THE "AERIAL BATTLE CRUISER." AT LEAST THAT was how the executives at Boeing referred to the airship when, in 1934, they entered an open competition to design a new bomber for the U.S. Army Air Forces.

Boeing had been founded in 1916, when its designers constructed their first canvas-and-wood aircraft. Since then, the company's engineers had been responsible for introducing a spectrum of aerial innovations into the U.S. military. Their successful implementation of an aircraft's tough, thin aluminum "skin," no thicker than a dozen sheets of notebook paper, was a major leap forward in aerodynamics. They were also pioneers in developing landing gear that retracted into a plane's wings during flight, greatly reducing drag.

So when the USAAF put out a bid to design a new, multi-engine bomber that could fly a minimum of 250 miles per hour, reach a ceiling of 25,000 feet, and remain airborne for six to ten hours continuously, the planners at the Seattle-based manufacturer intuitively recognized that they were being asked to build not only an aircraft that flew superbly, but a winged *weapon* to fulfill an international need. They also realized they were putting themselves at serious financial risk in the midst of the Great Depression. The young company had only $500,000 in its treasury, and it was committing more than half of that to build a single plane, which might not measure up to the ambitions of the USAAF. It went ahead anyway.

One new wrinkle Boeing initiated was to reconfigure the flight deck. To this point the cockpits of all bombers had been built flush with the plane's propellers. In order to improve the pilot's visual awareness, the developers of the prototype moved the cockpit forward ahead of its four engines. Then there was the problem of meeting the Army's speed specifications. At 75 feet long, with a wingspan of over 100 feet, the plane was a behemoth in terms of aerodynamic drag coefficient despite its thin skin and retractable landing gear.

In order to streamline the ship even further against wind resistance, Boeing introduced a bomb bay that, for the first time in aeronautical history, was moved inside the fuselage between the two wings. This allowed the plane to carry a maximum of 5,000 pounds of ordnance for an incredible 1,700 miles or, on longer round-trips of over 2,000 miles, a still-walloping 2,500-pound load.

Adding to the unique design was the tail, which went through several iterations. In earlier models it tapered into a bullet-like shape sporting a sleek, relatively small "shark fin." But this left no room for a backward-facing gun mount, virtually inviting enemy aircraft to attack from the rear. Later designs solved this problem by enlarging not only the tail gunner's position but the vertical fin itself to a towering 15 feet, prompting some Airmen to dub the plane their "big-ass bird." In any case, the aircraft now had more lateral stability at altitude as well as a lethal stinger in its tail.

By the time Boeing won the Army's competition and the first B-17s were introduced into service in 1938, they had already picked up their iconic designation as Flying Fortresses. The name, attributed variously to admiring Boeing hard-hat workers or newsmen astounded by the aircraft's five cupola gun stations, was more than appropriate—from the beginning it was obvious that the B-17 would completely revolutionize aviation warfare.

At first the B-17s rolled off the Boeing assembly lines at an agonizingly slow pace. When Hitler's forces invaded Poland in September 1939 there were only 13 operational Fortresses in service. But once the craft, destined to become one of the most powerful airplanes ever built, proved itself during trial runs, production went into overdrive. All told, nearly 13,000 Flying Fortresses would be put into action during World War II, and Airmen would come to love the plane for its inexhaustible ruggedness and its ability to absorb massive battle damage while remaining aloft. Further, given its maximum speed of close to 300 miles per hour—faster than most fighter planes of the era—flight crews were confident that they could outrun bogeys as well as outpace the sighting mechanisms of anti-aircraft gunners. Even if they could not, the plane had a ceiling of 35,000 feet—10,000 higher than the government had stipulated—and few weapons in any potential enemy's arsenal could reach that height. As a pilot of a B-17 would say in the years to come, "This was an airplane you could trust."

It was also badly needed. In June 1939 the United States had just under 2,500 total military aircraft in service, compared with Germany's 8,000 and Japan's 4,000. Eventually, as Fortresses began being produced by the thousands, the B-17 became almost every bomber pilot's object of desire. Jay Zeamer was no exception. His fascination with the B-17 remained sizable enough to need a tugboat escort.

WITH HIS OLD OUTFIT THE 43RD BOMB GROUP AND ITS B-17s LONG SINCE departed for New England, Jay resigned himself to flying B-26 Marauders out of Langley with the 22nd Bomb Group. Still, when the 22nd deployed on maneuvers—first to Texas, later to Georgia—he prowled the southern airbases seeking out Airmen who could teach him something, anything, about the Flying Fortress. He found most success among the maintenance crews. The wrench jockeys were accustomed to repairing and, on occasion, overhauling the planes, and some of them seemed to know even more than the flight crews about the aircraft's idiosyncrasies.

Jay was particularly curious to learn more about the latest version of the tachometric Norden bombsights just then being installed in Flying Fortresses. Before Joe Sarnoski had left for Maine, Jay remembered him practically swooning over the Norden's efficiency when the 43rd had been one of the first Bomb Groups to receive an early prototype of the Norden. Jay had been skeptical when Joe told him that the bombsight was so secret that the Army had instructed its bombardiers to use their .45-caliber handguns to destroy it in the event of a crash or ditch. He had since learned that this was indeed the case. The Norden bombsight was the kind of invention whose mechanical design would naturally captivate an M.I.T.-educated engineer.

The basic mechanics of the new bombsight, designed and developed by the Dutch engineer Carl Norden, had been around since World War I. But only recently had it been perfected to the point where the Army Air Corps had begun to boast of its ability to sink fast-moving ships, a valuable poker chip in the service's ongoing budget battles with the Navy. In the simplest terms, the key to the Norden's accuracy was a gyroscope-mounted analog computer that constantly calculated a bomb's trajectory based on current flight conditions. This allowed a bomber's autopilot to react quickly to changes in the wind and weather outside the plane and ensure greater accuracy.

As it happened, once aircraft equipped with the Norden were deployed in actual combat conditions, pilots and bombardiers discovered that the real-world vagaries of an enemy shooting back at them threw off several of the bombsight's calculations, and the precision of its targeting—

the "circular error probable"—enlarged from 75 feet to 1,200 feet. But for the moment, bombardiers who operated the Norden remained delighted by what they perceived as its pinpoint accuracy: Jay recalled how during those early beta missions out of Langley with the 43rd, Joe had been known to hone his aim by lobbing Hershey chocolate kisses onto his parents' farmstead after persuading his pilots to buzz the Pennsylvania property. His delighted siblings knew their brother was near whenever the sky rained candy.

Now, cozying up to ground crews while accompanying the 22nd on its southern deployments, Jay found his knowledge of the B-17's characteristics and quirks increasing well past his familiarity with the Norden. Sometimes he would invite the local maintenance boys to pile into one of the 22nd's old Bolos as payback for sharing their insights. Then, under the guise of "navigational training," he would take them up for a joyride or even ferry them to a nearby town to stand them to beers at a local tavern.

Once the 22nd returned to Langley, Jay got into the habit of flying to Boston on weekends with a passel of his new buddies, eager to show them his old college haunts. It was toward the end of one of these frolics when, nearly 6,000 miles away at just past seven a.m. local time, a different type of bomber pilot unobtrusively cruised his carrier-based torpedo plane down the leeward slope of the Koolau mountain range that formed the eastern shore of the Hawaiian island of Oahu. Banking west, the dive-bomber with the Rising Sun painted on its wings cruised over the remains of an ancient shield volcano called the Wai'anae as the sleepy city of Honolulu hove into view. When the aircraft approached Pearl Harbor its senior officer, a decorated commander in the Imperial Japanese Navy Air Service, counted 86 warships anchored in the snug lagoon, including eight battleships, the sum total of the American Pacific Fleet's battlewagons. To his consternation, the Japanese naval officer saw no aircraft carriers. Finally, as his aircraft swept over Hickam Airfield, he peeled back the canopy behind the pilot's seat and spun a green flare into the nearly cloudless sky.

Thirteen minutes later the dive-bomber's radio operator transmitted the code words "Tora! Tora! Tora!" The message was picked up by the 180 enemy aircraft trailing in his wake. Back in Japan, a fortunate confluence of weather and atmospherics allowed Adm. Yamamoto, the commander of the Imperial Japanese Navy's Combined Fleet and the mastermind behind the assault, to hear the signal for the attack.

DECEMBER 7, 1941, WAS A SUNNY, COLD SUNDAY AFTERNOON IN BOSTON, the temperature hovering just below freezing, when Jay lifted his Bolo into the air for the return trip to Langley. He was somewhere above Rhode Island when a news bulletin flashed over the radio. At first it was hard to decipher amid a loud buzz of crackling static, but when the Bolo's radio operator held a lead pencil near his signal gauge to boost the electronic arc the broadcast reception became clearer. Even at that Jay and his passengers could not digest it.

It was common knowledge among senior American military officers that the Japanese had for years been preparing for war. Tensions between the Empire and the United States had only heightened the previous summer when the Roosevelt administration imposed a trade embargo on Japan, denying the country in general and its Imperial Navy in particular vital oil shipments in a fruitless attempt to halt its march of aggression on China. But to someone like Jay the attack seemed unreal. He found it impossible to conceive that an island nation slightly smaller than the state of California had picked a fight with the United States. If he had been familiar with the term he probably would have agreed with the American ambassador to Tokyo, who called the prospect of war with America a form of "national harakiri."

But perhaps what stunned Jay the most was the decision by the Japanese to stage their initial assault at Pearl Harbor. It had been drilled into Airmen like Jay, as into the rest of the American public, that the naval base there was impregnable. Only a few months earlier a reporter for *Collier's* magazine had filed a story from "the fortress of the Hawaiian Archipelago," and that very adjective was used in the story's title—"Impregnable Pearl Harbor." Toward the end of his dispatch the author, a seasoned foreign correspondent named Walter Davenport, concluded, "You've got to be pretty pessimistic to envision any invader. Singly and in concert they'd come to swift grief where the Koolaus and the Waianaes rise starkly from the ocean. They'd have to sink our fleet and smash our last plane."

The Japanese came very close to doing just that. Within hours the simultaneous attacks on Oahu and the Philippines had sunk or badly damaged all eight American battleships (along with three cruisers and three destroyers) and knocked out an incredible 350 of the United States' 526 combat aircraft stationed in the Pacific.

Yet so ingrained was the idea of "impregnable Pearl Harbor" that Jay's lingering reaction was that this was a hoax similar to the alien invasion the actor and radio personality Orson Welles and his Mercury Theatre group had dramatized on Halloween three years earlier. The reality of the attack finally set in after Jay put down at Langley. Every vehicle attempting to leave the airbase was stopped at the flight line's exit gate, and each Airman was ordered to return to his squadron's hangar. Jay and his Bomb Group worked until midnight installing armored panels on their airplanes.

JAY DID NOT RETURN TO HIS QUARTERS JUST OFF LANGLEY UNTIL AFTER one a.m. He fell into bed, a million thoughts racing through his mind. His sleep was fitful, and when his telephone rang at three a.m. he nearly lurched for his sidearm. It was his squadron commander ordering him back to the airfield. The 22nd was deploying in two hours. Its destination was top secret. Jay threw his kit into a barracks bag, and by five a.m. he and the rest of the Bomb Group were in the air. His unit was not to return for years; some of Jay's comrades would never come back. A few weeks later his younger brother Jere picked up his car and drove it back to New Jersey.

Once aloft the Airmen were told that their destination was California. Jay, in the copilot's seat of his Marauder, was crossing the Mississippi

River when President Franklin Roosevelt's clipped voice broke the radio silence. The crew fell silent as Roosevelt intoned his famous phrase about the date, as the president put it, which would live in infamy. By the time his plane vaulted the Rockies and touched down at Muroc Dry Lake in the Great Basin of the Mojave, America was officially at war. The following day the 22nd took its first casualties when its commanding officer and his entire crew were killed when their B-26 crashed during takeoff. It would not be the last time, Jay wrote, that it struck him that the Roman poet had been mistaken. Though he could understand the *decorum* in *pro patria mori*, the *dulce* of the sacrifice eluded him.

6

THE WINDS OF WAR

OVER THE NEXT SEVERAL WEEKS THE 22ND BOMB GROUP'S PLANES ROSE from the desert each morning to vector low over the Pacific coast of Southern California and northern Mexico in search of Japanese submarines. As December progressed there was the occasional all-points alert—Point Conception shelled by a Japanese submarine; a lumber vessel torpedoed outside Long Beach Harbor; another merchantman damaged by one of the nine enemy submarines that had taken up positions along America's West Coast.*

---

* A simultaneous shelling of San Diego, Los Angeles, and San Francisco by all nine enemy boats scheduled for Christmas Eve, 1941, was canceled at the last moment after Japan's Imperial General Command deemed the assault too risky, owing to the American Navy's intensifying antisubmarine efforts.

Most of the flight crews felt the screening runs were a waste of time, effort, and aviation fuel. Bombardiers often dropped their ordnance on anything that looked like an enemy sub running just below the surface. Most of the Airmen believed they were actually targeting whales.

Jay and his fellow Airmen were housed by squadron in canvas pyramid tents set up in the Mojave, four officers to one billet, six enlisted men to another. The desert was a mélange of odd weather, and it was not unusual to wake to a blanket of snow being washed away by a hard winter rain that in turn ushered in wind gusts that kicked up a breathtaking sandstorm. Jay did remark, though, that he had never before seen such beautiful sunrises and sunsets. Meanwhile, as one long daylight flight rolled into another, Jay came to recognize the dusty contours and landmarks of the Baja peninsula by heart. He feared that this could be his home indefinitely—that he could be "left on the beach," in the military parlance of the era—while other Airmen were shipping off to fight. Worse, to Jay's everlasting disgust, he was still "frozen" in the copilot's seat.

The ennui he felt was relieved toward the end of December when the 22nd was issued new wool and leather clothing and transferred to the Sacramento Air Depot. There the men were ordered to disassemble and crate their bombers for shipment from San Francisco via two separate convoys which would carry the Group's ground personnel directly to Australia while the planes and their crews sailed for Hawaii. Most of the officers were peeved that the unit's new commanding officer, Col. Dwight Divine, refused to permit them to install temporary fuel tanks in their Marauders in order to make the 2,500-mile jump to Hickam Field. But someone up the chain of command had decided that since the 22nd had never trained with extra fuel tanks it was safer to deploy the aircraft by ship. Soon enough, however, the 22nd's Airmen would get their chance to fly long distances over the endless Pacific.

The early days of 1942 were a perilous time for the Allies. Guam, Malaysia, and the rich oil fields of the Dutch East Indies had already fallen.

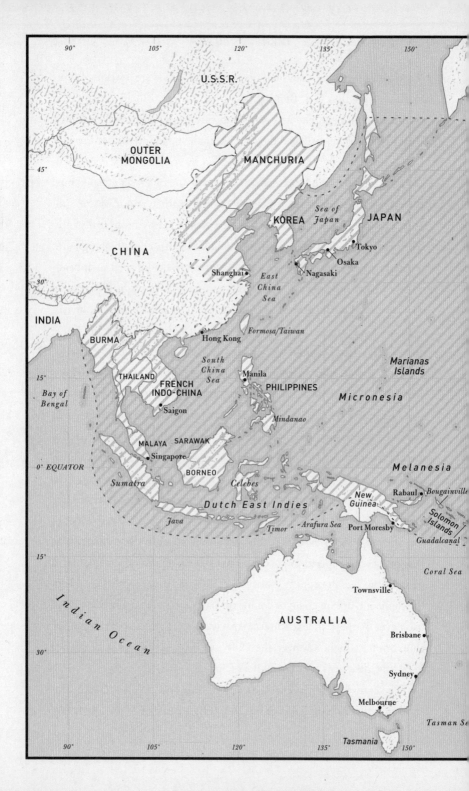

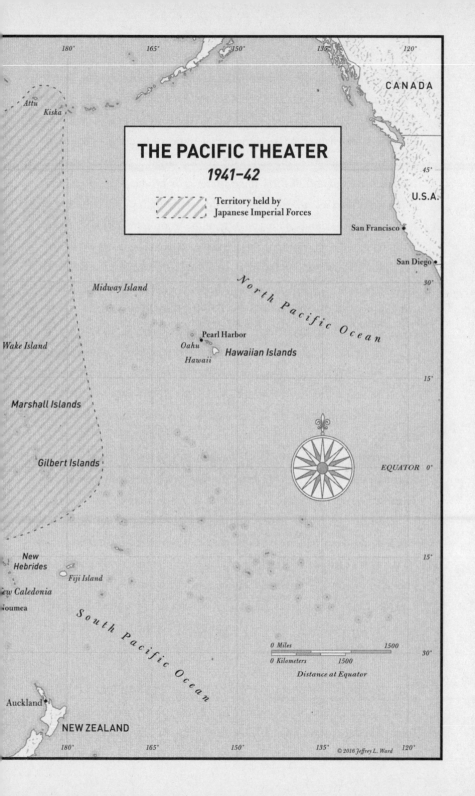

180°   165°   150°   135°   120°

CANADA

THE PACIFIC THEATER
1941–42

///// Territory held by
Japanese Imperial Forces

Attu
Kiska

U.S.A.

45°

San Francisco •

San Diego •

30°

Midway Island

North Pacific Ocean

Wake Island

Pearl Harbor
Oahu Hawaiian Islands
Hawaii

15°

Marshall Islands

Gilbert Islands

EQUATOR 0°

15°

New
Hebrides

Fiji Island

ew Caledonia

oumea

South Pacific Ocean

0 Miles   1500

0 Kilometers   1500

30°

Distance at Equator

Auckland •

NEW ZEALAND

180°   165°   150°   135°   120°

© 2016 Jeffrey L. Ward

In a few short weeks the banner of the Rising Sun would fly over 30 million square miles, about 15 percent of the earth's surface, from steamy Burmese jungles to snowbound Aleutian Islands to tropical Papua New Guinea. It was from the last of these that Imperial forces planned to invade and conquer Australia before turning the might of their war machine toward the mainland of the United States. For Jay, however, these concepts were abstract at best. He had only one thought on the morning of February 8 as he climbed the gangway of the troop transport USS *Grant* bobbing in the cool waters of San Francisco Bay: at last he would be seeing action. Below him, on the piers, men hugged and kissed sweethearts and wives, some hastily married only hours before; many no doubt were wondering if they would ever see the Golden Gate Bridge again.

Precisely 76 years earlier, Jay's grandfather Jeremiah had also stood at a ship's rail, not far from this San Francisco pier, likely contemplating his journey much as his grandson was now. It had taken Jeremiah nearly a year to reach California from Pennsylvania. He'd worked in the farm fields in what was then the far west of Illinois, and followed the Platte River by wagon train through the Indian Territory of Nebraska and up and over the Colorado Rockies. Jeremiah had passed through the new Mormon enclave fanning out from the big Salt Lake and traversed the Nevada Territory by stage. He'd paused at Virginia City to cut wood to replenish his grubstake before hopping an old side-wheeler down the Sacramento River and across the bay to San Francisco. And then when he'd finally reached his destination, he decided to return to Pennsylvania after all. He wanted to go home. Home was where Jeremiah's heart was.

Not Jay. For while Jeremiah had looked east to home and family, Jay's gaze was focused west. West to Hawaii, and from there to wherever the winds of war would take him.

THE USS *GRANT*—IRONICALLY, ORIGINALLY A GERMAN OCEAN LINER seized by the United States during WWI—was part of a small convoy that took eight days to steam the 2,300 miles to Hawaii. Three destroyers provided security for the line of ships, the gunboats zigzagging from port to starboard and back again on the lookout for Japanese submarines. Despite one false alarm—an Airman on a seaplane tender reported seeing a torpedo wake—the voyage was uneventful, consisting mainly of boat drills, queuing for inoculations, and endless card games and chess matches.

Jay thought he had battled rough seas off the coast of New England in his little dinghy, but he was not prepared for an ocean voyage across the Pacific. He often found himself squeezed between squad mates at the ship's rail, contemplating the Spam sandwiches served morning, noon, and night as the men regurgitated them into the sea. Finally, on the morning of February 15, the Airmen awoke to the sight of lush, cloud-crowned mountains rising on the western horizon. Within hours the *Grant* was steaming past the fabled cliffs of Diamond Head.

Jay and his fellow fliers were naturally excited—most of the men had never ventured out of their hometowns before, much less beyond America's shores. When they reached Oahu, however, their elation was numbed by the breadth and depth of destruction still in evidence. Even with newspapers back home heavily censored since the Pearl Harbor attack, it proved impossible to keep secret the full story of the devastation. Still, it was one thing to hear the scuttlebutt and quite another to see Hickam Field's smashed hangar line, the rooftops torn away, and the hundreds of shell holes that still pocked the landscape. The flight lines at Hickam Field remained littered with piles of bulldozed wreckage. Most alarming to Jay was the sight of the 151 army aircraft either badly damaged or completely destroyed on the ground during the surprise attack. None of the 22nd's Airmen were allowed near Pearl Harbor itself, where six of the eight burned and battered battleships were still being repaired and refitted.

It took some time for the Bomb Group's Marauders to be uncrated, reassembled, and flight-tested, and meanwhile Jay and his squadron took shifts flying both day and night patrols in a fleet of B-18 Bolos. They flew into and out of the army's nearby Bellows Field, whose dusty facilities reminded Jay a little too much of the base back at Muroc Dry Lake. Some of these reconnaissance flights lasted over 10 hours, the time it took to circumnavigate the island chain on the lookout for any sign of the Japanese. Jay had become accustomed to the speedy B-26s, so the Bolos struck him as lumbering and plodding. Some aircrews even experimented with waxing their fuselages, wings, and tails to see if that would add a few miles per hour to their airspeed. It did not.

Jay, who had been promoted to captain by this point, was billeted with the other officers of the Bomb Group in a tent camp adjacent to Hickam Field and later in barracks whose broken windows had been boarded up and whose walls remained pocked by machine-gun bullets. Their days were spent in makeshift classrooms where a succession of instructors drilled them in lesson plans ranging from aircraft and ship silhouette recognition to the geography of the South Pacific. Although they were officially kept in the dark about their next deployment, it was hard to miss the hints that the topograhy instructors offered when they placed particular emphasis on recognizing landmarks scattered about the Solomon Islands and the Bismarck Archipelago.

When Jay was not on submarine patrol or attending class, one of his favorite haunts was the base's pistol range, where ammunition for his .45-caliber sidearm was plentiful and free. He spent his off-duty nights playing cards and chess or viewing the Army training films shown nightly on-base. A treat was the occasional trip to the local movie house, which ran a steady string of B movie westerns. He managed to reach his parents several times through the base's telephone exchange, and one day he wangled a pass to visit Honolulu and Waikiki Beach, which had been strewn with barbed wire to protect against a Japanese invasion. He watched with great amusement as local surfers shimmied with their boards under the wire to ride the waves.

One highlight of the Bomb Group's stay in Hawaii came on February 24, when a shipment of beer and liquor arrived at the officers club. It was the first such delivery, Jay was told, since December 7. But the raucous celebration that followed was tempered by the news trickling out of the Philippines 5,000 miles to the west.

Prior to the attack on Pearl Harbor, strategists in the U.S. War Department had expected Japan's first strike against American interests to be on the Philippines, where the United States had maintained sovereignty since the Spanish-American War. Eleven days before the assault on Pearl, on November 27, Army Chief of Staff Gen. Marshall had even warned his forces at Manila, "Negotiations with Japan appear to be terminated to all practical purposes . . . hostile actions possible at any moment." To that effect Gen. Douglas MacArthur had been called out of retirement to organize the defense of the island chain and had immediately petitioned for, and been granted, a flotilla of over 225 American aircraft, including 33 B-17s, to beat back the expected Japanese invasion. This air fleet was, in the words of Gen. Marshall, the greatest concentration of heavy bomber strength anywhere in the world.

This did not stop the Japanese from invading the Philippines on December 8. Many of the veterans in Jay's 22nd Bomb Group had friends among the flight crews operating those Philippines-based bombers, and despite the Army's attempts at censorship, they were well aware of MacArthur's dire straits. What did come as a surprise was how quickly the Allied defenses across the Pacific crumbled. When the 22nd had departed from San Francisco, the British still occupied the vaunted "Fortress Singapore"—the "Gibraltar of the East," it was called—and the rump end of MacArthur's army was still holding out on Corregidor, an island in the mouth of Manila Bay. Singapore fell on the very day Jay's Bomb Group disembarked at Honolulu Harbor, and rumors swirled about MacArthur's imminent demise.

The unofficial military grapevine had it that even as MacArthur was transferring half a million dollars into his American bank account as a "reward" from Philippines President Manuel Quezon for his defense of the islands,* nearly 100,000 American and Filipino soldiers were fighting a doomed rearguard action across the Bataan peninsula. MacArthur had visited those troops precisely once in the interim, and they in turn had bequeathed him the disdainful nickname "Dugout Doug." Those who were captured and survived the notorious Bataan Death March offered harsher epithets.

In Hawaii, it was impossible for Jay and the others to ignore the reports that even some members of the general's own officer staff were put off by MacArthur's egocentricity. In his definitive biography, *American Caesar*, the historian William Manchester makes the telling observation that of the 142 communiqués dispatched by the general during the first three months of the war, 109 mentioned but one soldier: Douglas MacArthur. And after MacArthur escaped from Corregidor, he wrote to his starving subordinates still in the field in the Philippines, "If food fails, you will prepare and execute an attack on the enemy." This was too much for Gen. William Brougher, who complained to what was left of his staff that the order was a "foul trick of deception played on a large group of Americans by a commander-in-chief and his small staff who are now eating steak and eggs in Australia."

Naturally, Jay and his fellow Airmen of the 22nd followed intently the fate of their brethren under MacArthur's command. They were astounded to learn that during the first 48 hours of fighting across the Philippines, half of MacArthur's bombers and three quarters of his fighter planes had been destroyed—most while sitting on the ground. Particularly troubling to Jay was the fate of the 16 Flying Fortresses stationed at Clark Airfield on the island of Luzon. The planes constituted half of the 19th Bomb Group's fleet in the Philippines; the remainder, hangared farther south on Mindanao, had managed to escape to Australia's Port Darwin.

In the early hours of the invasion the Luzon B-17s had been ordered into the air without bombs to escape the fate of the American aircraft at Pearl Harbor that were caught defenseless on the ground. But when the

* Which was true.

expected Japanese air attacks on Clark Field were delayed by weather, the Fortresses had landed to refuel and, on MacArthur's direct orders, their crews went off duty for lunch. Moments later three waves of Imperial bombers arrived over Luzon, annihilating every Fortress.

As Jay patrolled for submarines off the Hawaiian coast in his lumbering old Bolo, the thought of those beautiful B-17s exploding in a pyrotechnic display as they sat defenseless before their hangars was almost too much for him to bear. So much for "the greatest concentration of heavy bomber strength anywhere in the world."

HALF A WORLD AWAY, JOE SARNOSKI HAD MORE IMMEDIATE MATTERS ON his mind as the converted steamship SS *Argentina* bobbed and groaned through a cyclone in the Indian Ocean. Two months earlier, while still stationed in Bangor, Maine, the 43rd Bomb Group had received a belated Christmas present—they were going to war somewhere in the Pacific. Some of the men, including Joe, found this odd. The 43rd had been hunting U-boats in the Atlantic since the onset of the war, and common sense dictated that they would eventually be folded into the 8th Air Force in England. But as one of Joe's fellow bombardiers noted, "Nothing in this war hardly ever makes any sense," and throughout January 1942 the Group gathered and crated its gear, with its deployment scheduled to be made in stages. A part of the Group's flight echelon had traveled to the West Coast, from where selected pilots and flight crews were assigned new B-17s to fly to Hawaii. Others, including Joe and all the Group's ground personnel, would sail from the East Coast. Joe's 403rd Squadron was chosen as the vanguard.

The 403rd traveled by train from Bangor to New York and sailed from New York Harbor on January 23 aboard the *Argentina*,* one of the larg-

---

* Four years later nearly to the day, on January 26, 1946, the *Argentina* would sail from Southampton, England, to New York carrying the first official contingent of 452 English war brides, 30 of them pregnant, and one war groom. The transport acquired several nicknames, including "The Diaper Run" and "Operation Mother-in-Law."

est and fastest vessels plying the New York–South America routes before being requisitioned by the government's War Shipping Administration and refitted into a troop carrier. Elements of the 43rd's three remaining squadrons—the 63rd, 64th, and 65th—were scheduled to depart about a month later from New York on the French liner *Normandie*.

The *Argentina* had been repainted a dull camouflage gray and designated the flagship of a seven-ship convoy capable of transporting 22,000 American troops. Its berths and suites, originally designed for 200 passengers, were reconfigured to carry well over a thousand men as well as over 200 tons of cargo. The 13-year-old steamship's first-class cabins had been reserved for officers, so Joe's home aboard for the next 35 days was a poorly ventilated second-class stateroom around which rows of triple-decker bunks fitted out with thin, lumpy mattresses were arranged like stacked tins of sardines. He slept with his barracks bag and an old Enfield rifle he'd been issued jammed under his bunk, and the only water to wash in was salt water sucked up from the ocean—freshwater was reserved for drinking. Because the American Airmen were well familiar with the frequent and deadly German submarine activity up and down America's East Coast, not much sleep was to be had as the vessel zigzagged south.

The mess room, one Airman wrote, "was like slopping the hogs," and whatever mystery meat constituted the hot meals—Joe could never quite figure it out—was plopped into their camp bowls from a huge metal pot. At first Joe tried to stick to the equally tasteless baloney and Spam, but soon came to rely almost exclusively on bread and jam. He just wished he had peanut butter to go with it.

Every Airman was expected to work during the voyage. Lookout positions were the prime assignments, drawn by selective servicemen who kept a constant watch for periscopes. Joe drew garbage duty. Since the convoy could not take the chance that an enemy sub might run across their debris slick, every evening just past dusk the loudspeakers would blare that it was safe to dump trash overboard. Joe knew enough about fish from his days of putting food on the family table to assume that there were great schools of sharks following them and feasting on their leavings. He would have liked to see that, but he couldn't. Each night the *Argentina* sailed under strict blackout conditions, with no lights on deck, all portholes covered, and lit cigarettes forbidden.

No one knew where the ship was heading. If the Airmen tried to pry information out of the Merchant Marines working belowdecks the answers would range from a noncommittal grunt to a knifelike finger drawn across a throat. The *Argentina* made refueling and resupply stops somewhere in Florida—Joe guessed Miami—and then at Cape Town, where they'd taken on mutton carcasses "stacked like cord wood." No one was allowed on deck, much less off the ship, during the layovers.

At some point in the mid-Atlantic they had crossed the equator, and the event kicked off an initiation rite. Joe and the rest of the novice "Shellbacks" were summoned topside and addressed by a deckhand carrying a makeshift trident and decked out in the crown and cape of King Neptune. At the end of his short welcoming speech each Airman was handed an "Ancient Order of the Deep" certificate attesting to the crossing. But any gods of the sea had saved the worst for last, as the rough weather in the Indian Ocean had the big liner rolling like a toy boat in shore surf. The only consolation was that by this point their anxiety over their destination had been eased; they were all fairly certain that it was Australia.

As part of his garbage duty Joe had been assigned to a kitchen police detail, which seemed to consist of washing every tin dish and cup that had ever been cast. Joe was no stranger to what he called "the dreaded KP," as he'd pulled the duty many times both at Langley and in Bangor. Now, however, as he dipped what felt like the millionth dirty cup into a tub of soapy salt water, he wondered if this was any way to fight a war. Within weeks he would have to wonder no more.

7

THE JAPANESE CITADEL

IT WAS NOT LONG AFTER THE FEBRUARY BEER BASH AT HICKAM FIELD when Col. Divine summoned Jay Zeamer and the other officers of the 22nd Bomb Group to a rare night briefing. They were assembled in a large classroom and, after being sworn to secrecy, given their flight orders. Their destination: Brisbane, Australia, via an island-hopping route that included refueling stops at Palmyra, Canton (Kanton), Fiji, and New Caledonia. Each man was handed a notebook containing Navy charts of the route—magnetic headings, distances, latitude, and longitude. The 22nd would be the first medium bomb group to fly across the Pacific and at this point in the war radio communications and navigation aids in that part of the world were virtually nonexistent. The pilots were also ordered to maintain radio silence unless they became separated and lost, in which case they were to use the command radio system to request "Lost Plane Procedure."

Over the next few weeks, 57 B-26 Martin Marauders lifted off from Hawaii in various stages to begin the six-day, 4,700-mile journey to Brisbane. Fifty-one arrived safely. Jay had seen men die in training mishaps before, the causes ranging from pilot error to equipment failure to sudden storms. Indeed, his first commanding officer and that officer's entire crew were one of the estimated 400 Army Air Force flight crews who would be lost to accidents over the course of World War II. But six bombers in one journey? Jay knew many of those men. He had shared beers with them, played cards with them, bitched with them. And now his outfit, yet to see a bullet fly, counted half-a-hundred dead. It was small consolation that the 22nd had become the first complete American Air Group to reach Australia. It was also a harbinger.

Only weeks before Jay landed in Brisbane, Gen. MacArthur had also alighted on Australian soil from the Philippines. As Jay would rapidly learn, if to err is human, to blame it on someone else was military politics. This was a strategy at which MacArthur apparently excelled. Australian newspapers, which many of the guileless American Airmen were surprised to find printed in English, trumpeted the story of MacArthur and his "Bataan Gang" being escorted off the Adelaide express train in Melbourne with the all the pomp reserved for a conquering hero. And in fact when MacArthur set up his headquarters in the city's swank Menzies Hotel, he bore the official title of the U.S. Army's Supreme Commander in the Far East.

Despite his famous promise to the Philippine people—"I came through, and I shall return"—his primary goal for the foreseeable future was the defense of Australia and New Zealand. "Hold Hawaii; Support Australia; Drive Northward" became the War Department's slogan. Unfortunately, the general had few troops with which to fulfill the mandate. So he was left to swanning about the antipodes in his garrison cap and khaki blouse holding press conferences, giving speeches to the Australian parliament, and making scores of radio broadcasts; a "Hero on Ice" in the words of a *Time* magazine headline writer.

If Jay and his fellow fliers' ardor for their new boss was somewhat less than enthusiastic, their feelings were not shared back in the States. For it was MacArthur's relentless self-promotion, aided not a little by the delight the Axis powers took in ridiculing his retreat from the Philippines, that prompted Congress to award him the Medal of Honor.* This made MacArthur and his father, Arthur, a Civil War hero, the only father and son to have received the nation's most prestigious military award. The general nonetheless stewed incessantly over his failure to be appointed supreme commander of the entire Pacific Theater. It was not for the Army's lack of trying.

As early as October 1941, two months prior to the attack on Pearl Harbor, Army Chief of Staff Gen. Marshall recommended to Secretary of War Henry Stimson that MacArthur be appointed the "Eastern Ike" and given overall authority over the American land, sea, and air forces in the Pacific. Marshall's proposal was rejected outright by the bluff and ornery Adm. Ernest J. King, chief of U.S. Naval Operations. King argued that the Navy had been preparing for two decades to wage war against Japan, and unlike the great land battles certain to be fought against the Nazis in North Africa and Europe, combat in the Pacific Theater would be primarily a naval and air campaign. He hated the idea of an Army general dictating orders to his admirals.

Thus in Washington's corridors of power a compromise was reached. MacArthur was designated Commander in Chief of the Pacific Ocean Areas west of the 160th meridian—Australia, New Guinea, and most important to the general, the Philippines—while Adm. Chester Nimitz would lead all U.S. forces stationed east of that line. Since there were so

---

* According to William Manchester's *American Caesar*, Hitler's Minister of Information Joseph Goebbels dubbed MacArthur the "fleeing general," while the Italian prime minister Benito Mussolini publicly labeled him a "coward." Manchester also reports that the "Jappie" radio propagandist Tokyo Rose predicted that MacArthur would one day be publicly hanged in Tokyo's Imperial Plaza for his perfidy.

few ground troops under MacArthur's command—of the 25,000 Americans in Australia, the vast majority were Airmen—for the moment any military objectives would have to be accomplished with airpower. This presented another major issue. MacArthur had no use for the officer whom the War Department had recently placed in charge of the Army's Far East Air Force, Gen. George Brett.

MacArthur well knew that Brett was a member of the Army's aviation contingent who were critical of the way he had handled both the Philippines debacle and his subsequent ignominious escape.[*] This "insult" to the Supreme Commander festered, and a full-blown feud developed when MacArthur discovered that while he was stranded on Corregidor, Brett had argued against sending any more supplies to his fighters on Bataan, considering the peninsula campaign a lost cause. In retaliation MacArthur confided to his aides that he was "disgusted with the unaggressiveness (sic) and disharmony manifest in the leadership of the American-Australian air organization in the Southwest Pacific Area."

The two generals' mutual enmity reached its breaking point when MacArthur learned that Brett had thoroughly ingratiated himself with Australia's politicians and service chiefs, who had unanimously recommended that Brett, and not MacArthur, be chosen to lead the Southwest Pacific Force. Thereafter MacArthur snubbed most of Brett's frequent requests for strategic and operational meetings, while instructing his chief of staff to fire off derogatory "eyes only" memos to Washington questioning the competence of his Air Force chief.

It was into these dual conflicts—the one against a surging enemy, the

---

[*] According to Bruce Gamble's authoritative *Fortress Rabaul*, after fleeing Corregidor to the island of Mindanao by PT boat with his retinue, including his wife Jean and his young son Arthur's Chinese amah, MacArthur was incensed with Brett for dispatching only one "rickety" B-17 to transport him to Australia. He fired off vitriolic communiqués to both Brett and Gen. Marshall in Washington demanding that they send the Army's three best planes to retrieve him.

other an intramural affair between MacArthur and Brett—that Jay and his 22nd Bomb Group put wheels down in Brisbane, each man seeking to begin to take his own personal revenge for Pearl Harbor.

DESPITE THE CONTINUED INFIGHTING BETWEEN MACARTHUR AND HIS AIR chief, the second and third tenets of the War Department's "Hold Hawaii; Support Australia; Drive Northward" strategy remained the Supreme Commander's priority. This, in essence and reality, meant securing Port Moresby, the lightly defended Australian base rising from the Gulf of Papua on the southwestern tip of New Guinea. The town, the Allies' only holding within air range of the Japanese bastion at Rabaul 500 miles away, boasted several airstrips as well as an excellent anchorage for Australia's few American-made Catalina flying boats.

The Japanese Imperial Command, however, also studied geography, and had scouted Port Moresby rigorously. Aware that the entire town was defended by a mere seven anti-aircraft guns and a scattering of Lewis machine guns, they bombed the base with impunity. These air raids became immeasurably more efficient in mid-March when, as MacArthur was still organizing his staff in Melbourne, Japanese troops landed at Lae* and Salamaua on New Guinea's northeast coast and captured both Australian bases virtually unopposed.

The loss of Lae in particular was a devastating blow. Enemy construction battalions rapidly transformed the prewar facilities, including the anchorage on the Huon Gulf, into a major airbase that the Imperial Command envisioned as a hub from which companies of infantry could spread into the island's interior. In a bizarre development, men of German stock posing as missionaries had laid the groundwork for these incursions by

---

* The port hamlet of Lae had been in the news five years earlier when the American aviatrix Amelia Earhart was last seen lifting off from its airstrip during her attempt to become the first woman to circumnavigate the globe by air. After departing from Lae for Howland Island, Earhart was never seen or heard from again.

circulating among the villages of northern New Guinea and encouraging the Papuans to welcome the Japanese as liberators, going so far as to teach and encourage the Nazi salute. Many natives volunteered as guides and porters for the newcomers. Those who did not, and could not manage to take refuge in the jungle, were rounded up and forced on to work gangs.

Meanwhile, as Imperial forces solidified their toehold on New Guinea, back in Washington the "Chief" of the Army Air Force, Gen. Hap Arnold, commissioned a trusted subordinate to undertake a secret fact-finding mission to Australia to assess the working relationship between MacArthur and Brett. The results were disheartening, if predictable. Arnold's man returned with a blunt report—their association was untenable. More important, it was hampering the war effort. One of them, he suggested, had to go. He doubted that Arnold planned to relieve MacArthur.

It was amid this complex arithmetic of war that the 22nd Bomb Group accustomed itself to evading enemy fighter planes over the Coral and Bismarck Seas and to dodging anti-aircraft fire in the skies above Lae and Salamaua. Yet as perilous as these missions would prove to Jay and his fellow Airmen, there was nothing that could prepare them for their bombing runs on the enemy's strongest redoubt, the Japanese-held town of Rabaul. For the Americans, even the name came loaded with awe and dread.

ON JANUARY 22, A MONTH BEFORE JAY'S ARRIVAL IN AUSTRALIA, 5,000 troops from the Imperial South Seas Force had executed a night landing on the crescent-shaped island of New Britain, the largest landmass in the Bismarck Archipelago. They were the first military units in Japan's history to cross the equator. Within hours they had overrun a small Australian garrison and seized the capital of Rabaul on the island's northern tip.*

---

* There is an adage in war that defeat and collapse are not the same. This was evidenced by one of the final radio messages received at Royal Australian Army headquarters in Melbourne from its commander in Rabaul as the Japanese approached the town. "*Nos morituri te salutamus*," he wrote—"We who are about to die salute you"—the phrase used by doomed Roman gladiators about to enter the arena.

Australia had administered the Bismarcks, a former German territory, since the conclusion of World War I under a League of Nations mandate. This mandate included a portion of what would become the country of Papua New Guinea as well as hundreds of atolls and islands dotting the Western Pacific. Some were mere specks of coral in the ocean, others home to thriving port towns. But Rabaul, with its two airstrips and large, natural harbor, was the strategic jewel in the crown.

Rising a mere 300 miles across the Bismarck Sea from New Guinea, Rabaul had been chosen by Tokyo as the ideal site from which to commence the campaign to extend the Empire's southern perimeter. On paper these expansion plans were simplicity itself—after securing Rabaul, Imperial troops would next seize control of the green puzzle of the Solomon Islands and New Guinea, then make landings on New Caledonia, Fiji, and Samoa. But the key to the entire enterprise was Rabaul. The town's deep anchorage, capable of handling up to 300,000 tons of shipping at one time, would be the hub from which the ferocious spokes of Nippon's South Seas Force would emanate. Then, with supply lines between the United States and Australia severed, the encircled southern continent would be eliminated as a military threat and ripe for invasion.

The Japanese high command, intoxicated by the ease with which its military machine had already conquered wide swaths of Asia, was confident in this South Seas campaign to the point of hubris. Yet wiser heads, particularly keen strategists such as Adm. Yamamoto, recognized that global conflict often tended to overturn the rosiest predictions. Prior to December 7, Yamamoto had suspected that the attack on Pearl Harbor would awaken a sleeping giant, and weeks after the strike he had written to a cousin, "The first stage of operations will, I am sure, prove no trouble; the real outcome will be determined after that, in the second stage. I wonder if we will have the men of ability to carry this through?"

Yamamoto had gone so far as to advise the Imperial General Command that if an armistice with the United States could not be reached by eighteen months into the war, Japan itself—heretofore "an octopus

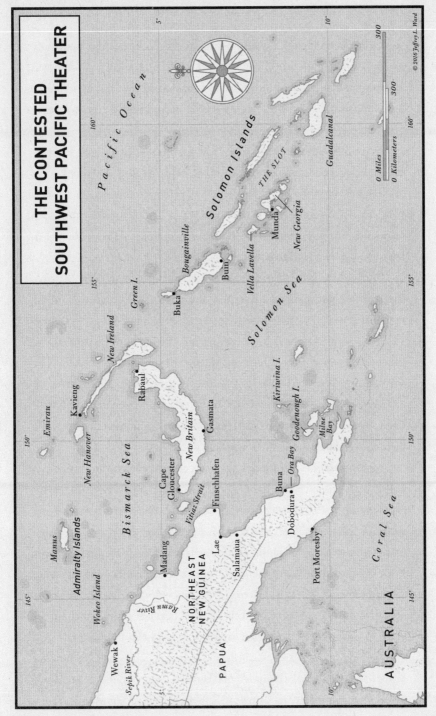

THE CONTESTED
SOUTHWEST PACIFIC THEATER

© 2016 Jeffrey L. Ward

Pacific Ocean

Solomon Islands

Guadalcanal

THE SLOT

Munda

New Georgia

Vella Lavella

Solomon Sea

Buin

Bougainville

Buka

Green I.

New Ireland

Kavieng

Rabaul

New Britain

Gasmata

Emirau

New Hanover

Bismarck Sea

Cape
Gloucester

Vitiaz Strait

Finschhafen

Manus

Admiralty Islands

Woleo Island

Madang

Lae

Salamaua

NORTHEAST
NEW GUINEA

Ramu River

Wewak

Sepik River

PAPUA

Port Moresby

Buna

Dobodura

Ora Bay

Goodenough I.

Kiriwina I.

Milne
Bay

Coral Sea

AUSTRALIA

0 Miles   300
0 Kilometers   300

spreading its tentacles"—would be in danger. So it was that Yamamoto and a few like-minded thinkers recognized that Rabaul's capture was as important to Japan as a defensive maneuver as it was as an offensive base. Specifically, Rabaul served as a bulwark against America's heavy bombers.

Since 1940 the Imperial Navy had berthed its Combined Fleet either in homeland waters or at the atoll of Truk, roughly 700 miles north of New Britain in the Caroline Islands. America's long-range B-17s and twin-tailed B-24 Liberators could not reach Truk from the Australian mainland. But they could from Rabaul's two airstrips. With Rabaul in Japanese hands, that threat was eliminated.

Situated a steamy five degrees south of the equator, New Britain's capital city—the name Rabaul means "the place of the mangroves" in the native Melanesian language—rests atop a rare seismic fault geologists call a ring fracture, essentially a subterranean kettle of churning magma that causes the ground to tremble with small earthquakes almost daily. The surrounding terrain is pocked with active fissures and fumaroles that emit a steady flux of noxious gases and steam, and units from the South Seas Force had even used the light from a minor volcanic eruption to guide them into Rabaul during their invasion.

But these modern eruptions paled in comparison with an event some 1,400 years earlier, when the magma blew through its fragile planetary capstone of earth and rock with such ferocity that every human being within a 30-mile radius was killed instantly. The explosion, recorded half a world away in the chronicles of the reign of the Byzantine Emperor Justinian I, rivaled that of the more famous Krakatoa six centuries later. All that remained after the discharge was an empty bowl on the northern tip of New Britain. It was into this caldera, 600 feet deep and about 20 miles in circumference, that seawater poured. The thumb-shaped body of water, three times larger than Pearl Harbor, is encircled by a serrated series of ridges and hills denuded of all growth and composed of both active and extinct volcanoes rising to 1,600 feet. Named Simpson Harbour by a self-aggrandizing nineteenth-century English sea captain, it was the finest deepwater anchorage in the Southwest Pacific Theater.

Within weeks of their landings the Japanese, exhibiting the terrifying thoroughness that much of the world was only beginning to confront, had transformed Rabaul into their most formidable advance base, surpassing even Truk. Naval engineers ringed Simpson Harbour with a series of modern wharves, piers, and coaling jetties extending into the anchorage's inner and outer bays, and laced its eastern entrance to the sea with a complex skein of underwater obstacles designed to obstruct enemy landing craft.

Simultaneously, native slave labor and more than 1,000 captured Australian soldiers and civilians were put to work repairing the town's two airfields that had been damaged during the softening-up bombings prior to the invasion. Scores of three-sided blast walls, or revetments, were erected to protect parked aircraft at Lakunai airdrome, a grass strip that bisected a finger of land separating Simpson Harbour from a smaller inlet called Matupit Harbour. As Lakunai was only long enough to accommodate fighter planes, across the harbor and farther south the runway at the larger Vunakanau airdrome was lengthened, widened, and paved with concrete. This was in anticipation of the arrival of several squadrons of land-based Mitsubishi G4M bombers—designated "Bettys" by the Allies—which had previously sown terror over China, Java, and the Philippines. Storage buildings, barracks, and another 150 revetments sprang up around the Vunakanau strip.

East of town, units of Imperial Army troops moved to improve and expand the primitive network of roads crosshatching the Gazelle Peninsula, guarding the harbor's mouth. They continued, brutally and illegally, to work to death the Australian prisoners of war euphemistically labeled "special details." The POWs considered too weak to continue on the labor gangs, accompanied by healthy captives singled out to pay for Allied bombings, were trucked to a garbage dump near the foot of the active volcano Mount Tavurvur. There they were forced to dig their own graves in the soft ash and pumice before being shot, bayoneted, or, depending on the whim of the detail's commanding officer, beheaded with katana swords. The graves were then backfilled by natives.*

At the same time, some 200 miles away on New Britain's southern coast, an Imperial Navy landing force secured the village of Gasmata, which had a smaller grass airstrip. There, engineers upgraded the runway to serve as a relay site between the island and the Japanese bases soon to rise on New Guinea's northern shores. A radar installation was also installed at Gasmata to act as an early warning system against Allied bombers en route to Rabaul.

Nearly overnight the once sleepy port town of less than a square mile took on the semblance of a modern citadel. All told, the Japanese tripled the number of existing structures, and the military complex that mushroomed around the wide boulevards and steep side streets extending from Simpson Harbour would grow to include four airfields, barracks for more than 100,000 troops, and scores of administrative buildings, hangars, machine shops, sawmills, armories, and fuel depots. This renovation included what were regarded as three of the "fanciest brothels east of the Netherlands Indies," staffed with over 500 Korean and Formosan "comfort women."

The antiquated Royal Australian Air Force had begun making bombing runs on Rabaul mere days after its capture, primarily with a tiny fleet of lumbering, American-made PBY Catalina flying boats. These raids had so far proved ineffectual. But the Imperial General Command could hardly fail to recognize that the base Japan was remaking on New Britain would be America's top target in the Pacific once the United States established an air presence in Australia. Thus nearly 400 anti-aircraft guns

---

* The same fate befell scores of American and Australian aviators forced to bail out over New Britain. These executed Airmen included the B-17 pilot and Medal of Honor recipient Capt. Harl Pease—the pilot who had flown to Mindanao the original "rickety" B-17 that had so enraged the retreating Gen. MacArthur.

were emplaced around the harbor, including dozens of 75-millimeter 88s and 80-millimeter 99s, whose shells could reach an altitude of almost 30,000 feet. These big guns were complemented by interspersed batteries of rapid-fire cannons, howitzers, mortars, and heavy machine guns, all positioned so that their kill zones, like the town's radar installations, overlapped. This, in theory, created a protective 360-degree cocoon that could cover the entire sky. The Japanese would need it. Soon.

AT PRECISELY MIDNIGHT ON FEBRUARY 22, SIX FLYING FORTRESSES COB-
bled together from disparate U.S. Army Air Corps units lifted off from the military base at Townsville on the northeast coast of Australia. Their target was Rabaul, 1,100 miles away. One of the B-17s flew into a storm over the Coral Sea and began shaking and bucking so violently—what the pilots called "porpoising"—that it was forced to turn back. The remaining five refueled and restaged at Port Moresby. They reached Rabaul at dawn.

The anti-aircraft batteries ringing the town erupted. As the bombardiers dropped their payloads from above 20,000 feet, one aircraft's wing was punctured by an unexploded shell. Another exhausted its fuel supply evading Zeros and was forced to crash-land in a swamp on the north coast of New Guinea. Its entire crew was recovered after surviving more than a month in the bush. The four remaining planes landed safely at Townsville 14 hours after takeoff. The results of the bombing run were officially recorded as "not observed." The lead pilot's After-Action report stated flatly, "We didn't hit anything." But if the raid was a tactical failure, a strategic point had been made to the Japanese. The first American long-range bombers had arrived in the Southwest Pacific Theater. There would be more, many more, to follow. These would include, within days, Jay's 22nd Bomb Group.

8

INTO THE FIGHT

ALTHOUGH GEN. MacARTHUR HAD BEEN PLACED IN OVERALL COMMAND of Allied forces in Australia, by unofficial custom the American Airmen arriving in-country during the early stages of the war were considered guests of the Royal Australian Air Force, or RAAF. When in early April two squadrons of Jay's 22nd Bomb Group settled in at the Garbutt Field airbase some 600 miles north of Brisbane, the locals' hospitality initially buoyed and surprised the "Yanks," some of whom were surprised that English was the Australians' native tongue. The Aussie fliers were delighted to show the newcomers the local "swimmin' hole" where they could bathe, fish, and wash their clothes. They helped them set up a horseshoe pitch and cut, trimmed, and donated the logs with which the Americans constructed a crude officers club complete with generator-powered electric lights, shortwave radio, card tables, and a small bar whose taps spewed Australian lagers.

The same bonhomie was demonstrated by the civilians in the nearby port city of Townsville. The hamlet, with a population of just over 20,000, was an oasis amid a swath of cattle and sheep farms. With its wooden sidewalks, hitching posts, and swinging-door saloons, it struck the American Airmen as a town out of a Gene Autry movie. Once the visitors got the hang of exchanging their dollars for the local currency, a few shillings would buy them a bus ride into town, a hearty breakfast of steak and eggs, all the coffee they could drink, and a tall glass of cold milk. Australians did not have the same affinity for milk as American boys, and pub countermen were amazed at the Yanks' ability to put down glass after glass as if it were beer. But most gratifying to the newcomers were the shy smiles and waves from the gorgeous "sheilas" whose men were off waging war on the other side of the globe. These often resulted in clandestine relationships, and a few of the 22nd's officers even kept rooms in local hotels for the purpose of what they dubbed "recreation."

Though Australia is roughly the same size as America's Lower 48 states, there were only seven million people living on the continent in 1942, and the Australian Imperial Forces (AIF) had lost 16,000 at the fall of Malaya alone. With the rest of its small army, including its two most professional divisions, currently being chewed up by the Germans in North Africa, nearly everyone in the country had been affected by the war. Families who had lost fathers and sons, or who had not heard from them for months, came to treat the American boys as not only saviors but surrogates who filled a dark void. This was particularly true in a small places like Townsville. "If you happened to be downtown on Sunday morning, folks would stop you on the street and invite you to dinner," wrote one of Jay's fellow Airmen from the 22nd. "I can't say enough about the people of Townsville. Kind, caring, extremely generous."

The inhabitants' cordiality, however, masked an anxiety that lingered just below the surface. Like their British cousins after most of Europe was overrun by the Nazis, Australians saw themselves as the lone holdouts—in their case, against Japanese aggression in the Pacific. And in reality, just as so many Englishmen and -women feared an imminent invasion, the idea of Japanese landings on Australian beachheads was by no means far-fetched. Enemy bombers had already struck the continent, inflicting particularly heavy damage on the port city of Darwin. In the winter months of 1942, as the American correspondent John Lardner put it, Australia was staggering and "wiping blood from her mouth."

Lardner, a son of the acclaimed writer Ring Lardner, was part of the first wave of adventurous reporters sent to cover the war in the Southwest Pacific. His description of unopposed enemy dive-bombers virtually "lounging over their targets, calling their shots, at will" was particularly evocative to the American troops pouring into the country. Those troops, Lardner wrote, "found the thought of invasion in the air." They were in fact merely taking their cue from Australian government leaders, who Lardner added, "knew how thin were Australia's resources to meet a full-dress attack by a foe prepared for the job."

What this meant for the United States was apparent to the country's defiant Prime Minister John Curtin, who was left to declare what had become frighteningly obvious: "Australia is America's last bastion between America and Japan."

True as that was, the country's unsettled mood inevitably caused cracks in the goodwill between Australian servicemen and their American counterparts. For Jay and the U.S. Airmen at Garbutt Field, it was only a matter of time before trifling national tics blossomed into larger annoyances. Thousands of miles of air travel had left the 22nd Bomb Group's B-26s in need of substantial repair, for instance, and the lack of maintenance personnel throughout the theater became a point of contention. The 22nd's ground support teams, around 600 men, had sailed directly for Australia from San Francisco eight days before Jay and the other pilots and flight crews departed for Hawaii. But most were still delayed in a makeshift camp converted from a racetrack outside Brisbane by the time the B-26s began flying their first combat missions. It did not take long before the Americans began to sense that the RAAF mechanics regularly prioritized their own planes with the few spare parts allocated to the Garbutt Field base.

This was a far cry from the situation in Europe. American bomber flight crews stationed in England could count on having their own crew chief, and often an assistant crew chief, responsible for tasks as disparate as recalibrating an engine's prop speed and patching up bullet holes. In the European Theater these maintenance men were often complemented by a small platoon of sheet metal specialists, grease monkeys, armorers, and refueling crews. But in the Southwest Pacific, with Australian mechanics suspected of favoring their own aircraft, American flight crews were left to perform tasks ranging from the basic to the complex.

Jay and his fellow officers became adept at overhauling balky engines, patching blown fuel lines, and refurbishing broken electronics systems with Rube Goldbergian ingenuity. They discovered, for instance, that women's sanitary napkins, Kotex in particular, made excellent air filters. And in a pinch the Australian sixpence coin provided just the right spark for an engine's ignition magneto. Given the urgency imposed by the Japanese advances, the anxious Yanks were particularly galled by the Aussie habit of dropping everything twice a day for a leisurely smoke and a billy-can of tea. As one of the 22nd's navigators complained, "Of all the damn nonsense! These screwball Aussies and their tea!"

It came as something of a release valve for explosive tempers in both camps when the Yanks were finally allowed to take their frustrations out on the Japanese. Sundry formations of the 22nd's Marauders scrambled almost daily, and though Jay had yet to be assigned to a specific crew, he was designated as either a fill-in copilot or a flight engineer for the first of the Group's squadrons to become combat-ready. So it was that on April 6 he eased into the right-hand seat of one of eight Marauders taking part in the 22nd's first combat mission, a night raid on Rabaul. It would be the first American combat operation of the war by a B-26.

In Europe and North Africa, American bomber runs were accompanied by fighter protection as often as possible, but a variety of circumstances precluded this in the Southwest Pacific Theater. The most obvious was the vast distances flown on missions, generally 1,000 to 1,400 miles, well beyond the range of the Allies' fighter planes. The harsh, unpredictable weather was also a factor. Fighters like the American P-39s and P-40s could not stand up to the heavy storms and turbulence a bomber often encountered over the Coral, Solomon, and Bismarck Seas. Finally, the exigencies of the war itself played a part. Port Moresby, for instance, was the ideal location for attack and pursuit fighters to fuel and stage. Yet most of the Allies' available fighters could not be spared to screen bombing missions when they were so desperately needed to defend the continual enemy air attacks on the base.

So on his initial combat mission, Jay's bomber formation flew without a fighter escort. As a sop to the inexperienced Americans, and as a show of solidarity, the Australians did volunteer to send along the pilot who had led the RAAF's first PBY Catalina raid on Rabaul two months earlier. The offer was accepted, and the Aussie Airman joined the Marauder squad leader, Lt. Albert Moye, in the cockpit of his B-26.

Earlier in the day the flight crews had been briefed on primary and secondary targets—the largest ships in the harbor and parked aircraft, particularly bombers—as well as where they were likely to confront the heaviest anti-aircraft fire over the town. In essence, that was *everywhere.* Then, while the navigators were called together to map out the best route home should their aircraft become separated from the formation, the bombardiers headed out to the runway to oversee the loading of the ordnance. All the pilots had been warned to expect rough weather, and that night, after topping off their fuel tanks and staging at Port Moresby, the fleet of bombers encountered trouble almost immediately. Two of the planes were forced to turn back for Australia when a curtain-drop of whiteout fog prevented them from locating the passes through the Owen Stanley Range, the cloud-shrouded cordillera that forms the miles-high spine of the Papuan peninsula. The remaining six emerged from the mist on the

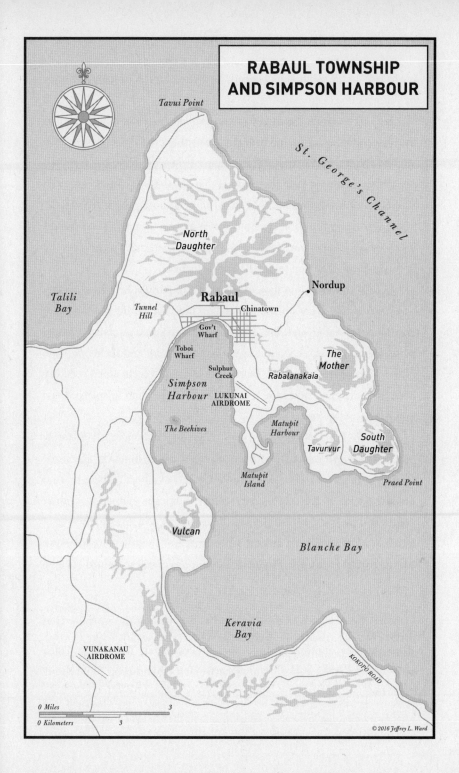

RABAUL TOWNSHIP
AND SIMPSON HARBOUR

Tavui Point

St. George's Channel

North
Daughter

Rabaul

• **Nordup**

*Talili
Bay*

*Tunnel
Hill*

Chinatown

Gov't
Wharf

The
Mother

Toboi
Wharf

Rabalanakaia

Sulphur
Creek

*Simpson
Harbour*

LUKUNAI
AIRDROME

The Beehives

*Matupit
Harbour*

*South
Daughter*

Tavurvur

*Matupit
Island*

Praed Point

Vulcan

Blanche Bay

*Keravia
Bay*

VUNAKANAU
AIRDROME

KOKOPO ROAD

0 Miles   3

0 Kilometers   3

© 2016 Jeffrey L. Ward

north side of the mountains beneath a palette of random stars, as if they had flown into a Miró painting.

Hoping to evade the enemy radar installations at Gasmata as well as the observation stations and listening posts that crosshatched New Britain, the formation flew well east of Rabaul before doubling back and approaching the target from the channel that separates the northeast coast of the island from the southwest coast of neighboring New Ireland. As the sun rose over Simpson Harbour the ring of enemy anti-aircraft batteries threw up a hailstorm of what American Airmen called ack-ack as the bombers droned on and released their ordnance.

One B-26 was said to have exploded a troop transport, although this was never verified. Jay's plane claimed no hits, but neither did it sustain any damage from ground fire. Not so Lt. Moye's lead aircraft. Shrapnel penetrated his fuselage, wounding his radio operator and slicing into one of the Marauder's fuel lines. Before Moye could reach Allied territory both of his engines quit from a lack of fuel, forcing him to splash down into the Solomon Sea.*

Back at Port Moresby the five remaining Marauders had barely touched down to refuel when a formation of enemy bombers accompanied by a flight of Lae-based Zeros appeared overhead. There was no time to get the B-26s into the air, so the Americans jumped from their planes and ran for the bush. Jay was being buffeted by pressure waves of bursting bombs when he saw the tail gunner from another aircraft cut in half by machine-gun fire. Moments later he was crawling toward his own

---

* One member of Moye's crew was killed when the lieutenant's plane crashed just north of Kiriwina Island in the Trobriands about 100 miles north of New Guinea's eastern tip. The rest struggled to shore in a single life raft. Hours later an alert pilot of a patrolling RAAF Catalina flying boat spotted three flares fired by one of Moye's crewmen from his Very pistol. The Aussie flier, Pilot Officer Terence Duignan, put down in a lagoon and picked up the Americans as well as the Australian guide who had flown with them. In doing so, Duignan became the first pilot of an RAAF flying boat to perform an air-sea rescue.

plane's navigator, who had taken a bullet in his arm, when he heard the whine of different engines overhead.

He looked up to see a squadron of at least eight Australian P-40s from a nearby airbase streaking across the dove-gray sky. They had no hope of reaching the high-altitude Japanese bombers, so they instead engaged the Japanese fighter escort. The furious aerial battle that followed seemed to last hours. But in fact when Jay looked at his watch he realized only a few minutes had passed. Watching the Australian fighters chase the Zeros back toward the Owen Stanleys, Jay realized how odd it was that his formation had not encountered any Zekes patrolling the skies during the run over Rabaul. He was unaware, given the predawn timing of his mission, that despite the enemy's numerical advantage, it would be months before Japanese fighters were equipped for night combat.

It was a different story only a few days later when Jay, again in the co-pilot's seat, was assigned to a formation bound for a second night raid on Rabaul. The mission again got off to an inauspicious start when the aircraft were separated by severe thunderstorms over the Solomon Sea. The Aussies had cautioned the Americans about flying into these treacherous "monsoon troughs." The warning did not do the reality justice.

Jay's briefings back in Hawaii had included classes on what was known at the time as an intertropical front,* known to sailors as the Doldrums; in the equatorial latitudes, this is essentially where the northeast and southeast trade winds converge. But sitting in a classroom studying wind charts was a tame experience compared to flying through the center of the semipermanent weather system he was now traversing. This atmospheric vortex was notorious for its strong, erratic gusts and its violent, lighting-laced thunderheads, which can top out in the lower reaches of the stratosphere at 40,000 feet. Tonight his squadron was confronted

---

* After the war, new technology allowed meteorologists to recognize the significant effect wind field convergence had on tropical weather, particularly near the equator, and the term "intertropical convergence zone" replaced "intertropical front."

by a storm so thick and visibility so reduced that the intermittent throbs of jagged lightning flashes momentarily blinded him. No B-26 was capable of vaulting above this weather—no World War II aircraft was—and all Jay could hope for was that his plane's navigator could plot a course skirting the worst of this convective activity. As it was, his aircraft's crew was holding tight to anything bolted down in the bucking bomber as if they were flying through the inside of a paint mixer. By the time the squad of Marauders regained formation on approach to Rabaul their mission had been delayed to the point where the sun was breaking over the Eastern Pacific.

Jay's bombardier emptied his ordnance over the target—again, the pilot recorded no hits—and the plane began to race southwest when it was intercepted by three Zeros. This was Jay's first encounter with the notorious A6M1 Type 0 Japanese fighter that ruled the skies during the early stages of the war. He was astonished.

The single-engine fighter plane was designed with an emphasis on speed and agility. It was referred to, for short, by its pilots as the *Rei-sen*, or Zero, for the last digit of the Japanese equivalent of the date when it was introduced, the Imperial Year 2600, or 1940. Weighing just over a ton fully loaded, it had a 950-horsepower radial engine that allowed it to outclimb and outrace any aircraft the Americans could as yet put into the air. The Zero also combined a long-range capability with its uncanny maneuverability. Some U.S. Army Air Force pilots noted the bitter irony that during its development the aircraft's Mitsubishi engineers had largely followed specs initially conceived by the American aviator Howard Hughes.

By 1942 the Zeke,[*] as the Allies designated the plane, had already at-

---

[*] U.S. Intelligence eventually gave code names to 122 different makes of Japanese aircraft, including "Rufe" for the AM62-N Zero-style floatplane and "Hamp" for an upgraded version of the original Zero model that came on line in mid-1942. By then, however, the Americans had bestowed such an iconic stature on the plane that most enemy fighters continued to be referred to by American Airmen as Zeros or "Zekes."

tained legendary status as an acrobatic dogfighter, achieving a kill ratio of 12 to 1 in air-to-air combat. Its seasoned pilots were well trained, with an Imperial Navy aviator averaging close to 650 hours of flying time before entering combat and an Imperial Army pilot close to 500 hours. These men, venerated throughout Japan as the "Wild Eagles," disdained parachutes and sometimes even radios as accoutrements of the cowardly that would shred their *Bushido* concept of honor. Nor would they allow the by now commonplace self-sealing gas tanks to be installed in their planes. Though the foam-and-rubber liners could prevent a single bullet from exploding the aircraft, Zero pilots felt that the extra weight would slow them down.

Although they were eager for fighter-to-fighter combat, the truly big game for Zero pilots was America's bombers, the B-17 in particular. They referred to the B-17 simply as a "Boeing" and held it in respect verging on awe. Since the beginning of the war, when Zeros had pumped round after round of cannon and machine-gun fire into Flying Fortresses over the Philippines only to watch them remain aloft, the highest achievement for an enemy flier was to take down a B-17. But flaming a B-26 Marauder was nearly as much of an accomplishment, and as time went on Japanese fighter pilots became experts at culling a single American bomber from its formation, especially one wounded and trailing smoke, and attacking it like baying wolves dragging down an injured caribou.

For Jay, however, a Zero's reputation was one thing. Coming face-to-face with the wasplike whine of the fighter's radial engine and its two 20-millimeter wing cannons and the brace of 7.7-millimeter machine guns that spit fire from its nose was quite another.

During stateside training, Jay and his fellow bomber pilots had become accustomed to their twin-engine Marauders outrunning American fighter planes. Thus, when the three Zeros broke from the clouds to the east of Rabaul using the sunrise as camouflage, Jay expected that all the Americans had to do was "pour on the coal" in order to leave the bogeys in their wake. But right after his B-26 went into a dive at 350 miles per hour Jay was astounded to see the little yellow-green fighter planes actually gaining on them, the red balls on their wings glowing and growing.

Within moments machine-gun fire shredded the B-26's fabric-encased ailerons that shrouded the trailing edge of the wings' aluminum ribbing, pocked across the wings themselves, and punctured the equally thin fuselage.* When the war began it was an American article of faith that Japanese Airmen were handicapped by a "national weakness": their eyesight. But that morning their aim appeared just fine to Jay. At first the sound of the bullets reminded him of the patter of hail hitting the roof of his old Whippet during a winter storm. But as the shells ricocheted through the metallic airframe he began to feel as if he were trapped inside a huge bass drum.

Jay's pilot finally lost the bogeys by ducking into a thick, flat-bottomed cumulus cloud formed by condensation rising from the warm sea. They had escaped unscathed, but Jay's recollection of his first encounter with Zeros hung over him like Banquo's ghost. Over the next weeks the 22nd flew seven more daylight missions against Rabaul, targeting shipping in the harbor with dozens of general-purpose 500-pounders or swooping in low on enemy aircraft parked at the two airdromes to release scores of 100-pound demolition bombs. The Japanese took notice, and after a particularly successful raid that wiped out several parked bombers at Vunakanau and sparked a munitions-dump fire, one Imperial Navy rear admiral even noted "conspicuous signs of defeat in the air war."

These early raids may have been portents, yet as the remainder of the 22nd's Air Group squadrons became operational Jay was often the first man to pull aside a novice pilot to offer a warning that despite the racist caricatures perpetrated back home of the Japanese as bucktoothed, slit-eyed man-apes, they should never, ever, be taken lightly. That this Asian

---

* Most American bomber flight crews did not even realize that the hinged flight control surface at the tip of their wings—aileron is French for "little wing"—was constructed primarily of cloth.

enemy was smarter and more clever than such depictions implied was driven home just weeks after Jay's first encounter with a Zero. A few days earlier, on April 18, Col. Jimmy Doolittle had led 16 B-25s on a 600-mile trek across the Pacific to drop incendiary bombs on Tokyo. The secret mission, accomplished by the near-impossible launching of the twin-engine land-based bombers from the aircraft carrier USS *Hornet*, had been a tremendous morale booster that reverberated across the Pacific to America's shores. Now, as Jay and a group of pilots and copilots from the 22nd were milling about the Ready Room at Garbutt Field awaiting a briefing, someone began fiddling with a radio in hopes of hearing more news of Doolittle's daring raid.

But that morning, they did not find Walter Winchell or even an Australian newscaster updating news of Doolittle and his Raiders; instead the voice cutting through the static belonged to Tokyo Rose. When the lyrical propagandist had nearly completed her broadcast with her typical invective—"You Americans will all die"—she surprised the Airmen by promising a particularly hideous end for the fliers from the 22nd Bomb Group newly stationed in Australia. She then proceeded to recite their names in alphabetical order. Jay's was last.

PART

II

*It is probable that future war will be conducted by a special class,
the air force, as it was by the armored knights of the Middle Ages.*
—Brigadier Gen. William "Billy" Mitchell,
"Winged Defense," 1924

9

BREAKING THE CODE

REAR ADM. FRANK JACK FLETCHER WAS AN UNLIKELY HERO. IN FACT, HE was probably lucky to still have a job. Five months earlier, in late December 1941, Fletcher had been placed in command of the relief task force charged with delivering reinforcements to the 1,500 beleaguered Marines, sailors, and U.S. civilian construction workers garrisoning Wake Island in the Western Pacific. The Americans had been under constant air bombardment since the day after Pearl Harbor, and had even repelled several small landings attempted by the Japanese. By the time Fletcher arrived, however, a larger enemy invasion force had already killed or captured the island's defenders, and secured Wake.

Fletcher was criticized heavily in Washington for what the Navy brass felt were unnecessary refueling stops that compromised his mission. On the front lines, however, the admiral's immediate superiors cited a series of unavoidable storms as the cause of the delay and refused to blame him for the loss of Wake. Such was Adm. Nimitz's faith in the man that he made a point of retaining Fletcher as commander of the flotilla, consisting of an aircraft carrier, three heavy cruisers, and eight destroyers. This proved to be a wise decision.

Five months later, in May 1942, the Imperial General Command initiated a series of campaigns in the Southwest Pacific that Japanese war planners presumed would knock Australia out of the war. They hoped that with the fall of its Australian ally, an isolated United States, still reeling from Pearl Harbor, might be forced to rethink its entire Pacific strategy. A major aspect of this Japanese push south was to capture the Allies' bare-bones installation at Port Moresby. This would not only eliminate the staging area for American bombers attacking Rabaul—"Japan's acknowledgment of the needle in her flank"—but move the Empire a step closer to invading Australia.

The Port Moresby operation was to consist of a two-pronged amphibious landing centered on the base's two airfields. Two thousand Japanese troops would come ashore southeast of the town and engulf the Kila Kila fighter strip while another 3,500 landed to the northwest and drove on Seven Mile airdrome, used for staging bombing missions. The town would be encircled and devoured. Nearly simultaneously, the seizure of Guadalcanal and its key airfield in the southern Solomons would serve both a tactical and a strategic purpose—Japanese bombers would now be housed less than 1,400 miles from Brisbane, while the shipping stem from America would be severed.

As for the Port Moresby assault, as far back as 1938 the Japanese Imperial Command had planned to effect this separation of Australia from its powerful American ally by using New Guinea as a jumping-off point. With the forces of the Rising Sun achieving their goals across the South Pacific with efficient and brutal precision, all that needed to be added to the Port Moresby operation were specific dates. In the spring of 1942 this was easily done; the Japanese Navy predicted that its amphibious landings would take place on May 7.

Australian Prime Minister John Curtin was not the only politician to recognize the severity of the situation. If Australia was lost, the Roosevelt administration might even have to consider abandoning all of the United States' Pacific holdings and make protecting Pearl Harbor and the American mainland a priority even above defeating Germany. That was, at any rate, the Japanese thinking behind the assault on Port Moresby. If it was carried out with speed and stealth, the Americans and Australians would never know what hit them. How could they? They would have had to break the most secure code the Imperial Navy used to send messages . . . which is exactly what the Allies had done.

Well before the war began, American and Australian intelligence officers had been working on intercepting and decoding Japanese radio messages. Since the attack on Pearl Harbor several breakthroughs had been made, with American cryptologists partially deciphering the enemy's main naval encryption system, known as JN-25. Although the code breakers had yet to completely crack JN-25, their methods had become proficient enough to provide fair warning that Port Moresby was in peril. Reconnaissance flights reporting an increase in shipping traffic at Simpson Harbour and an influx of land-based bombers to Rabaul's Vunakanau airdrome further solidified the strong circumstantial case.

By early May the Americans were well aware that a large enemy naval force had departed from Rabaul and was steaming into the Coral Sea with Port Moresby its likely objective. MacArthur's staff in Brisbane was even hinting to reporters that a major Japanese offensive was imminent. This intelligence breach outraged Adm. King back in Washington: as King knew, the Japanese read American and Australian newspapers, and they might easily deduce that their codes had been broken. King even buttonholed Gen. Marshall at a meeting of the Joint Chiefs to remind him to keep MacArthur's loose lips sealed.

But Japanese military intelligence seemed not to have picked up on the public hints. This was fortunate for a variety of reasons, the most crucial being that the U.S. Navy had so few ships in the Western Pacific—had the Japanese suspected that America was covertly tracking their movements, they could have prepared to take advantage of this imbalance. At his headquarters in Hawaii, Adm. Nimitz second-guessed himself for dispatching Adm. William Halsey to transport Doolittle's bombers; there was now no way Halsey's two carriers could reach the Coral Sea in time to intercept the Japanese force. Nimitz was left to order whatever vessels he had available to counter the strike. The most readily available in the area was the task force under the command of Adm. Fletcher. Though Fletcher had acquired a second carrier, he remained severely outgunned. He could not fail to recognize that in a fight on the open sea, his ships wouldn't stand a chance. He would have to rely solely on his carriers' airpower.

Meanwhile, Fletcher's Japanese counterpart, Adm. Shigeyoshi Inoue, began to receive Imperial intelligence reports indicating that American ships were somewhere in his vicinity. Inoue welcomed them; the Allied ships presented a golden opportunity. Fletcher's two carriers, the USS *Yorktown* and the USS *Lexington*, represented half of America's entire carrier force. If Inoue, while landing his 5,500 troops at Port Moresby, could also cripple or even destroy those carriers, the war in the Southwest Pacific might be as good as won.

Bad weather delayed the meeting of the two fleets for several days. On the morning of May 7, the date set for the invasion, reconnaissance flights from both flotillas found each other, and attack planes were launched. Over the next two days the Japanese managed to sink an American destroyer and oiler.* The Americans sent a cruiser and a light carrier to the bottom of the sea.

---

* In a preview of air warfare to come, the oiler USS *Neosho* was swarmed by a flight of Japanese dive-bombers. When one of the enemy planes was hit with crippling anti-aircraft fire, its pilot deliberately crashed it into the oiler's deck, hastening the ship's demise.

The next day the Americans suffered their most grievous loss when the *Lexington*, having endured a succession of withering Japanese bombing runs, detonated in a cloud of black smoke. It sank rapidly, taking 26 officers and 190 sailors with it. Only the heroic maneuvers of Fletcher's destroyer skippers resulted in the rescue of over a thousand men. The *Yorktown* was also damaged, but it fared better than the large Japanese carrier *Shokaku*—the lead ship in its class—which sustained crippling damage from American dive-bombers.

What came to be known as the Battle of the Coral Sea was the first naval engagement in history in which enemy ships did not directly fire on one another. The entire fight had been waged by aircraft, with American fliers destroying more than 100 enemy planes while losing only 35 of their own. When these startling numbers were reported to Imperial General Headquarters, the Japanese high command decided that without adequate air cover, Adm. Inoue's remaining ships were too vulnerable, and the Port Moresby invasion force was ordered to turn back for Rabaul.

What official reports and newspapers back in the States celebrated as Fletcher's "victory" was in truth more stopgap than turning point. Indeed, in comparing the ship losses on both sides it could be argued that the Japanese had achieved a tactical triumph. Further, American aircraft out of Australia had performed dismally, with less than half of the bombers finding enemy targets. In one formation the bombers mistakenly dropped their ordnance on a task group of Royal Australian Navy cruisers and destroyers; luckily, and typically, these payloads all missed. But there is not much doubt that the Battle of the Coral Sea was a strategic success for the Americans if for no other reason than the fight forestalled the invasion of Port Moresby.

Perhaps more important, though Allied forces in the Pacific remained thoroughly outmanned and outgunned, for the first time since the surprise attack on Pearl Harbor the Rising Sun's seemingly unstoppable juggernaut across Asia had been slowed. The Imperial General Staff, however, was far from cowed. For even as pilots from each side bombed

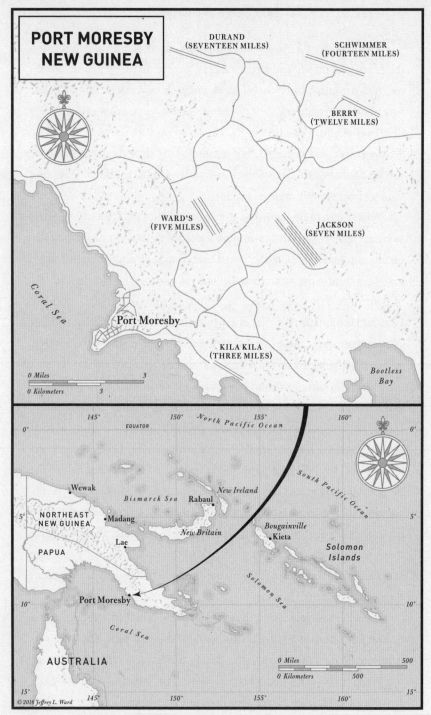

PORT MORESBY
NEW GUINEA

DURAND
(SEVENTEEN MILES)

SCHWIMMER
(FOURTEEN MILES)

BERRY
(TWELVE MILES)

WARD'S
(FIVE MILES)

JACKSON
(SEVEN MILES)

Coral Sea

Port Moresby

KILA KILA
(THREE MILES)

*Bootless
Bay*

0 Miles   3
0 Kilometers   3

145°   150°   *North Pacific Ocean*   155°   160°

EQUATOR   *North Pacific Ocean*

0°   0°

Wewak

Bismarck Sea   Rabaul   *New Ireland*

South Pacific Ocean

5°   NORTHEAST
NEW GUINEA   •Madang   5°

New Britain   *Bougainville*
•Kieta

•Lae

PAPUA   *Solomon
Islands*

Solomon Sea

Port Moresby

10°   10°

Coral Sea

AUSTRALIA   0 Miles   500
                             0 Kilometers   500

15°   145°   150°   155°   160°   15°

© 2016 Jeffrey L. Ward

the other's shipping on the Coral Sea, Japanese scouts were mapping the tiny island of Guadalcanal in the southern Solomons, a little over 700 miles to the northeast. In mid-June, the van of Japan's invasion force came ashore there unopposed.

The landing force quickly scattered the island's smattering of Caucasian cattle ranchers and rubber harvesters. A few would subsequently volunteer to remain behind as spotters, or coastwatchers, as the Royal Australian Navy called them. The native Melanesians of Guadalcanal who were not captured and conscripted as slave labor fled into the jungle. By early July a full complement of Japanese soldiers and marines had arrived with over 100 trucks of construction equipment with which to refurbish the island's grass airstrip.

As Commander in Chief of the U.S. Pacific Fleet, Adm. Nimitz was already planning a counterinvasion of both Guadalcanal and the even smaller Japanese-held island of Tulagi for an as yet undetermined date in the future when he began to receive reports from the coastwatchers informing him that the enemy effort to recondition the airfield on Guadalcanal was proceeding faster than expected. The new airdrome taking shape, he was told, appeared both sturdy enough and long enough, at 3,600 feet, to allow for the operation of long-range bombers that could reach Australia. Nimitz was taken aback.

Tall, courtly, and strikingly handsome, Nimitz carried himself with an aristocratic mien that lent an air of confident gravitas to his office. He was also an ardent map hobbyist whose profound interest in military literature was reflected in his principle of taking only what he called "calculated risks." He recognized that it would take time, probably at least a year, for America's factories, mills, and assembly lines to achieve a practical war footing to begin driving back the Japanese via an island-hopping campaign. Until then he was prepared only to execute a twofold battle plan—to surprise and confuse the enemy with quick and stealthy strikes against their holdings while also overburdening the Imperial Navy's ability to protect its lengthening supply lines and shipping lanes. But now, with the enemy on Guadalcanal virtually knocking on Australia's door, Nimitz exhorted his invasion planners to send him a timetable for landings no later than August.

As the admiral's staff rushed to meet this deadline, they were more than buoyed by news of a battle that had just taken place near a small island far off to the northeast.

THE TINY ATOLL OF MIDWAY, AS ITS NAME IMPLIES, BREACHES ALMOST the exact center of the Pacific Ocean, dangling from the northwestern tip of the Hawaiian Islands chain like the smallest charm on an unclasped bracelet. Prior to the war, the U.S. Navy had constructed a crude airstrip of perforated steel matting on the lagoon-fringed spit of land with the intention of establishing a forward submarine base that would allow its boats to range deeper into the Western Pacific.

But the Imperial Navy, particularly Adm. Yamamoto, also had eyes for Midway. Yamamoto considered it the ideal location for the decades-old plan to lure the American fleet into an ambush. Yamamoto's strategy was simplicity itself: threaten Midway, await the arrival of America's aircraft carriers to defend it, and destroy them. Yamamoto himself would personally lead the Combined Fleet when he sprang the trap. With Midway in their possession, Japanese forces would not only have eliminated the threat of another embarrassing—like Doolittle's—raid on the homeland, but also have secured their own forward base a mere 1,300 miles from Oahu.

But first Yamamoto had to convince his superiors in Tokyo that this was the right time for an epochal showdown with the Americans. He faced strong opposition from influential members of the Imperial Navy General Staff, who instead argued for employing the Combined Fleet in a broader South Pacific offensive. Even more ambitious than the landings at Port Moresby, this sweeping drive would entail invasions not only of New Guinea and the Solomons, but also at New Caledonia, Fiji, and Samoa.

In the end, however, Yamamoto's renown and track record prevailed, and the admiral pressed forward with his Midway plans. He scheduled the assault for early June when, taking no chances, he planned to sail with more than 200 warships, including two battleships and four aircraft carriers carrying over 500 planes. It would be the largest combined tonnage ever assembled in the history of naval warfare.

And it was indeed a well-planned venture. Except that, as with the Coral Sea, American code breakers knew all about it.

Thanks to this foreknowledge, Adm. Nimitz was also aware that his Pacific Fleet, with three aircraft carriers and no battleships, was outnumbered. Under normal circumstances this discrepancy in firepower between the competing flotillas would have given the American admiral pause. But on this occasion there was also a mitigating factor to consider. Some months earlier, Adm. King had sent Nimitz an editorial from the *Saturday Evening Post,* suggesting that Nimitz make it required reading among his staff. Written by a vice president of research at General Motors and titled "There Is Only One Mistake: To Do Nothing," the article argued that "taking risks, even accepting intelligent mistakes with tragic consequences, was a recipe for determining and solving *real* problems amid the distractions of *apparent* problems."

There was no doubting King's intentions in forwarding the story, and it served its purpose. Nimitz decided to buck the long odds his ships would face at Midway. After all, his code breakers had provided him with the element of surprise. He wagered that this would give his 233 aircraft more than a fighting chance. His bet paid off.

The four-day battle produced a devastating U.S. victory that stunned the Japanese. Wave after wave of American planes swept over the enemy fleet, knocking Zeros out of the sky and feasting on the ships below as their captains desperately, and unsuccessfully, attempted evasive maneuvers. Back at Garbutt Field in Australia, tremendous whoops and hollers went up in the 22nd Bomb Group's Ready Room when Jay and his fellow Airmen learned that four of their Marauders had taken part in the assault. The bombers had been held up in Hawaii for repairs when the rest of the Group had flown on to Australia, and now they became the first U.S. Army aircraft to ever complete a torpedo attack. It was a proud moment.

In the end, U.S. losses amounted to a single aircraft carrier and one destroyer while all four Japanese carriers—the *Akagi, Kaga, Soryu*, and *Hiryu*—were among the vessels destroyed before a humiliated Yamamoto ordered the remnants of his Combined Fleet withdrawn. In a bitter irony for the Japanese, each of those four carriers had been among the half dozen to carry out the attacks on Pearl Harbor. It was not lost on the Americans that the last day of the fighting at Midway, June 7, also marked the six-month anniversary of that dreadful day.

Of equal importance, more skilled enemy aviators were killed in one day than the Japanese could develop in a year. As one Army Air Force general observed in the aftermath of the Battle of Midway, the Japanese Army and Navy might be able to "hold their own in any league, but he simply cannot train Airmen to compare with ours in a hurry. His original highly trained crews were superb, but they are dead."

Although neither side could have foreseen it at the time, losing a quartet of aircraft carriers was a blow from which the Empire would never quite recover. For the moment, however, the catastrophe at Midway forced the Japanese to accept that, for the first time, they were now on a defensive footing. Their earlier Southern Strategy regarding New Caledonia, Fiji, and Samoa was restructured in favor of consolidating their holdings in the Bismarcks, in the Solomons, and on New Guinea. Moreover, there was now a much greater urgency to secure and stabilize these bases. Despite their defeat at Midway—or perhaps because of it—to Imperial General Headquarters this meant another assault on Port Moresby, this time from a different direction.

WITH THEIR PREVIOUS ATTACK ON PORT MORESBY THWARTED BY THE Battle of the Coral Sea—and with no carriers left to provide support for another amphibious landing directly on the Allied base—the Japanese decided on another tack: to land a force on New Guinea's opposite coast and march overland, traversing the buttresses of rock that formed the Owen Stanley Range.

On July 21, as reconstruction was nearly completed on Guadalcanal's new airfield, 13,000 Imperial Army troops accompanied by 1,000 conscripted indigenous bearers came ashore at Buna, on New Guinea's north coast. After establishing a beachhead, the five enemy battalions immediately began the 100-mile trek south, up and over the Owen Stanleys along a serpentine pack trail that had been tramped out of the rain forest over centuries and was known as the Kokoda Track.

Their march was stalled the very next night when the Japanese advance party—hacking its way with machetes through the jungle-choked footpath—mistook an ambush by a small company of Papuan militiamen for a much larger resistance party. These New Guinea Volunteer Rifles, recruited by the Royal Australian Army from the area's best hunters and marksmen, continued to harass the invaders over the next 24 hours, enough time for swarms of American B-17s and B-26s to get into the air. The aircraft initially had difficulty locating the Japanese troops in the thick rain forest, but with the Papuans radioing location coordinates, they finally found the main body of infantry and began bombing and strafing them as they cut across the face of a steep-sloping forest of eucalyptus and allspice.

The Allied counterattack was enhanced by the fact that the Americans had swiftly expanded Port Moresby's facilities. Two new runways had been graded and matted, including one 6,000-foot strip capable of accommodating heavy bombers. Now, with four airstrips operational for planes arriving from Australia, the Americans started a campaign of near-constant bombing runs against the Japanese soldiers gingerly picking their way along what came to be known as the "Bloody Track," as well as against the steady stream of resupply ships sent from Rabaul.

Despite their continuing losses in the mountains and on the coast near Buna, the enemy managed to land thousands of reinforcements, crest the Owen Stanley Range, and begin a slow descent toward Port Moresby. Admiral Nimitz, desperate to relieve the pressure on New Guinea, chose this time to unleash Operation Watchtower, landing 11,000 Marines on the beaches of Guadalcanal at just past dawn on August 7. It was the first amphibious landing by U.S. forces in nearly half a century, and within 24 hours the Marines had captured the airstrip that was to become known around the world as Henderson Field.

This small victory was merely a presage to five months of hard fighting on Guadalcanal. The assault on Port Moresby proved similarly vicious, particularly as it dragged on through New Guinea's rainy season. Although the Japanese attack down the south slope of the Owen Stanleys advanced to within 25 miles of the town, it was slowed by swollen streams and sodden turf. After a final firefight whose gunshots could be heard at the U.S. bomber base at Jackson Airfield, Imperial troops were beaten back by a combination of U.S. airpower and Australian and American infantry reinforcements flown in on American cargo planes. The fighting at Buna, however, was destined to rage for months.

Stateside newspaper reports of even such minor victories, coming as they did on the heels of the successful sea battles on the Coral Sea and at Midway, gave the folks back in America a spark of hope after so many months of depressing dispatches from the Pacific. And when another attempted Japanese landing on New Guinea was thrown back into the sea, this time at Milne Bay on the thin neck of Papua's eastern tip, some Americans stationed in the Southwest Pacific experienced a slight quake of excitement, as if the war's filament had shifted ever so slightly. A few cocky U.S. politicians even began to speak of getting their boys back home in time to see spring flowers blooming in the victory gardens that more than 20 million people were tending in their backyards.

The War Department knew better. Despite the loss of four carriers at Midway, Japan's Combined Fleet still greatly outnumbered the U.S. Pacific Fleet in destroyers, cruisers, and battleships. And the confrontations on the Kokoda Track, at Buna, at Henderson Field, and at Milne Bay had been skirmishes at best, opening gambits in a much larger chess match expected to end well over 3,000 miles away in the streets of Tokyo, where President Roosevelt and his generals assumed "the last battle will be fought."

Meanwhile, during the Battle of the Coral Sea, Jay Zeamer's exhausted 22nd Bomb Group had run nearly continuous bombing raids over Rabaul to keep enemy planes there occupied while the two task forces slugged it out. Then the Group had taken the lead on nearly as many of the daily runs over Buna and, later, at Milne Bay. Now, after catching their breaths, they were striking even farther north, stabbing at Lae and Salamaua with regularity.

Jay was personally witnessing the dents in the mighty Nippon Empire's armor. Back in Australia, on the Reid River satellite airbase close to Garbutt Field, one of his colleagues expressed these emotions in a personal diary: "We feel we are not only defending Australia, but our own U.S. as well," he wrote. "This latter thought, above all, heartens us. It helps make our aerial attacks more vicious. We eat, sleep, loaf, drink, and fight like hell together. We've already repulsed two invasion attempts, and believe me, the Aussies are happy to have us here."

Jay, in turn, marked this shift in attitude with a simple, one-word entry in his own journal: "Turnaround?"

10

THE RENEGADE PILOT

IN THE AFTERMATH OF WHAT CAPT. JAY ZEAMER HAD LABELED A "TURN-around," the metaphors flew fast and furious across the United States. This was most apparent in the medium that was perhaps the most popular form of political communication for the era, the editorial cartoon. The Japanese caricatured as subhuman creatures—dogs, snakes, "beastly little monkeys"—were a predominant theme.

"Well, well, seems to be a slight shifting of the Japanese current," read the caption to one widely circulated political sketch depicting a worm-like Asian being knocked cold by a brawny American sailor wielding the "Midway Tide-Stick." Drawn by Theodor Geisel, then the chief editorial cartoonist for the New York newspaper *PM*, this was one of more than 400 lampoons, many of them breathtakingly racist, produced by the author and illustrator who would soon become known by his nom de plume, Dr. Seuss.* In fact the subhuman Asian being knocked cold in the sketch bears a striking facial resemblance to the title character in *The Cat in the Hat*.

Geisel was far from alone in his relentless visual attacks on the enemy. American cartoonists could not resist portraying Uncle Sam punching a Japanese soldier, usually bespectacled and bucktoothed, in either the face or the solar plexus with his giant fist. The caption for one such cartoon in the *Buffalo News*—"Losing Face"—was emblematic, as was the *Kansas City Star*'s "Jolt the Japs at Midway." General MacArthur also benefited from the pen-and-ink onslaught. One caricature, captioned "The Exterminator," depicted his giant hands pumping a bug spray device shaped like an American bomber to kill hordes of the tiny "Japanese Beetle." And in London, *Punch* published an editorial cartoon of MacArthur standing in the prow of a boat and spearing enemy-held islands like so many sponge fish as he sailed toward the Rising Sun. The point, however crude, was nevertheless accurate: the United States was indeed lifting itself up off the Pearl Harbor canvas and starting to counterpunch.

At Garbutt Field this muffled elation was somewhat tempered by Jay's quirks, which continually puzzled his fellow Airmen of the 22nd Bomb Group. Jay's laissez-faire attitude toward authority was particularly bewildering. Little did his fellow pilots know that this was the very renegade quality to which Jay's mother and father had reconciled themselves so long ago. As one family member put it, "Jay never took his superiors

---

* Jonathan Crowe's *Open Culture* reports that Geisel was also a vocal proponent of the internment camps for Japanese-American citizens in the western United States during the war. Geisel's racialist views took a 180-degree turn when he visited Hiroshima in 1953 and observed the aftermath of the atom bomb's destruction. The following year, when his book *Horton Hears a Who!* appeared in print, it was dedicated to "My Great Friend, Mitsugi Nakamura of Kyoto, Japan," and the narrative's refrain is a pointed: "A person is a person no matter how small."

very seriously, at least externally. Even when he was reprimanded severely for doing things *his way*, he just didn't seem to care."

"His way" often manifested itself in odd behavior. Even in the tropics, for instance, bombing runs at extremely high altitude usually necessitated flying in arctic temperatures that could fall well below zero degrees. Airmen wore so many layers of clothing that it was not unusual for them to have to be hoisted into their aircraft by helpful ground crews. When the brass back in Australia discovered that not all aircrews were adhering to standard dress codes, however, instructions came down from Bomber Command that no Airman was to lift off on a mission without donning his "boilersuit"—the loose-fitting, one-piece coverall with a zip-in fleece lining that was standard USAAF issue. The 30-pound flak suits remained optional.

Jay blithely ignored these orders. Particularly on shorter missions, he figured that his bomber jacket was enough to protect him from the frigid temperatures, and in essence he went native, preferring to slide into the right-hand seat clad only in a pair of Australian bush shorts and boots, packing a sandwich, thermos, and his .45 sidearm in an Aussie haversack slung over his shoulder. On occasion he would deign to add a pair of long woolen socks to the ensemble.

It was almost as if he were two different men. On the ground he was known as the lanky guy with the effervescent grin as wide as a badger's stripe—a smart, well-liked, and respected officer. On one occasion, when a malfunctioning Marauder crashed on takeoff, killing all eight crew members, Jay was among the first on the scene to help remove the charred corpses and remained until the last of them had been recovered. Yet in the air he was viewed as a lazy pilot, too self-absorbed to be bothered to follow everyone else's rules. He wrote later that he did not mean to come off as a troublemaker. He was bored, but it was more than mere ennui. It was a malaise, a free-floating despair associated with the feeling that he was in the war but not a part of it. It had settled into his soul and detached him from his surroundings. Perhaps with good reason.

After the few inaugural missions by the 22nd over Rabaul, it was decided that the B-26 lacked sufficient range to continue bombing runs over New Britain. Fuel consumption increased dramatically when the plane flew over the Owen Stanley Range with a full bomb load, and too many of the Marauders were being forced to ditch on the return flight. This left the Bomb Group consigned almost exclusively to raids on Japanese bases on New Guinea and to antishipping patrols over the Solomon Sea.

Barring emergencies on these shorter runs, a B-26 copilot like Jay was expected to take control of an aircraft only during the brief period when its commander decided to crawl down into the nose to double-check the bombardier's flight headings and sightings. Jay wanted more responsibility. He wanted the left-hand seat. Before the war he didn't have time to watch the world go by because he was too busy moving through it. Now he felt as if the biggest moments of his life were passing him by.

He had beaten the odds through pure resourcefulness and strength of will on so many occasions, whether it was facing a prep school disciplinary hearing or a recalcitrant university admissions board, or even overcoming a failed eye test. Now those odds seemed to be catching up with him. As his petulance grew, so did his reputation as a slacker. It reached a point that when he drew a copilot's assignment in the Operations Hut, a collective groan would rise from that aircraft's crew.

The situation came to a head one day in late summer 1942 during a mission over Lae. The 22nd had been making daily runs on all Japanese holdings in northern New Guinea in order to keep as many enemy aircraft as possible "at home" to prevent them from attacking the Marines digging in on Guadalcanal. On this run Jay was again assigned to the right-hand seat, flying with a new pilot named Joe Seffern, recently transferred into the squadron. After staging at Port Moresby and clearing the Owen Stanleys, the mission became what the fliers had taken to calling a milk run as Seffern's B-26 soared north along the New Guinea coast. Since this was Seffern's first combat mission with the Group, the squadron commander wanted to see how the new man handled himself. So he had instructed Seffern to remain close to him in the formation.

With almost nothing to do, Jay drifted off to sleep. An alarmed Seffern thumped him on the chest several times, but Jay barely stirred. On
the approach to the enemy base at Lae, with thick bursts of ack-ack black-
ening the sky about them, Seffern's thwacks finally woke Jay—who casu-
ally strapped on his Mae West life preserver, buckled into the parachute
he had been sitting on, donned an old World War I helmet he'd picked up
in Townsville, and shut his eyes again.

Though their Marauder loosed its payload and returned to Garbutt
Field without damage, Seffern had briefly fallen out of formation while
trying to wake Jay, and his frustration with Jay's bizarre behavior had
boiled over. Although it may sound like a minor transgression, breaking
formation during a bombing run can have dire consequences. It not only
negates the meticulously planned crossfire that bomber gunners plan well
in advance but also strings out a bomb drop, making it easier for defending fighter planes to single out individual attackers.

Back on the ground, Seffern wrote a scathing report to the squadron's
flight commander. "The flack was really thick over the target, and then this
guy goes to sleep," Seffern reported. "I hit him in the chest to wake him
up. That's why I couldn't keep up with the rest of the formation. He woke
up and then went back to sleep again! We got hit by everything they could
throw at us and Zeamer sleeps his way through it. The guy isn't human."

Joe Seffern's complaints kicked into motion a series of consequences
that would change Jay's life forever. Jay would later gloss over the incident,
writing to a friend that he had merely "finagled a transfer." But the truth was
that Seffern's report packed such an emotional wallop that when Jay heard
about it he demanded a move to another outfit. Meanwhile, Col. Divine,
the 22nd's harried CO, had finally had enough. He was fast running not
only out of airworthy B-26s but also out of patience with the Eagle Scout
whose evident intellectual brilliance was offset by what a magazine writer
called Jay's "screwball stunts." Today the adjective "screwball" does imply
a minor transgression, perhaps a light, comic breach of etiquette. But at the
time, and given the context, it was a serious charge to level.

Col. Divine was under a lot of pressure. His outfit seemed almost jinxed from the outset of its deployment, having lost six bombers during the jump from Hawaii. He had also presided over a string of mishaps that included losing three more of his planes and their entire crews to tropical storms during training exercises before the Group had even reached Garbutt Field. Adding to his woes, Divine had the dubious distinction of being the commander of the first Americans from MacArthur's Southwest Pacific Command to be captured by the Japanese, when two noncommissioned officers—a technical sergeant and a corporal—bailed out of their damaged B-26 near Rabaul.

Even after the 22nd's runs over Rabaul were scaled back and limited to missions over northern New Guinea, the Group had the misfortune to face the toughest opposition of any American air unit based in Australia when the Japanese Navy's famous Tainan Wing, a handpicked unit of aces, moved its base of operations from Rabaul to Lae. During a bombing run over Lae on which Divine flew as an observer, Zeros from that squadron had so badly damaged his plane's landing gear that he was forced to take over the controls and belly-land. No one was seriously hurt, but the Marauder became one of the nearly half of Divine's original 51 aircraft that had been either lost or semipermanently hangared since their arrival in Australia.

The outfit's travails had reached a point where even other units felt sorry for it. After two of the 22nd's bombers crashed on takeoff on successive days, the official combat diary of the 8th Photo Squadron noted, "The B-26s are receiving a lot of unjust criticism because they are cracking up so often. But it must be remembered, these are 1940 planes flying combat. Because the U.S. considers this front secondary, the finest B-26 pilots and crews are losing their lives."*

---

* Even Divine's apparent triumphs came with an asterisk. On June 9, two days after the successful conclusion to the Battle of Midway, a Texas congressman named Lyndon Baines Johnson used his political connections to wangle his way onto a bombing run over Lae as an observer. Johnson, a commissioned U.S. Navy officer who had persuaded President Roosevelt to send him on an inspection tour of the Pacific The-

In fact, over 100 men from the 22nd Bomb Group had already been killed in just two months of fighting, and by this point Col. Divine was not averse to jettisoning one more. The colonel sensed that Seffern's complaints were emblematic of the general bitterness his men were beginning to feel over being, as one pilot wrote, "picked off one by one, nearly alone." Another pilot from the 22nd added that "observers from the States and from the High Command were relatively few and far between, [and] the lonely manner from which the Group operated had created the conviction among our crews that we were carrying the war load in the Southwest Pacific."

One of the Bomb Group's senior officers summed up quite succinctly the dreadful miasma that had encompassed the 22nd's Airmen: "If they do not relieve us we'll all be dead, the whole Group, in another six months. We need rest and some help. We hear and we read in the papers of great fleets of planes to come over here to fight, but we never see them. We do the suicidal work, and I guess I'm getting a little bitter."

If the transfer of one man, even an inherently good man like Jay, would ease even an iota of the duress his Airmen felt, Col. Divine was more than happy to accommodate the request. That is how and why, in September 1942, Jay was cut lose from the 22nd and reassigned to the 43rd Bomb Group. The 43rd consisted of four squadrons, and as it happened the first of those was just then touching down in Australia with its brand-new B-17 Flying Fortresses.

---

ater, saw the raid as a means to burnish his combat résumé. But before the Marauder in which the future president was flying could reach its target the plane's generator failed, forcing the pilot to turn back. MacArthur, no stranger to politics, nonetheless awarded the congressman the Silver Star, citing Johnson's coolness under fire after his aircraft was intercepted by "eight hostile fighters." Most of the 22nd's Airmen at Garbutt Field knew the story was baloney, but Divine and the rest had little choice but to go along with the tale.

• • •

JAY WAS OVERJOYED. THE IRONY OF HIS REDEPLOYMENT WAS NOT LOST on him. Back at Langley he had originally been assigned to the 43rd after graduating from Advanced Flight School. But the unit's heavy bombers were slow to arrive in Virginia, and in the interim he had been ordered to Ohio to test-fly the new B-26s. By the time he returned to Langley, the 43rd had been officially activated, or "stood up," but because of Jay's experience with Marauders he had been folded into the 22nd.

While he had flown west with his new Group, the 43rd had taken up its own submarine screening missions along the New England coastline and, later, in the Panama Canal Zone. But Jay had always missed the B-17 Group. Even the acronym formed from the outfit's motto—"Willing, Able, Ready"—resonated with Jay's desire for combat in a Flying Fortress. Now he was back with the Bomb Group and his anticipation ran high.

Four-engine bombers like the Flying Fortress and, later, the B-24 Liberator—which the Airmen dubbed the "Big Boxcars"—would prove the only aircraft capable of reaching targets in the Pacific Theater that the Japanese assumed were beyond America's range. In an effort to attack Japanese installations even farther afield, the Allies' plan was for several of the 43rd's squadrons to eventually be housed at Port Moresby. For now, however, with Port Moresby so close to enemy airbases and so lightly defended, the risk to the Bomb Group was too great. Gen. MacArthur understood that his first priority was to secure Port Moresby.

To that end, the War Department was finally forced to confront the fact that it could not allow the feud between Gen. MacArthur and Gen. Brett to continue. The sniping between the Southwest Pacific's Supreme Commander and his top Airman had become more vociferous in the months since MacArthur's arrival, and so it was that in the summer of 1942, Army Chief of Staff Gen. Marshall consented, fairly or not, to MacArthur's fevered demands to dismiss Gen. Brett. As Brett's successor was later to admit, "[Brett] had not had much to work with, and his luck had been mostly bad." But as military leaders since Napoleon had known, in war you make your own luck.

In the peculiar manner in which military organizations often operate, Gen. Brett was awarded a medal—a Silver Star for "gallantry in action," pinned on by MacArthur himself—before being sacked. The next day Brett boarded a B-17 and, with his medal, flew from Australia for the final time. Within weeks he took up his up his new command as head of the Army Air Force's Caribbean Defense Command, the ultimate backwater.

11

THE BULLDOG

FINDING GEN. BRETT'S REPLACEMENT WAS NOT EASY. FEW COMPETENT officers viewed the prospect of working under MacArthur as appealing. After Chief of Staff Marshall's old friend and first choice, Gen. Frank Andrews, turned him down flat, Marshall submitted two candidates to the Supreme Commander. One was Gen. Jimmy Doolittle, by now famous worldwide for his raid on Tokyo and soon to receive the Medal of Honor for the bombing mission. But the last thing "Dugout Doug" needed in Australia was the spotlight shining on a man who had actually taken the fight to the enemy. And it is doubtful that Doolittle, headstrong himself, would have found the offer compelling. Instead he successfully lobbied for an assignment to the European front. Doolittle was placed with the nascent 8th Air Force, based in England, from where he was rapidly promoted to commanding general of the 12th Air Force, soon to be operating in North Africa.

This left the job under MacArthur open for a comparatively unknown 53-year-old general, George Churchill Kenney. It was a serendipitous selection. Like Jay Zeamer, Kenney had caught the aviation bug while studying engineering at M.I.T., in his case prior to World War I. When the United States entered combat in Europe in 1917, Kenney, again like Jay, wanted nothing so much as to fly. He got his wish when, after enlisting in the U.S. Signal Corps, he was assigned to a reconnaissance squadron of the newly formed Army Air Service that specialized in photo flights behind enemy lines. These were dangerous runs; Kenney flew 75 missions and was shot down twice, earning both the Distinguished Service Cross and the Silver Star.

Kenney's combat experience gave him a keen sense of the chaos and uncertainty of war: and the fact that he was one of only four pilots from his unit to survive the conflict left a lasting impression regarding the importance of adequately training young men, many of them still in their teens, before sending them into actual combat. After the armistice, Kenney, by then a captain, opted to make the military a career. He proved both an able strategist and an innovative tactician, and as his star rose he acquired a reputation as an engineering wizard whose grasp of the new science of aeronautics was responsible for helping to modernize the Army's aviation wing. In the early 1920s, while test-flying several versions of prototype bombers for the Air Service's Engineering School, he not only studied how aircraft were actually built but immersed himself in the possibilities of modifying them to be more effective in combat.

He then went on to teach classes on low-altitude attack techniques at the premier military school for Airmen, the Air Corps Tactical School in Langley, Virginia, where he emphasized the destructiveness of forward-firing guns against a variety of targets. It was at the tactical school that he drafted and devised the concept of mounting two fixed .30-caliber machine guns on the wings of an old de Havilland bomber. His engineering background was also integral to the development of both the leakproof fuel tank and a bomb fuse that would explode ordnance in the air, showering a greater area with deadly shrapnel.

While experimenting with these tactical aeronautical improvements, Kenney also honed his reputation as a strategist. It was during a teaching stint at the Army's War College that he published a groundbreaking paper, years ahead of its time, detailing how the service's air wing should be composed and used. And during his 1940 deployment to France as a military observer he angered some of his superiors when he went on record predicting that the U.S. Air Corps "as presently constructed" would never compete "with the kind of war the Germans are going to have here." Blunt opinions were typical of the man.

Kenney stood only five feet, five inches tall, which perhaps lent credence in some circles to a theory that his boundless energy was fueled by a Napoleon complex. Even George Churchill Kenney's name swaggered, and relaxing with him, a colleague once noted, was an exhausting experience. Despite his relatively short stature he supercharged any room he entered with a Cagney-like energy. This aura was enhanced by his deep-set hushpuppy eyes and the jagged scar that ran across his teardrop chin, a vivid souvenir from one of the crash landings he barely survived.

Newspapermen and magazine writers consistently used terms such as "feisty," "tenacious," and—no doubt in homage to his protrusive lower lip—"bulldog" to describe Kenney in their dispatches. There is no evidence, however, that the general displayed any of the overly aggressive or domineering behavior commonly associated with the so-called short-man syndrome. At bottom, he was known throughout the service as an officer more concerned with the welfare and morale of his men than with his own advancement. In contrast to what had been predicted for Doolittle, Kenney would prove able to work with MacArthur.

By the time Kenney's plane touched down in Australia on a cold winter day in late July, MacArthur had moved his headquarters from Melbourne to Brisbane. At their first face-to-face meeting, Kenney listened patiently as the Supreme Commander ranted for a good 30 minutes about Brett, Brett's staff, and the overall sorry state of Allied airpower in the Pacific. The ineptitude of the Allies' airpower during the Battle of the Coral Sea was a particular grievance. When MacArthur was angry his voice could scour a stove, and he ended his tirade with one overriding demand. His highest expectation for Kenney, he said, was utter and complete loyalty to himself, Gen. MacArthur.

When it came Kenney's turn to speak he assured the Supreme Commander that he recognized who was in charge and would certainly respect the chain of command—as long as, he added, the respect flowed both ways. "I didn't ask to come out here," he told MacArthur. "You asked for me. My gang is always loyal to me, and through me they will be loyal to you. You be loyal to me and my gang and make this fifty-fifty, or I'll be calling you from San Francisco and telling you that I have quit."

At this MacArthur rose slowly from his chair and walked around his desk. Kenney had no idea what to expect. At first the Supreme Commander's face, a patrician mask, betrayed no hint of emotion. Then the corners of his famously downturned mouth rippled into a smile. As Kenney recalled in his diary, "He grinned and put his hand on my shoulder and said, 'I think we are going to get along all right.'"

Kenney, reacting instinctively, had played to the general's massive ego in order to thaw what the eminent naval historian Bruce Gamble describes as MacArthur's "frosty shell of mistrust. Perhaps his small stature was a contributing factor, but it was probably Kenney's infectious blend of intelligence and energy that won over the Supreme Commander."

In either case, the new man in charge of MacArthur's air force would need to put those qualities to work immediately. Before leaving the States, Kenney had been briefed by Gen. "Hap" Arnold not to expect much in the way of reinforcements. Arnold admitted to Kenney that the weight of America's airpower was being dedicated to defeating Germany, and that he would have to make do with the 600 or so aircraft already in the Pacific Theater. He could expect no more. Now, on his first day on the job, Kenney also learned from his new boss of the enemy landings that had just occurred at Buna. True to his reputation, Kenney wasted no time and flew to Port Moresby the next morning. What he found there was an Allied force whose morale had hit rock bottom and which was convinced that New Guinea was lost.

During briefings at the Kila Kila airstrip, Kenney was dismayed by the poor if not crippled condition of so many Allied fighter planes—fewer than 50 of the 245 in-theater were combat ready. He stewed silently as frontline officers groused about the glacial pace of a supply line that had left them without spare parts. Similarly, he had no answer when a maintenance crew chief showed him an entire cabinet of requisition forms that had been rejected and returned because they contained minor filing errors. One mechanic even said that he and his crew were forced to bring filthy and nearly spent spark plugs to their tents each night to scrape them clean with pocketknives before plugging them back into aircraft engines at first light.

The Airmen, Kenney discovered, assumed that most of the parts and materials they requested were being shipped to the European Theater. At first the general suspected that the searing heat of previous months at Port Moresby had encouraged such fevered anxieties. In any case, even if he agreed with them, he dared not say so, but he made a mental note to look into the matter.

On a more personal level, Kenney was also appalled by the wretched food being served in the chow halls at Port Moresby. So many mess cups were encrusted with strange green algae that the Airmen had simply stopped washing them; the powdered milk tasted like liquid chalk; and the barely edible potatoes and rice were often rancid and contaminated with dead flies and rat droppings. So awful was this daily regimen that the men had begun to recall with fondness the cracker-dry Spam and baloney sandwiches served for breakfast, lunch, and dinner on the transports that had delivered them to Australia. As a result of the terrible food the troops were losing an average of 30 pounds each per combat tour, and the occasional delivery of a shipment of canned corned beef, the once-despised "corn willy," was now treated as an occasion to celebrate.

Spirits fell even further with each Airmen brought down by malaria, dysentery, and the ulcerous cuts and scratches that the men simply called jungle rot. The daily rations of quinine were constantly running out, and the medical tent not only smelled like the inside of a leper but reverberated with a weird, scrofulous coughing, deep and percussive, as if something was trying to claw its way out of the chests of the patients splayed across the cots.

The shoddy state of the equipment, the lousy food, the rampant illness: it was no wonder, Kenney realized, that an eerie despondency had settled over the base. Even the poker games seemed listless.

His inspection of the new Seven Mile airfield was even more distressing. Kenney was astounded to learn that raids on Rabaul had been such haphazard affairs that no flight leader had ever been designated to guide a bombing formation because a combination of bad weather and the shoddy conditions of the planes had left the Airmen doubtful that they would even reach the target anyway. The general was also told that when attacking aircraft did manage to reach the Japanese stronghold, primary targets were never predetermined. Pilots and bombardiers merely dropped their ordnance helter-skelter.

Even the weather forecasting proved slack, with the Army's aerologists providing stormfront predictions based on historical seasonal weather patterns in lieu of reconnaissance flights. More troubling, no one seemed to find anything amiss with this lack of organization. Perhaps, Kenney began to suspect, MacArthur's analysis of his predecessor's shortcomings was not so far off.

Kenney remained at Port Moresby all day listening to complaints and making notes. Before departing he ordered several quick fixes—each bombing mission would now be flown in formation with a lead pilot; primary targets and at least two backup targets would be designated beforehand; weather forecasts would be based on real-time analysis whenever possible. He also promised to untangle the kinks in the inefficient supply line that was keeping planes grounded.

Once back in Brisbane he signed an order relieving most of Brett's "deadwood" generals of their assignments, and he instructed that refrigerators, mosquito screens, and sacks of cement to pave the mess halls' dirt floors be immediately shipped to Port Moresby. Finally, in an effort to speed the movement of supplies, he also ordered the commanders of the Army Air Force supply depot in southern Australia, over 2,000 miles away from the front lines, to move their entire warehouse complex nearer to the continent's north coast and begin releasing the spare parts they had been hoarding on the assumption that New Guinea would soon fall.

Kenney explained his thinking to a reporter, beginning with the admission, "The Jap is a hell of a tough boy." Then he inserted a caveat. "But he's best when he's attacking. That's why our cue is to attack him. The attacker always has the advantage of surprise, and the Jap has not got any crystal ball."

Only then did Kenney approach MacArthur with his strategic vision. The two agreed that Rabaul would remain the Allies' primary bombing target. That, however, was easier said than done. With the Japanese on the Kokoda Track knocking at Port Moresby's back door, any raids on Rabaul would have to be made by Australian-based aircraft. Even when it was safe enough to restage and refuel at Port Moresby, this required allocating anywhere from one to two days to make a single run. Who knew when enemy aircraft might suddenly appear overhead?

Moreover, the two generals agreed that for the moment the Allies had more pressing concerns. The enemy landings at Buna would have to be repulsed. Or, as Kenney noted in his diary, "There was no use talking about playing across the street until we got the Nips off our front lawn."

Within days Kenney had every aircraft at his disposal aloft over New Guinea. These planes bombed and strafed the enemy troops bogged down on the Kokoda Track from treetop level, and blasted the Japanese forces assembled on the beachheads near Buna. But what really turned the situation around was Kenney's understanding that if the enemy was without food, ammunition, and reinforcements—without a supply stem— its assault could be stopped cold. To that effect Fortresses and Liberators, Marauders and Mitchells, even A-20 Boston dive-bombers and old Australian Beauforts—screened by waves of American P-39 Airacobras, P-40 Warhawks, and Australian Beaufighters—darkened the skies over New Guinea's north coast and the sea-lanes leading to Buna.

It was also Kenney's groundbreaking masterstroke to employ the 43rd Bomb Group's cargo planes as the first heavy military airlift in history. Kenney was aware that Germany had transported troops by air from Africa to Spain during the Spanish Civil War, and before his arrival Down Under small contingents of mostly Australian infantry had been ferried to specific hot spots throughout the Southwest Pacific Theater. Six months earlier, for instance, the RAAF had commandeered commercial airliners to insert a company of 300 riflemen into the New Guinea bush to stop a Japanese advance.

But now, with no seagoing troop transports or cargo ships at his disposal, Kenney ordered nearly two regiments of American infantry-men flown to emergency strips hacked out of the pit-pit grass that grew wing-deep southeast of Buna. This flanking maneuver not only eased the pressure on the Aussies making a stand on the Kokoda Track, but allowed for safe perimeters to be established around Buna. Once these bases were secure the same cargo planes were put back into the air delivering tons of food, ammunition, artillery pieces, bulldozers, mules, and even a 250-bed hospital tent to the area. It was a move that turned the tide for those the general called "my youngsters up there."

As Kenney's grasp of the local terrain and the logistic hurdles it pre-sented evolved, he rapidly discerned that the air forces under his com-mand faced a fourfold task: negating the multiple Japanese air threats that emanated in an arc from northern New Guinea to the Bismarcks; harassing Japanese shipping both on the high seas and in Simpson Har-bour; providing close air support for Allied ground troops striking enemy positions in New Guinea and the lower Solomons; and airlifting troops and supplies to wherever they were most needed at the moment. Quite often these multiple challenges appeared to loop back on themselves in a deadly parabola, as when he reasoned that bombing raids over the enemy airfields at Rabaul were in fact supporting the American offensive on Guadalcanal not only by destroying aircraft, but also by keeping the enemy "home" to defend the base.

Prioritizing these efforts required continual face-to-face interactions with his commanders on the ground, and Kenney became such a frequent flier between Australia and New Guinea that every day two lunch tables were set for him, one in Brisbane and one in Port Moresby. His memories of flying missions over Western Europe during World War I were never far from his mind. During his shuttles to and from the front lines he could not help noticing that while his bullet-catching air squadrons were being commanded by green captains and even greener lieutenants, MacArthur's desk jockeys back in Brisbane were displaying enough stars, bars, and fruit salad to stock a commissary. He remedied this by wrangling from the Supreme Commander the authority to hand out decorations up to and including the Distinguished Service Cross without having to go through MacArthur or his staff.

"Our only excuse for living was to help them," Kenney wrote of the "youngsters" who were actually fighting the war. "The payoff would be Jap ships sunk and Jap planes shot down. As far as I was concerned, the ones accomplishing that job were going to get top priority on everything."

He was true to his word: a rash of field promotions and combat-ribbon awards ensued, and even maintenance crew chiefs were presented with wristwatches, donated by Arde Bulova himself, for keeping their planes in the air.

The food, however, never got any better.

12

A MICROSCOPIC
METROPOLIS

THE JAPANESE RETREAT OVER THE OWEN STANLEY RANGE AND BACK TO Buna proved both a psychological and a tactical victory. The setback, however minor, was the first land defeat the Empire had suffered since the war began. Perhaps more important, the Americans now considered Port Moresby secure enough to permanently house B-17s. Among the initial planes to arrive in September 1942 for one-week "cycles" was a heavy-bomber squadron from the 43rd Bomb Group. Accompanying it was Capt. Jay Zeamer.

Although Port Moresby was the capital of Papua New Guinea, its pre-war population had barely topped 4,500, divided between a small band of hardy Australian and European copra and rubber traders living near the snug little harbor and a larger contingent of indigenous Papuans hunting wild pigs and farming small plots of pawpaw and yams in outlying villages composed of thatched bamboo huts built on stilts six feet off the ground. The traders had since been evacuated by military order, and to the arriving American Airmen their new base seemed an alien world. In Australia the Yanks had split their deployments between coastal enclaves such as Townsville, surrounded by a fertile and temperate plain; and, beyond the low, rugged Queensland mountains, the vast inland area known as the "outback." The palettes in this hot, bone-dry environment ran to rusty ochers, dull umbers, and smoky taupes—with the occasional ruddy glow of a blood-orange sunset shattering the dusty monotony. It was no wonder that the rum sights, sounds, and aromas of New Guinea were guaranteed to confound the Americans, whose conception of the mysterious South Pacific might have been formed by equal parts *King Kong* and Dorothy Lamour.

More than 40 species of birds-of-paradise wandered Port Moresby's outlying rain forest, their honeyed whistles combining with the scraggly carillon cries of dazzling companies of hookbill parrots to produce a sound track melodic enough for one of Lamour's "Sarong Girl" pictures. Amid this cacophony seemingly endless flocks of magnificent birdwing butterflies flitted between the twining branches of towering fig trees, their pink-and-white canopies shading groves of scarlet orchids. And the native Papuan women sported more color than most Americans were accustomed to seeing on their girls back home. They used a mixture of berries and betel nuts to dye their hair and clothes in an electric mélange of greens, blues, purples, and reds, while their teeth glowed scarlet from betel nut juice. At first glance nothing was missing but hurricanes, tidal waves, and headhunting cannibals (some of whom, in fact, still practiced anthropophagy, mostly for revenge, in remote corners of the bush).

Jay was familiar with the base from his staging and refueling stops while he was flying with the 22nd, and he cautioned his new mates in the 43rd not to be fooled by the exotic if superficial beauty of Port Moresby's blooming frangipani and hibiscus, its dazzling waterfalls, its frolicking

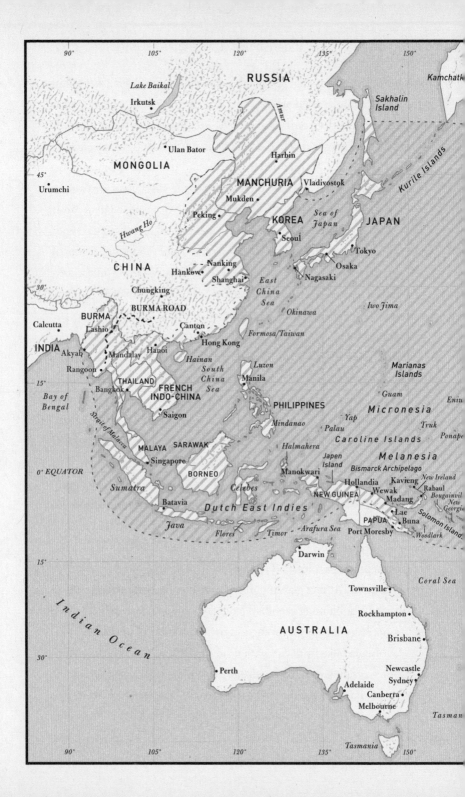

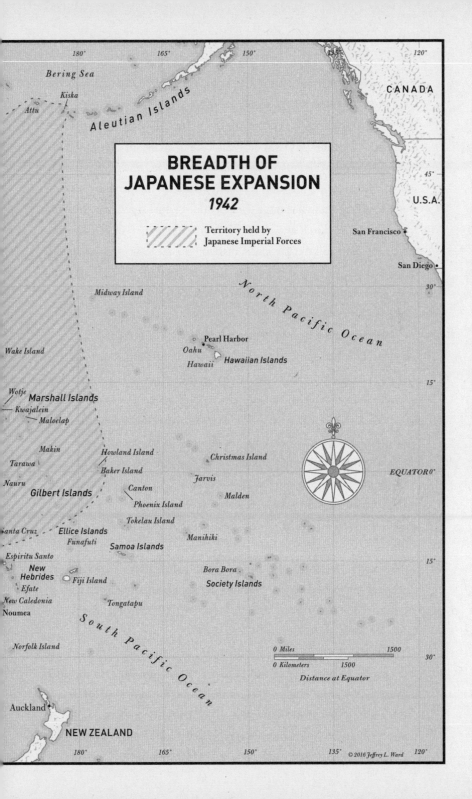

BREADTH OF
JAPANESE EXPANSION
1942

Territory held by
Japanese Imperial Forces

tree kangaroos and fuzzy-eared koalas that resembled nothing so much as plush toys. They were, he told them, about to stake billet in a mosquito-infested hellmouth that was encompassed on three sides by malarial jungle, and where the main dirt road dead-ended at the edge of a leech-infested swamp crawling with crocodiles and deadly snakes. The entire coast, he added, was a humid inferno alternately baked by the parching sun—"it was like walking into a shower with all your clothes on," wrote one Fortress pilot—or scoured by walls of wind-driven rain that could split rocks. It was the kind of heat, Jay knew, that could melt reality into unfamiliar shapes, and it was not for nothing that a melancholy English navigator had christened the waters that flanked Port Moresby's jug-handle harbor Caution Bay and Bootless Inlet.

Clouds of mosquitoes competed with hordes of black flies for insect primacy. The crunching of their dead husks underfoot after the nightly DDT spraying reminded some Airmen of the sound of walking on popcorn in a filthy movie theater. The base's "Diggers," as the Aussie soldiers had been known for at least a century, taught the Yanks how to rig the mosquito tenting over their cots "as tightly and handsomely and complexly as a three-master under full sail," as one war correspondent put it. Still, there was no escaping the "New Guinea Salute"—the constant gesture of brushing away the hovering swarms of biting and stinging pests. It was not unusual for a single swipe of the hand to kill three or four insects, and at one point over a third of the 43rd's aircrews were hospitalized with either malaria, beriberi, or dengue fever, a particularly pernicious viral disease characterized by fever, debilitating joint pain, skin rash, and searing headaches. Disease ran so rampant at Port Moresby that the Americans soon nicknamed the base "Death Valley."

After the 43rd's forward echelon settled in, Jay was officially posted to the Group's Headquarters Squadron as a "supernumerary" to the intelligence staff. He was also unofficially instructed to begin roaming among the bomber crews as a "pilot-at-large," filling in for fliers grounded by injury or illness. Given the attrition rate, Jay found plenty of work among the patchwork crews, usually flying as either copilot or flight engineer, but in a few cases commanding one of the Group's B-17s. Although construction had begun on at least five more airdromes around the town, Port Moresby's primary airstrips remained the two Kenney had visited months earlier, Kila Kila and Seven Mile. Both were still in deplorable condition, with the latter proving particularly problematic for the 43rd's bomber pilots.

The searing equatorial sun baked the runways so dry that billowing eddies of sand kicked up by the propellers blinded pilots taking off and landing, engulfing their windshields like great, amorphous tumbleweeds. And when it rained, as it did almost daily for a good half of the year, many a skipper fought to avoid skidding off the slick, muddy track and into the mangrove swamps that lined the coast. More ominously for American fliers trained on the flat, forgiving surfaces of spacious runways back in the States, the foreboding Owen Stanley Range rose only a few miles from the end of Seven Mile, shouldering the near horizon like a natural backboard.

About a third of the way up the steepening slopes, the lowland rain forest gave way to a thick tanglewood of oak, beech, and red cedar before it abruptly ended at the tree line in what must have appeared to the Airmen as a precipitous blade of granite peaks soaring to 13,000 feet—if they could see them at all, for these jagged declivities were almost invariably hidden by thick clouds and luminous swirling mists. Though Australian cartographers had mapped the few passes bisecting the towering mountaintops, rare was the day when the clouds parted long enough for a pilot to actually see where he was flying, and this lack of visibility forced all but the luckiest navigators to rely entirely on instruments when negotiating the heights. The crew would go dead silent as a pilot listened to the sound of radio beam signals bouncing off the mountains to make his bearings—"flying on the beam," this was called, and it was at times more harrowing than the idea of any enemy gunfire.

Prior to the 43rd's arrival, Port Moresby had been occupied by a small

Royal Australian Air Force contingent and maintained by a skeleton staff of ground crews. So primitive were the conditions that these men were often forced to chase loitering wallabies from the runways before takeoffs and landings. Aside from a refueling depot and staging area between the Australian mainland and Japanese targets farther north, the base had been used by the Americans primarily as an emergency landing site for disabled planes or flights socked in by weather. Bombers like the Townsville-based Marauders of Jay's former 22nd Group would put down at Port Moresby and, while flight crews scrambled to roll out 55-gallon drums of high-octane aviation fuel to hand-pump into the tanks, their pilots would scan the sky with engines idling. Since the Japanese bombed the port almost daily, these "top-offs" were performed with alacrity.

Now, with American Airmen moving in permanently, Navy Seabees overseeing a company of African-American stevedores arrived to grade and extend Seven Mile—soon to be renamed Jackson Field in honor of an RAAF fighter pilot killed the previous April. Incredibly, with Australian cities such as Darwin being bombed with regularity and a Japanese invasion looming just over the northern horizon, the Australian government continued to hew to the maintenance of a "white Australia" policy.

As the U.S. Army Air Force *Historical Study No. 9* noted (somewhat matter-of-factly), "The establishment of barriers against the immigration of black, brown, and yellow races has received the support of all [Australian] political parties, and could not be ignored by American military authorities." This law was in fact responsible for barring two "Negro" companies of the U.S. Army's 31st Truck Battalion from entering the country, and it was only the personal intervention of President Roosevelt that calmed the racial storm.

Yet even the American president was forced to accept a caveat stating that in exchange for the Australian government's permission to admit the urgently required "colored troops," they were to be withdrawn immediately after they were no longer needed. To the African-American stevedores, it must have appeared much ado about nothing, as after they installed interlocking steel planking known as Marsden matting over the rough dirt and brown grass of Jackson Airfield, their work came to little avail. Despite the metal overlay, nature prevailed, and the strip remained as dangerous as ever to navigate. Even a third parallel runway built by the construction crews was, in Jay's words, "a tire swallower. As sandy as a beach or as mucky as a swamp depending on the weather."

Many of the rickety white and yellow wooden houses that overlooked Port Moresby's tiny harbor still stood—albeit with most of their windows blown out from explosive concussions. However, the military "bases" that rose farther inland on the coastal lowland were bombed-out shells. Since capturing Rabaul the Japanese had, with impunity, launched continual air raids on the town, attacks that proliferated with the taking of Lae and Salamaua. During the month of May alone Jackson Field withstood no fewer than 21 separate attacks. During these assaults scores of enemy bombers dropped their loads against minimal resistance. Zeros swooped in to strafe at all hours of the day and the enemy's own version of flying-boat seaplanes, reconfigured to carry earthshaking 2,000-pound bombs in their large fuselages, were a continuing presence in the skies above.

After each attack, work crews would fill the bomb craters with non-compacted gravel, sand, and earth to create a soft, dry mush that proved a further hindrance to the sinking wheels of a fuel-and-bomb-laden B-17. One of Jay's fellow pilots recalled, "A number of times we had to take off downwind and we'd clip grass for a mile or more getting the wheels up and bleeding up the flaps before we really could figure we were flying. Nothing like a good thrill first thing—why wait to get to the target?"

Jay had never seen it happen, but he heard credible stories about Japanese pilots on bombing runs also releasing bundles of letters written by Australian POWs at Rabaul. These communications, though certainly comforting to forlorn families back home wondering if their sons, husbands, and fathers were still alive, had no impact on the Australian veterans of the fighting, particularly those who had hidden out in the jungles of New Britain before making their escape. They had witnessed Japanese atrocities firsthand, and a few handwritten notes dropped from the sky were certainly not enough to put them in a forgiving mood.

The Japanese, after all, could afford such magnanimous gestures. Their bombing runs over Port Moresby had destroyed every permanent structure around the airstrips, leaving the Americans to make do with storehouses and all manner of huts thrown together by native "camp servants" paid in forks and spoons, the occasional ax, and even an aircraft's broken engine rods, from which they fashioned hunting spears. These shacks—which served as headquarters, operations, and intelligence centers—were constructed of jungle grass and rough planking that rotted and mildewed within weeks. In a dubious attempt to hide their aircraft the Americans were forced to construct palm-frond revetments, as flimsy as they were obvious.

There was no electricity except in the mess hall, which finally had a concrete floor thanks to General Kenney. And a filthy tent city that served as the men's living quarters sprouted like green-tarp mushrooms around this motley collection of edifices. Latrines consisted of a long trench on the base's outskirts or, for bowel movements, a walk to the jungle with a spade or a shovel. One of the 43rd's pilots recalled another officer from his squadron initiating a letter-writing campaign, with each Airman imploring his family back home to send cedar chips to offset the stench. "When those packages finally started to arrive it was like living in a huge hope chest," he said. "But at least it masked the vile smell."

Amid this desolation and devastation one makeshift building shone like a beacon. The RAAF officers club—dubbed the "Oasis"—had been erected far enough away from the Kila Kila airfield to have escaped the Japanese bombs. The Australian Airmen welcomed their American counterparts, and by the dim light behind blackout curtains the two groups sang familiar songs and clinked pints of beer and the occasional whiskey glass if a bottle or two happened to be in stock. The Yanks taught their hosts the words to "The Whiffenpoof Song" ("We're little black lambs who have gone astray . . .") and the Aussies were fond of "Waltzing Matilda." Both sides knew the words to "Bless 'Em All" ("the long and the short and the tall . . .") by heart.

Many of the Australian fliers had fought with the Royal Air Force over England and the Channel before trading in their Spitfires and Hurricanes for Airacobras and Kittyhawks when the war lapped onto their own country's shore. Jay found them a reticent group, more reserved and "decorous and old-school" than the Australians he had encountered back in Townsville. Their voices betrayed a world-weariness that he decided was only natural. Jay understood that these men had experienced years of war on both sides of the globe, and their officers club was where they reluctantly counted heads, where the man you drank with one night might not be there the next.

Port Moresby may have been a town built on mud and wrath, but every man stationed there recognized that it remained the Allies' last stronghold in the Southwest Pacific. And though the enemy may have been defeated on the Kokoda Track, just across the Owen Stanleys still stood thousands of Japanese troops receiving regular supplies and reinforcements from Rabaul. Despite Port Moresby's isolation, both the American and the Japanese high commands recognized its strategic importance. A "microscopic metropolis," the correspondent John Lardner called it, "standing in bold relief on the map of the world at war."

To Gen. MacArthur, the "microscopic" Port Moresby was the springboard from which he would sweep the Japanese out of northern New Guinea and then from the entire Southwest Pacific. For its part, Imperial General Headquarters viewed the Allied presence in southern New Guinea as the final impediment to Japan's invasion of Australia. War strategists in Tokyo calculated that their forces were capable of launching amphibious operations in the area up to a maximum of 500 miles. This was the distance not only between Rabaul and Port Moresby, but also between Port Moresby and the most suitable invasion site on Australia's northeast coast, near the city of Cairns. It was obvious to the Allies that the constant air attacks on Port Moresby were a precursor to another ground invasion by the Japanese.

Making matters worse, Port Moresby lacked any significant radar installations. The only two stations up and running were severely lacking in range and had multiple blind spots, and, of course, spare parts were in short supply when the machinery inevitably broke down. This made the base's early warning air raid system extremely primitive, since it relied almost entirely on radio reports from Australian coastwatchers camped in the bush on the other side of the mountains. Given the range's near-constant cloud cover and thick rain squalls, these lonely lookouts could scarcely be counted on to spot every enemy formation heading south. Japanese planes were often atop the Americans well before the red flag could be raised over the crude Operation Tower constructed of logs.

Jay and the rest learned soon enough that seconds after the three rifle-shot signals fired by the air raid sentry echoed through the camp, every crew had best rush its plane aloft lest the aircraft be turned into smoldering hunks of metal or chopped to pieces by Japanese fragmentation bombs. "Daisy Cutters," the Americans' term for this frightening ordnance, sent scores of jagged shards of metal whizzing through the air at eye level. Some thought the enemy bombs, spinning as they dropped, sounded like a piercing whirlybird. To others it was a shrill whistle. In either case, if a man heard those terrifying sounds, it was probably too late.

This was just another reason why many of the American aircrews at Port Moresby eschewed the base's tent city and instead slept (or tried to sleep) on sodden blankets beneath their bombers, with only wings for roofs. Even so, one of the pilots and another crewman always remained inside near the cockpit, ready to kick over the engines at the first thrum of enemy aircraft reverberating off the nearby hills. It was not unusual to see planes with cold motors reeling down the runway and clawing for air as bombs and machine-gun fire rained down among them.

The Australian government in Melbourne recognized that Port Moresby remained the last, precarious line of defense for the country, and had already made secret plans to cede the top half of the southern continent, from Brisbane up through the Northern Territory, should the Japanese use it to stage an invasion. To Airmen like Jay Zeamer, however, such grand strategies were well beyond their pay grade. He and his squadmates had only one priority—to keep themselves alive and inflict enough damage on the enemy until the United States could devote its full might and resources to the war in the Pacific.

13

KEN'S MEN

IN 1942, AND FOR MUCH OF THE REMAINDER OF WORLD WAR II, PRESS coverage of the "Mighty" 8th Air Force in Europe overshadowed that of George Kenney's ragtag outfit in the Pacific. Kenney's assemblage, which had been redesignated the 5th Air Force shortly after his arrival in Australia, was generally considered to have been thrown together from leftover Airmen and other replacement parts and hurriedly deployed to the Southwest Pacific Theater almost as an afterthought.

This was not far from the truth. Early on, even MacArthur described the airpower allotted to his Southwest Pacific Command as "a rabble of boulevard shock troops whose contribution to the war effort was practically nil." And though to some extent the force would remain the "Forgotten Fifth" for the remainder of the war, the Airmen's achievements throughout the theater were gradually gaining notice within the halls and planning rooms of the War Department. Much of this was due to Kenney.

Unlike the 8th Air Force, which flew strategic offensive strikes against the Nazi war machine, Kenney and his 5th had been tasked merely with waging a war of containment while the European campaign took priority. Chief of U.S. Naval Operations Adm. Ernest King estimated that only 15 percent of all Allied war resources were being distributed throughout the Pacific Theater. Worse, this trickle of equipment and weapons being shipped southwest had to be shared with the defenders of India and China. Fortunately, King's sharp public hints that further Japanese advances might prompt a reevaluation of America's commitment to the European Theater so alarmed the British that they did not put up much of a fight when in late 1942 President Roosevelt agreed to at least attempt to double the amount of men and matériel dedicated to the Pacific. This was a comparatively small triumph, as there remained no doubt that victory in Europe was foremost in Roosevelt's, and America's, thoughts.

The perception of the 5th Air Force as a second-class unit did not stop Kenney from using his distinctive combination of energy, personality, and intelligence to turn it into a feared and respected fighting machine. Even MacArthur, the die-hard infantryman, came to regard Kenney as his most important tactician, and the Supreme Commander once remarked that had his air general been born three centuries earlier he would have made a fine pirate. Accordingly, MacArthur, rarely a man to bestow nicknames, made an exception for Kenney by dubbing him and those under his command "Buccaneers."

It happened when Kenney called MacArthur late one night to report that he had ordered his planes into the air to disrupt a supply convoy of five enemy destroyers heading for New Guinea. After apologizing for waking the general, Kenney told him that, so far, it was "one down, four to go."

"Don't apologize for news like that," MacArthur replied. "Call me any time you can tell me that you're making some more Japs walk the plank."

An hour later, Kenney again telephoned. "Two down, three to go," he reported.

MacArthur laughed and said, "Nice work, Buccaneer."

Gradually the sobriquet was expanded to encompass all of Kenney's Airmen.

All in all, following Gen. Brett's disastrous tenure, Kenney's effect on the once listless 5th was no less than astonishing. He was well aware that according to unofficial statistics, an Airman serving in the Pacific Theater stood a 50 percent chance of being killed before fulfilling the fluctuating combat-mission requirement assigned to bomber crews.[*] Group and squadron commanders tried to give their flight crews short respites after a dozen or so missions, but the lack of trained Airmen in-theater made that difficult. Kenney's reputation as the enlisted man's friend was clearly confirmed when, several months after his arrival, he proposed that flight crews should be granted a week of R&R in Sydney for every 20 missions flown. MacArthur agreed, apparently warming to his air chief's way of doing things.

Kenney's presence brought out a heretofore well-masked sense of humor in the Supreme Commander. Once, when asked at a press conference where the 5th Air Force was bombing that day, MacArthur suggested that the newsman ask Kenney.

"General," the reporter followed up, "do you mean to say you don't know where the bombs are falling?"

---

[*] The actual number varied widely from theater to theater. When America entered the European war, for instance, the requirement was first set at 25 missions before the USAAF raised it to 30, then 35, and finally 50 missions for heavy bombers. In the more chaotic Southwest Pacific Theater with its lack of adequate replacement crews, however, 25 missions may have been the standard early in the war, but Airmen, particularly veteran pilots and bombardiers, routinely surpassed that number.

MacArthur allowed himself a smile. "Of course I know where they are falling," he said. "They are falling in the right place. Go ask George Kenney where it is."

This magnanimous attitude toward his air commander extended to Kenney's Airmen. On another occasion, a group of American fliers on leave were picked up in Sydney for starting a bar brawl. When a seasoned quartermaster complained to Kenney that it was about time "these brats grew up and behaved themselves," the general exploded at the officer. The last thing he needed, Kenney said, was for his "kids" to grow "too old, fat, and bald to shoot down Nip planes and sink Nip ships."

In the middle of his lecture Kenney looked up to see a grinning Mac-Arthur standing in his doorway. "Leave Kenney's kids alone," MacArthur said. "I don't want to see them grow up either."

Of course, not all of Kenney's charges qualified as "kids." Age did not matter, as long as they brought new ideas to the table. This was never more evident than in the innovations to the 5th Air Force proposed by the aviator Paul Irvin Gunn, an "ancient" 43-year-old flier who had served in World War I as a Navy aircraft mechanic. After he was demobilized and returned from Europe, Gunn acquired his pilot's license and reenlisted in 1923 to become a naval aviator. He distinguished himself as a member of the "Tophatters," one of the U.S. Navy's first fighter squadrons, and later as a flight instructor at the naval base in Pensacola, Florida. But with no war to fight, Gunn grew bored, and upon his retirement he opened up a business flying freight throughout the Philippines.

After Pearl Harbor, Gunn's fleet of cargo planes was commandeered for evacuation missions, lifting American civilians and military officers to safety as the Japanese advanced on Manila. He later flew transport runs carrying medical supplies to MacArthur's beleaguered forces on Bataan, and for his actions he became one of the rare civilians to be awarded the Distinguished Flying Cross. In April 1942, weeks before America's official surrender in the Philippines, Gunn again reenlisted, this time in the

U.S. Army Air Force, and was commissioned a captain. He became one of the USAAF's oldest B-25 bomber pilots and, naturally, acquired the nickname "Pappy."

Gunn had a sharper enmity than most against the Japanese. He was piloting an evacuation flight to Australia when Manila fell and his wife and four children were taken prisoner. From that point on he made it a personal mission to ensure that as many of the enemy were killed as possible, and when Kenney arrived in Australia later that summer he discovered the gray-whiskered Gunn experimenting with attaching an extra four .50-caliber machine guns to the noses of the light, fast A-20 Havoc bombers of the 3rd Bomb Group. Gunn had collected the machine guns from damaged fighter planes that would never fly again, and rather than see the armaments go to waste, it was his idea to convert the A-20s from bombers to gunships capable of strafing the hell out of their targets.

Kenney was mightily impressed with Gunn's innovation, and when the upgraded A-20s subsequently proved devastating in combat, he pulled Gunn from his squadron, appointed him staff Supervisor of Special Projects, and assigned him an entire maintenance crew to help him similarly convert a dozen of the Group's B-25s from medium bombers into pure strafers. With mechanics and supplies now but a phone call away, Gunn no longer needed to cadge stray machine guns from disabled fighter planes, and he soon hit upon the idea of modifying the B-25s with tail gun turrets welded onto their noses. After flight tests gauging the balance and weight of this new kind of "cargo buster" proved successful, Gunn's initial demonstrations so delighted Kenney that he awarded Gunn the Silver Star.[*]

For all Gunn's innovations with the 3rd Bomb Group, the tip of Ken-

---

[*] By the time the old aviator retired at the war's end as a colonel, he had added the Legion of Merit, the Air Medal, the World War II Victory Medal, and nine Purple Hearts to his Distinguished Flying Cross and Silver Star. Gunn remained in the Southwest Pacific after the war, restarting his freight-hauling company, and was killed in 1957 when his plane crashed in the Philippines during a storm.

ney's spear remained the 43rd Bomb Group, whose aerial feats and innovations were to become integral to creating the legend of "Ken's Men." It was the 43rd's transport planes that had conducted the momentous troop airlift which helped blunt the Japanese advance on Port Moresby from Buna, and it was the 43rd's bomber crews who had perfected the method Kenney had first proposed back at the Air Corps' Tactical School of dropping parafrag bombs over enemy airfields on New Guinea.

These small bombs were attached to parachutes and timed to explode into thousands of pieces of shrapnel that, like the Japanese Daisy Cutters, would shred enemy planes in their revetments. The first time Kenney experimented with their use, ordering 240 of them dropped during one of the Allies' initial attacks on Buna, 17 of the 22 enemy planes observed on the airstrip were reported destroyed, as well as all of the antiaircraft batteries. "You've got to devise stuff like that," Kenney boasted to a war correspondent from *Time* magazine. "I've studied all the books on these different goddam campaigns, and Buna was not in any of them."

In private Kenney was more circumspect. Once, after advising MacArthur that only two thirds of the 74 heavy bombers, 82 medium bombers, 36 light bombers, and 258 fighter planes that composed his 5th Air Force were actually flightworthy, he remarked to one of his aides, "I am having an interesting time inventing new ways to win a war on a shoestring."

For all of the "stuff" Kenney devised, the 43rd Bomb Group's greatest breakthrough was the adoption of an attack technique against Japanese shipping known as skip bombing. As combat raged on Guadalcanal through the summer and fall of 1942, Japanese supply convoys steamed from Rabaul almost daily, transporting reinforcements, ammunition, and precious food to what Japanese soldiers had come to nickname "Starvation Island." The final two thirds of this 650-mile route took the enemy ships through a passage, which the Americans had labeled "The Slot," that bisected the Solomons chain. This was a natural interdiction site for the Allies, but it became apparent early on to MacArthur and Kenney that conventional high-altitude bombing was having little to no effect on the enemy's speedy cruisers and destroyers.

What was called Battle Damage Assessment, or BDA, was greatly inflated by all combatants during the war, but in fact secret official reports indicated that of the 416 sorties flown against Japanese shipping in the month of September, only two vessels had been sunk, and three more damaged. The 5th Air Force, unlike the "Mighty 8th," simply did not have enough aircraft to blanket-bomb these moving targets from on high; and despite its early promise, the Norden bombsight was proving to be not as accurate as first thought. A tactical overhaul was clearly in order.

Enter a 33-year-old major named Bill Benn, a rail-thin officer whose resemblance to the young Frank Sinatra was enhanced by the rakish tilt of his peaked forage cap. Benn was an aide on Kenney's operations staff, a polymath who brimmed with the energy of a live grenade. While studying at Temple University in the late 1920s he had won a national essay contest in which the first prize was two weeks of flying lessons. He became so infatuated with aviation that he temporarily dropped out of college to fly mail routes for the U.S. Post Office, often with nothing more than a compass to guide him through the roughest of Northeast blizzards.

After returning to Temple and earning his degree, Benn signed on as the aerial spotter for an American archaeological dig in Iran led by a German-born U.S. citizen named Eric Schmidt. It was during this foray to the Mideast that he became convinced that a world war was inevitable, particularly after the shah, believing Schmidt to be a Nazi spy, expelled the expedition. Back in the States, Benn enlisted in the Army Air Corps and met Kenney when the two were both stationed in California. The general was so impressed with the adventurous young pilot that when war did indeed break out he offered Benn a job on his staff. By the time they flew to Australia together to take up their new posts, Benn had become Kenney's top confidant.

Despite his executive position, Benn remained at heart a pilot who chafed to get out from behind his desk and into a cockpit. During their

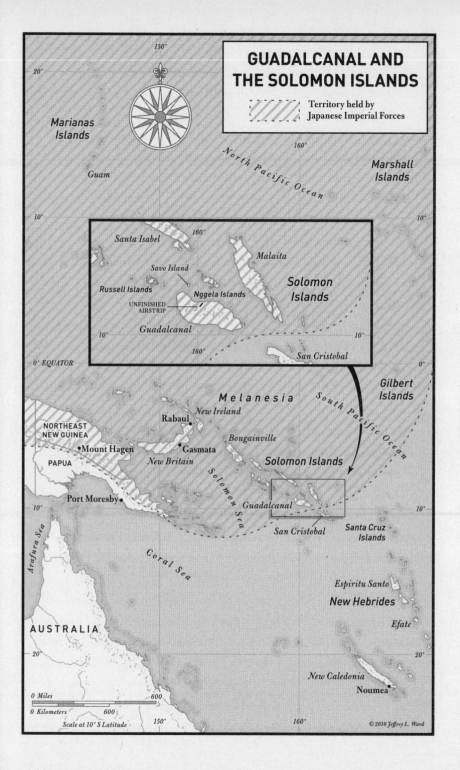

GUADALCANAL AND THE SOLOMON ISLANDS

▨ Territory held by
Japanese Imperial Forces

Marianas
Islands

Guam

North Pacific Ocean

Marshall
Islands

Santa Isabel

Malaita

Savo Island

Solomon
Islands

Russell Islands

Nggela Islands

UNFINISHED
AIRSTRIP

Guadalcanal

San Cristobal

EQUATOR

Gilbert
Islands

M e l a n e s i a

New Ireland

South Pacific Ocean

Rabaul

Bougainville

NORTHEAST
NEW GUINEA

Gasmata

Solomon Islands

Mount Hagen

New Britain

Guadalcanal

PAPUA

Solomon Sea

Port Moresby

San Cristobal

Santa Cruz
Islands

Coral Sea

Espiritu Santo

New Hebrides

Arafura Sea

Efate

AUSTRALIA

New Caledonia

Noumea

0 Miles   600
0 Kilometers   600
Scale at 10° S Latitude

© 2016 Jeffrey L. Ward

long, segmented flights across the Pacific, he and Kenney often discussed how best to improve the 5th's dismal bombing record against enemy shipping. Benn suggested borrowing a tactic from the old British Royal Air Force: low-level skip bombing. The RAF had experimented with skip bombs against German convoys in the North Sea earlier in the war, but had discarded the technique as too dangerous and difficult. But Benn was certain it could work in the Pacific, particularly against vessels at anchorage in Rabaul's Simpson Harbour and the heavily laden supply transports riding deep and fat as they steamed down The Slot.

To make his point, during a layover in Fiji he commandeered a B-26 Marauder, loaded it with dummy bombs, and invited Kenney up for a demonstration. With a coral reef as his target, he made several low passes and "pickled" the inert ordnance from distances ranging between 200 and 440 yards. The experiment was close enough to a success to fire the general's interest.

Certainly there would be kinks to work out: on slower approaches the bombs sank like rocks; if the plane came in too high they would ricochet right over the target; and on hot approaches below 50 feet the bombs would nearly bounce back and clip the plane. Moreover, live bombs would need to be equipped with a five-second delayed fuse, about the time it would take for them to reach the target. But enough of the dropped ordnance "skipped along just like flat stones," as Kenney wrote, to convince him that his aide was on to something. "The lads in Fiji didn't think much of the idea," Kenney noted in his postwar memoirs. "But I decided that as soon as we got the time I would put Benn to work on it."

In August, shortly after Kenney set up shop in Australia, he dismissed Benn from his staff with a wink and a nod. This freed the major to command the dozen planes from the 63rd Bombardment Squadron, the first of the 43rd Bombardment Group's squads to come on line. In his new role Benn singled out several pilots eager to be molded into a skip-bombing unit. Over the next two months, between regular high-altitude bombing missions, Benn's chosen few made run after run skipping dummy bombs on the rusting hull of a partly submerged British merchantman that had run aground on a reef beyond the harbor off Port Moresby. There were problems, of course, but none proved insurmountable. Benn experimented with different approach altitudes depending on the size and weight of the ordnance to be dropped, and he used his personal connection to Kenney to ensure that manufacturers sent him delayed fuses timed to detonate down to his four-to-five-second specifications.

Benn also recognized that the Norden bombsight's groundbreaking feature—the analog computer that calculated a payload's trajectory based on current flight conditions such as wind shear at high elevation—would be of no use to his planes attacking shipping at mast height. Instead his crews came up with the technique of marking an X on a plane's windshield precisely six and three-quarter inches from the top and using the bombardier's Plexiglas nose blister—the "Greenhouse"—as the pilot's forward point of reference. "Just as one would use the sight on the nose of a shotgun barrel to shoot a flying duck," wrote one of his pilots.

After a pilot and his bombardier decided on a target, preferably a ship backlit by the sun or moon, Benn instructed them to throttle back to an approach speed of no more than 220 miles per hour. He explained that the enemy's anti-aircraft batteries were generally pointed skyward, and coming in so low and slow would catch them off guard. Then the bombardier would release his load, usually a 100-pounder, when the X on the windshield lined up with the middle of the vessel anywhere from 60 to 100 feet away. If all went successfully—as, after weeks of practice, Benn expected—the bombs armed with their delayed fuses would bounce across the water's surface and explode beneath, above, or, ideally, against the hull.

In mid-September, when Benn's squadron became the first from the 43rd to move into Port Moresby, Kenney flew in from Brisbane to personally oversee a skip-bombing exhibition. Knowing that the general carried a pair of small wooden dice in his fob pocket as a good-luck charm, Benn awarded the honor of leading the exercise to another man not unfamiliar with a craps table, his handsome and popular wing man Capt. Ken Mc-Cullar.

In an earlier time the broad-faced, 24-year-old McCullar might have been a riverboat gambler plying the Mississippi with what Mark Twain called "the confidence of a Christian with four aces." Beloved in his outfit for his sophisticated charm and easy smile, McCullar was an avid poker player whose deep, booming laugh usually signaled that he was raking in a pot. When the squadron had lain over in San Francisco en route to the Southwest Pacific, he had purposely chosen as his aircraft a B-17 whose serial number ended with 21. Naturally, he had the ace and jack of spades painted on its nose. He named the bomber *Black Jack* and drove the plane with the same reckless abandon with which he bluffed his way through high-stakes card games.

That morning, as Benn, Kenney, and the general's entourage observed from the beach, McCullar's *Black Jack* made 10 runs against the scuttled British merchant ship at 200 feet above the water, dropping a single 100-pound dummy on each approach. Six times the ordnance skipped across the waves and smashed dead-on into the old vessel's hull.

Afterward, Benn explained to Kenney that despite the demonstration, the B-17's enormous size and wingspan rendered daylight skip bombing practically suicidal. The big bombers were just too easy to spot from a distance. But, he added, he and his men had perfected night runs by following the reflective slick of moonshine across the water to their target when the moon was 20 degrees or less above the horizon. In an inside joke, Benn referred to this as his *gekko* experiments—using the Japanese honorific term for moonlight. Kenney flew back to Brisbane impressed.

Not so his top aide, Gen. Kenneth Walker. Walker was, in fact, dead set against employing the young major's novel tactics.

14

A PLACE WHERE
TROUBLE STARTED

BRIGADIER GEN. KENNETH NEWTON WALKER WAS A BIT OF A WILD CARD, a rawboned and laconic Gary Cooper to Kenney's frantic Yankee Doodle Dandy. A sophisticated ladies' man and something of a prima donna in Kenney's eyes, Walker at 44 was one of the Army's youngest generals. The scion of New Mexican ranchers, he found the Brisbane social scene a bit sedate for a man who was known to enjoy a cocktail. There were in fact more than a few eyebrows raised around the bluenosed* at MacArthur's headquarters when Kenney appointed the two-time divorcé to be his head bomber commander. But Kenney liked and admired Walker's rap-

---

* William Manchester reports in *American Caesar* that MacArthur took but a single alcoholic drink for the entire duration of the war—a glass of brandy, which he did not finish.

port with the enlisted men, and his deployment to Port Moresby meshed perfectly with Kenney's leadership to send morale soaring.

Walker was not afraid to get his hands dirty in the maintenance shed before heading to the chow tent to wait in line just like any other grease monkey—his tie draped over his shoulder, his wire-rim spectacles askew. On one such occasion, while Walker stood at the back of a line so long it curled like a cobra, a newly arrived second lieutenant entered the mess tent and elbowed his way to the front. "General Walker stepped up from the end of the line," wrote one observer, "took the upstart by the arm, and led him to the rear of the line to wait his turn, demonstrating to the offender that it sometimes takes more than an act of Congress to make a gentleman."

And if Walker's penchant for hitching rides on dangerous bombing runs annoyed Kenney no end, it endeared him to the lower ranks. As one of the 43rd's flight officers told a reporter, "The general figures he can't tell the boys to go out and get shot at unless he's willing to get shot at too."

As for his opposition to skip bombing, it no doubt irritated Walker that Maj. Benn, technically one of his own subordinates, had such a direct line to Kenney's ear. More important, Walker had long been a vocal proponent of high-altitude daylight bombing. This was due in large part to the fact that he had been integral in developing the tactic, which had subsequently been widely adopted by the USAAF. Walker was known as the "high priest" of the Air Force's strategic "Bomber Mafia," and to him there was a no more beautiful sight than a close-run bomber formation approaching a target from the west, hidden by the fading night and using the sun's first light to silhouette a ship's outline far below. Accordingly, he argued that skip bombing and even parafrag bombing were a waste of the Army's time and resources.

There was, however, a flaw in Walker's premise. He had developed his bombing theories for use against the stationary industrial complexes of the European Theater—munitions factories, steel mills, airplane assembly plants. Such targets did not exist in the Southwest Pacific. As Kenney explained to a reporter, "Shipping and planes are our two chief targets and our own planes should be designed with that in mind. If the same weapon can be used against both, you're sitting pretty. The weapon is a question of skip bombing and lots of .50 caliber gunfire."

Ten months of war against the Japanese had demonstrated that the high and tight formations Walker favored, with bombers unleashing their payloads from 25,000 feet, did not work against shipping. Saturating a target area with bombs, usually in a rectangular pattern, was out of the question, as Kenney had neither the aircraft nor the manpower to engage in what would come to be known as carpet bombing. Moreover, as opposed to carpet bombing, conventional precision-bombing tactics held that a high-altitude formation would have to include at least nine aircraft to hit a vessel zigzagging in evasive maneuvers. That figure was based on statistics compiled by analysts studying planes employing the Norden bombsight under perfect training conditions. Yet the efficacy of the Norden was fast becoming academic, and rare was the day, Kenney soon learned, when he could even put that many bombers in the air at one time.

In the end, neither Walker's popularity with the troops nor his reputation as an aviation combat theorist put him in a position to argue with his superior officer when, one night late in October, Kenney sent Benn's skip bombers aloft on their first combat mission, a run over Rabaul.

BILL BENN'S FORMATION OF SIX FLYING FORTRESSES REACHED SIMPSON Harbour just before sunrise on October 23. One by one the pilots cut back their engines, descended to mast level, and let loose their 1,000-pounders. The lead bomber took out a merchant ship (which he mistook for a troop transport), as did the second plane in the formation.

Ken McCullar, flying through the staccato flashes of anti-aircraft fire at 200 feet off the deck, buzzed what he took to be a Japanese destroyer.

He estimated that *Black Jack* was 300 yards from the vessel when his bombardier released his payload. Seconds later fires and explosions threw smoke and debris high into the air. The ship sank within moments, and the 63rd's trailing aircraft also claimed numerous hits.[*]

Back at Port Moresby the entire base awaited the results. When word began to spread of what came to be known as Benn's and McCullar's "jackpot night," one pilot in particular on the 43rd's intelligence staff was intrigued and enthusiastic. Jay Zeamer pored over the skip bomber's After-Action report the next morning and, as Benn and McCullar took on more and more missions, over the many mornings to come.

McCullar's combat diaries in particular read like rough drafts of the action-adventure novels Jay had devoured as a child. This, for example, was recorded in the aftermath of a night run on a speedy flotilla resupplying Lae during which *Black Jack*, perforated by anti-aircraft fire, still scored hits on both a torpedo boat and a destroyer: "We spotted the convoy and climbed to about 3500 feet, cut our throttles and RPM back, and made the first skip-bomb run at 200 feet with a speed of 255 miles per hour. The bombs hit just off the end of the boat and anti-aircraft shrapnel hit in the tail gunner's ammunition can, exploding about 70 [machine-gun] shells and starting a fire. On the next skip-bombing run our #1 engine was hit. However our bombs hit directly, starting a fire on the starboard bow; on run three, also skip-bombing, #1 engine was hit again and all the controls shot away.

"The engine could not be feathered as the switch did not work. We climbed to 1500 feet and made a run from 1200 feet, this time the bombs hitting close and we were hit again. We climbed to 4000 feet as #1 engine was now gone. Another run was made dropping our last bomb and #3 engine cut out, having received a hit in some part of the fuel system. We feathered this engine but found that we could not keep altitude with only

---

[*] A U.S. Navy postwar analysis posited that McCullar's target was more likely a WWI-vintage cruiser.

two engines. We flew for a while and tried to bring #3 engine in again. In the meantime we sent in our position, condition and course.

"Number 1 engine got red hot from the windmilling of the prop and it looked like any minute the whole thing would catch fire and blow up. We placed the navigator and bombardier in the back compartment of the plane in case the prop flew off. Then something broke in the prop gear and the engine soon cooled off. Still losing altitude, work was kept up to try and bring #3 engine back. Finally the engine worked to the extent where it would pull 25 inches [of manifold pressure]. All excess weight was thrown overboard, including all our ammunition."

McCullar's next obstacle was the Owen Stanley Range, a dicey climb even with three working engines. With only two, McCullar knew that his Fortress would never gain the lift to clear the peaks. Luckily, as they neared the range's foothills his number 3 engine suddenly sputtered back to life. McCullar spent the next two hours looking for a gap between the highest mountains. In a pithy if nonchalant coda that encapsulated life and death in the Southwest Pacific Theater of War, McCullar reported, "We found a pass to sneak through, landed o.k. and forgot about it."

Reading this After-Action report, Jay had one thought: this was how the war was intended to be fought. He began frequenting the 63rd Squadron's Operations Hut, hoping someone would be grounded so he could fill in. It was during this period that he became friendly with McCullar, who, like Jay, was acquiring a reputation as a place where trouble started.

McCullar was no stranger to a good fistfight, and back in Australia stories were legion of his brawls with locals who took exception to their women succumbing to his charms. But one night at Port Moresby his hot temper nearly got the best of him. The incident occurred at the shabby officers club outside Kila Kila when McCullar and some friends from the 43rd overheard an army doctor, a full bird colonel attached to the infantry, loudly and profanely berating the Army Air Force. When the medical officer denigrated Gen. Kenney by name, McCullar challenged him. The infantry officer not only outranked McCullar, but topped him in height, weight, and reach. But when his antagonist stood up, McCullar launched him through the club's front window and left him sprawled in the mud.

When word of McCullar's hooley reached Kenney, accompanied by reports that the battered colonel was seeking to press charges, he reacted immediately. In order to head off the more serious possibility of a court-martial, Kenney ordered his chief of staff to issue a prompt, formal reprimand. With his pilot shielded from harsher discipline, and with the straightest face he could muster, he also personally ordered McCullar "to lay off the colonels from now on." The punishment was a slap on the wrist compared with what could have been, no doubt because the dashing McCullar had always been one of the general's pet fliers. As Kenney was to put it, "Hitler might have had a secret weapon as he claimed, but I'd bet it wasn't as good as Ken McCullar."

McCullar was precisely the type of pilot to sense in Jay a kindred free spirit, and he offered to take Jay up with him whenever he had a crew opening. In October they flew three missions together, with Jay serving twice as copilot and once as flight engineer. On their first run, *Black Jack* was one of nine Fortresses patrolling the Solomons in search of a Japanese convoy that coastwatchers had reported running for Guadalcanal. After hours of patrolling, Maj. Benn in the lead plane was the first to spot the phosphorescent wakes from the line of vessels snaking down The Slot.

As per Benn's operational instructions, the first six Fortresses attacked the ships with standard, high-altitude bombing procedures to distract the anti-aircraft gunners. They dropped nearly 50 500-pounders. There were no recorded hits. Meanwhile the planes in Benn's formation, with McCullar on his wing, glided down in silence through the "moonlit darkness" and released their skipping payload from below 250 feet.

"Violent explosions and flying debris were observed, with the result that the experiment was considered a success," Benn wrote in his After-Action report. The squadron claimed a cruiser, a destroyer, and two cargo vessels while two more cargo ships and a troop transport were badly damaged. Jay was ecstatic.

To Jay, the competence and grace exhibited by pilots like McCullar in the face of great peril were seemingly contagious. On their last flight together, a daylight raid over Japanese holdings on New Guinea's north coast, McCullar was torqing *Black Jack* across the sky to avoid the mushrooming black puffs of anti-aircraft fire when they were jumped by five Zeros. Jay, in the copilot's seat and still more accustomed to flying the B-26, was amazed at the B-17's maneuverability. Unable to outrun the bogeys, McCullar threw the plane into a swiveling dive and successfully avoided presenting it as a target as he "hedgehopped" from cloud to cloud. His dazzling evasive action left an indelible impression on Jay. With the right man in the pilot's seat, he realized, a Flying Fortress could move like a fighter plane.

That final run with McCullar constituted what Jay later called his "graduation ceremony." He was, he wrote, confident that he had acquired both the flying skills and the leadership qualities to skipper his own Fortress.

15

"CLEAR AS A BELL"

IN EARLY NOVEMBER, JAY LEARNED OF GEN. KENNEY'S DESPERATE NEED to photograph Rabaul. October had been a particularly brutal month for the Marines battling the Japanese on Guadalcanal, and reports from Naval Intelligence indicated that something big was happening in Simpson Harbour. Over the previous two months, B-17s had flown 180 sorties against Rabaul, and recent missions appeared to confirm a buildup of ships in the thumb-shaped harbor. The weather had been so consistently lousy, however, that no firm estimates could be made.

MacArthur, Kenney, and the Allied intelligence reports guessed that a large convoy was being assembled to move massive shipments either down The Slot or across the Huon Gulf to reinforce the Imperial Army's toehold on Buna. Japan's defeat at Midway, combined with the setbacks on the Coral Sea and the Kokoda Track, had lethally interrupted the enemy's great Southern Strategy. The planned invasions of Fiji, Samoa, and New Caledonia would have to be postponed, which meant that any hope of taking Hawaii in the near future was on hold as Imperial General Headquarters delineated a strategy for the recovery of Guadalcanal and perhaps even a third ground assault on Port Moresby.

In either case, the Americans needed to know precisely how large a force was being mustered in Simpson Harbour. And they wanted more than eyeball estimates. They needed hard photographic evidence.

The United States had horribly neglected to innovate and upgrade its reconnaissance aircraft between the wars, and as a result nearly all its spy planes were jerry-rigged combat planes. The only dedicated photo unit available to Kenney was a ragtag outfit, the 8th Reconnaissance Squadron, whose three primitive flight units consisted of specially modified Lockheed P-38 Lightning fighter planes modeled on the British Spitfire. The Lightning fighters were reclassified as F-4s; their cannons and machine guns were removed and replaced with camera equipment and additional fuel tanks. As fighter planes, the F-4s were faster and flew higher than anything the Japanese could send up into the skies, yet for most of 1942 the only such aircraft available to Kenney were the five F-4s of the 8th Reconnaissance Squadron's "A" flight unit, four of which were consistently grounded for lack of spare parts.

During this period the recon squadron's commander, 33-year-old Maj. Karl "Pop" Polifka, did yeoman's work with the one plane the outfit could usually get into the air. Polifka, a former Oregon lumberjack, nearly single-handedly photo-mapped the coasts and interior of Papua New Guinea and the surrounding islands at great personal peril. The main drawback of the F-4 was its limited range, and the 5th Air Force was less than enthusiastic about lending out its long-range bombers for reconnaissance flights. Yet when time and necessity allowed, Polifka and his pilots were always on the lookout for a B-17 and its crew that they could "borrow" for longer-distance forays.

On three separate occasions that November, lone Fortresses from the 43rd, carrying cameramen from the 8th Reconnaissance Squadron, were sent up to get the photos of Simpson Harbour that Kenney required. Each time they returned empty-handed—the cloud cover over Rabaul was too heavy for their cameras to penetrate. On the eve of the fourth attempt the pilot scheduled to skipper the photo flight turned up in sick bay, and Jay volunteered for the mission. Following unofficial protocol, the first thing he did was meet with the bomber's regular flight crew to request permission to lead them. Each man nodded his assent. None of them was aware that Jay had never been officially checked out for the left-hand seat. But, as Jay wryly put it, "they didn't ask either."

During the flight briefing Jay was ordered not to descend below 25,000 feet, and the next morning at just past dawn his Fortress approached Rabaul from the southwest at 28,000 feet. The harbor was socked in by a thick cloud cover, but Jay noticed that a corridor of clear air stretched northwest perhaps 150 miles to the Japanese base at Kavieng on New Ireland. There was something odd about that. Pacific storms, he knew, usually covered hundreds, if not thousands, of miles.

Then it hit like a cartoon lightbulb going on over his head. He double-checked the wind's direction to be certain. Sure enough, Mount Tavurvur, the active volcano abutting the harbor, was emitting a stream of hot air blowing northwest and clearing a passage. That's why he could see Kavieng protruding from the weather mass. He also realized that the same vaporous corridor would keep the airspace clear directly over the harbor if he could only get below the medium cloud cover.

Jay conferred with his navigator, who plotted a course to swing around and approach Rabaul from the north. As they neared New Britain's coastline Jay eased back his throttles and descended slowly into the cloud bank. Aside from the navigator, the rest of the crewmen were bewildered; they were aware of the command not to go low. Yet a few moments later the Fortress popped out of the soup at 8,000 feet on the north edge of the harbor. Visibility, Jay wrote, "was clear as a bell."

Jay oriented his position using the two volcanic rocks encrusted by razor-sharp kunai grass that protruded from the middle of the harbor like enormous stelae. American pilots had nicknamed them the "beehives," and they were all that remained of an indigenous enclave that had disappeared beneath the water during a volcanic eruption six years earlier. In the opening weeks of the war the rocks had occasionally been mistaken for enemy ships and erroneously bombed during night missions over Rabaul. Most American Airmen, including Jay, now knew better. Off his port side, perhaps a mile east and safeguarding the entrance to Blanche Bay like a menacing sentry, the squat, gaping crater of Mount Tavurvur belched plumes of gas and steam.

The photographer clicked away as the bombardier marked 110 vessels beneath them, from cruisers to destroyers to scores of cargo ships lining the wharves and jetties. Anti-aircraft gunners on the vessels opened up within seconds—it seemed as if every ship was firing at them—and the gauntlet of exploding shells shaded the sky outside the cockpit with a Bosch-like tapestry of ugly black smoke. Then the waist gunner's voice crackled over the interphone: "Zeros above."

The top turret gunner counted 16 Zekes circling like vultures. Jay pushed forward into a paint-peeling dive so hard and steep that the suction ripped the belly gunner's hatch off its hinges. The descent took the aircraft through even thicker ack-ack, but Jay felt as if they were safe for the moment. The enemy fighters, he knew, would not follow him into that hellspout. He also understood that shrapnel from anti-aircraft shells exploded outward and upward, so he needed to get below those detonations before the enemy gunners had a chance to recalibrate their aim. Once closer to the deck, he leveled off at 3,000 feet so his photographer could get the last of the pictures he needed.

When the photographer reported his mission accomplished, Jay sent the B-17 screaming south over the harbor, shoving all four throttles wide open and throwing the plane into a series of violent S-turns at 300 miles per hour. Not only were the Japanese ships firing at will, it seemed as if every shore battery had turned its guns on them. But the bomber was losing altitude faster than the gunners could wheel their sights. After two minutes "that seemed more like two hours," Jay again leveled the aircraft. At this the anti-aircraft operators ceased fire to allow the Zeros to attack.

As the Fortress neared the southern end of Simpson Harbour, Jay's tail gunner reported three Zekes closing fast. Jay kicked the rudder hard, hurtling the bomber into a vicious midair skid to one side, and then to the other, at the same time the three bogeys dived. Streams of pink tracers flashed outside his cockpit windows.

Jay banked the plane right and his port waist gunner flamed the closest fighter out of the sky. Then he banked hard left and his starboard waist gunner blew the tail off a second. As the third Zeke swooped in from above and behind, two rivulets of .50-caliber machine-gun fire from the top turret gunner and the tail gunner converged on the fighter's fuselage. The Zero did not so much blow up as disintegrate. The crew barely had time to see the aircraft's remnants swirl into the sea before Jay pointed the bomber toward a lone cumulus cloud a few miles south of the harbor.

Some pilots might have thrown their aircraft into a steep climb to make for the wispier cloud bank almost directly above them, the same bank through which they had descended. But Jay knew that if he tried to duck into that bluish-gray altostratus sheet, the Japanese fighters would be able to spot his shadow while he remained blind to their whereabouts. Instead he reached the fat cumulus cloud and vanished into its Rembrandt gloom. He spent the next 50 miles jumping from one dark cloud to another until the remaining Zeros finally turned back.

Ken McCullar had taught Jay well, but the day's adventures were hardly over. In that morning's briefing the American crews had been told that the airstrip at Buna had been captured by Allied ground forces. When Jay's B-17 neared Buna he lined the plane up with the airstrip in order to offer a congratulatory flyover. Suddenly, however, his bombardier screamed over the interphone that there were eight Zeros below strafing the American and Australian troops. Within moments the Japanese spotted the lone "Boeing" and peeled away to attack.

Jay was unaware that his belly gunner had squeezed back into his now hatchless station, and dived for the trees to protect his underside. The tops of most of the coconut palms had been blown off by naval gunfire during the previous weeks of fighting, but their gnarled and sickly trunks would at least keep the fighters from getting under him. The ensuing dogfight was waged only several feet above the ground, with the wash from the bomber's props creating a vacuum that lifted huge whirlpools of earth and gravel, which eddied behind the plane in smoky vortexes.

On the enemy's first pass Jay's tail gunner scored a direct hit, blowing the engine cowling and wings off a trailing Zeke. The fighter's fuselage spun languidly, as if in slow motion, before its fuel tanks exploded, salting the Solomon Sea with a million shards of glass, metal, and flesh. Jay's entire crew "whooped like Dodger fans."*

Their cries faded when they spotted two more bogeys racing to overtake them in order to execute a sort of midair pincer movement. Jay caught the glint of one Zero on his port side; his copilot reported the other to starboard. Jay assumed that they were trying to get out in front of him before turning for a coordinated head-on attack. He dived his plane even lower while speeding through and around a dragon's back of low-lying hills. The maneuver threw off the pursuit enough for Jay to notice that the enemy pilots were now out of sync—the Zeke on his left had fallen perhaps 30 seconds behind the plane to the right.

When the lead Zero finally overtook him and turned to attack, Jay wheeled the Fortress on its left wing and lunged straight into him as his

---

* After years of futility, the Brooklyn Dodgers had won the National League championship in 1941, sending the borough into a frenzy. Alas, the infamous ball dropped by Mickey Owen contributed to "da Bums'" loss to the New York Yankees in the World Series.

nose gunners opened up. Jay and the Japanese pilot found themselves playing a high-speed game of chicken. The Japanese pulled up first, and as he swooped above the bomber the top turret gunner raked his exposed belly with his .50-cals. The fighter plane exploded in a bright orange ball of aviation-fuel flames.

Handling his aircraft "like a peashooter," Jay now rolled his bomber directly toward the lagging Zero. Again he found himself on a collision course. Again the Japanese pilot pulled up. Again his machine gunners flamed the bogey. The fighter plane hit the water in a vicious spin. At this the remaining five Zekes, probably running low on fuel and ammunition, peeled north and disappeared over the horizon. Not until Jay's B-17 landed hard at Port Moresby did its crew realize one of its front tires had been shredded by machine-gun fire that had punctured the fuselage.

For their actions that day Jay and the entire crew were awarded the Silver Star, the nation's third-highest award for valor. Not everyone was thrilled. As the turret gunner recorded after Jay put the plane down, "I got out, went up to the pilot, asked his name, and told him I wasn't ever going to fly with him again." More important was the lesson Jay took away from the running gunfights. If his final flight with Ken McCullar had served as his graduation ceremony, this photo run had been something of an awakening, like the first day at a new job. "That mission," he wrote, "instead of scaring our crew, made us really believe that we would never get into a situation where there wasn't some way out. I believe other crews developed the same feeling."

It was a wonderful thought to carry through Christmas and the new year. Twelve months of desperate fighting, however, had provided ample evidence that a flight crew's esprit de corps—or its honor or loyalty or kindness or obedience or fortitude or any of the other virtues Jay had sworn to uphold as a Boy Scout—often counted for little in a combat zone. Sometimes it all came down to luck. A few weeks later, on the fifth day of 1943, Gen. Ken Walker's ran out.

16

THE MISSING GENERAL

BY ANY METRIC, DECEMBER 1942 WAS A VAST IMPROVEMENT ON THE AL-
lies' plight of a year earlier in the devastating and confusing aftermath of
what President Roosevelt called the "dastardly and unprovoked" attack
on Pearl Harbor. Still, even after their debacle at Midway the Japanese
retained the upper hand throughout the Southwest Pacific. And with Rabaul as a virtual Tintagel from which to launch landings on New Guinea—
as the enemy did in mid-month, at Wewak and Madang, where airdromes
sprouted immediately—they could hardly be viewed as giving ground.
Imperial troops also continued to ramify south, establishing firmer foot-
holds in the upper Solomon Islands of New Georgia and Bougainville.

The enemy's seeming superiority on paper, however, masked the
fact that between the Allied counterattacks at Guadalcanal and Buna,
Japan had also lost more than 30,000 troops killed and tens of thousands

wounded, a dispiriting sacrifice. The war in the Southwest Pacific Theater was close to becoming one of attrition for the Japanese. Vice Adm. Nobutake Kondo, second in importance only to Adm. Yamamoto in the Imperial Navy, appeared to admit as much when, noting the setbacks, he wrote that if the Americans continued to press their accumulating advantages "enemy air attacks consequently would result in sacrificing our important striking force which could hardly be supplemented afterward." Or, as another aide to Yamamoto put it more succinctly, Japan's ambitions for rapid and total conquest throughout the theater "have all scattered like dreams."

Perhaps it was this growing sense of confidence that led Gen. Ken Walker to begin accompanying his bomber crews on more and more raids. After all, the recent Japanese setbacks had shifted the initiative for Allied operations in the Pacific from a purely defensive posture into at least a limited offensive mind-set. And if future plans included taking back more and more territory from the enemy, its precious airbases in particular, Walker was just the sort of general officer who would want to be in the van. This attitude, however, did not sit well with Gen. Kenney.

As far back as October a Fortress in which Walker was flying as an observer had taken heavy flak during a raid on Lae. Kenney had warned his bomber commander then that he did not want him going up on any more combat missions. He was too important to lose.* But when Walker blithely ignored what he considered his superior's "suggestion," Kenney made it official, ordering him in November to stand down.

Whether Walker's continued disobedience stemmed from arrogance, an inflated sense of his own infallibility, or even his long-held belief that it was only fair play to confront the same danger as his aircrews—there is ample evidence to suggest it was a combination of all three—he continued

---

* In a touch of irony, Kenney had been chastised by MacArthur back in August for doing precisely the same thing, after Kenney had personally scouted a site for a new airfield inland from Buna from a bomber that flew 100 feet off the ground.

to fly without informing Kenney. The situation came to a head early in the new year when Kenney, having rolled his wooden dice and watched them come up six-one, ordered Walker to plan an "all-out attack" against yet another convoy assembling in Simpson Harbour. The raid, on Kenney's instructions, was to take place at daybreak on January 5.

There were problems from the start. Despite the proven success of the 43rd's skip-bombing missions, Walker remained a vociferous proponent of high-altitude bombing. Like a stubborn dog worrying a bone, he decided that the only way to fulfill Kenney's mandate for an "all-out attack" on Rabaul was from 8,000 to 10,000 feet. In other words, no skip bombing. The timing of the raid also bothered him. In order to reach the target at Kenney's prescribed dawn hour, his bombers would have to take flight soon after midnight. He feared that the darkness would play havoc with the aircraft attempting to rendezvous into formation once they had cleared the Owen Stanley Range.

To that end Walker asked that the time of the raid be delayed several hours, so that his planes would arrive over Rabaul at noon. Kenney denied the request. He knew that Japanese fighter planes patrolling the skies over the harbor were rarely in the sky at dawn. He would, he told Walker, rather risk a loose formation than the certain interceptors a midday strike would face. Incredibly, Walker decided to go ahead with a midday strike anyway.

When Walker laid out his plans during an operational meeting, Bill Benn became angry. A daylight raid, he argued, was tantamount to being led to slaughter. The next day Benn discovered that his 63rd Squadron had been excluded from the mission. This was more than odd. Not only had the 63rd racked up a stellar combat record, but what kind of major attack could Walker be carrying out without employing every serviceable bomber at his disposal? It is likely that Walker was afraid that Benn would use his personal pipeline to Kenney to voice his objections. For their part, Benn and his Airmen—including Jay, who was scheduled to copilot one of the 63rd's bombers—blamed Walker's vindictiveness.

From this inauspicious beginning the situation deteriorated. On the

day of the mission, heavy storms over the theater grounded several bombers scheduled to take part in the raid. Three of the 90th Bombardment
Group's four squadrons of B-24 Liberators, which had been rotated back
to Australian bases as a safety precaution, found themselves socked in
by bad weather. Also scratched were a scattering of Fortresses that had
relocated to Queensland bases for maintenance. With Benn's squadron
inexplicably grounded, this left Walker with a grand total of 12 planes at
Port Moresby—six B-24s and six B-17s from the 64th Squadron. Hardly
enough to constitute Kenney's "all-out attack."

In a final show of either disrespect, frustration, or insane bravado, at
eight a.m. on January 5, Walker hoisted himself into the hatch of a Fortress nicknamed the *San Antonio Rose* piloted by the 64th's executive officer, Lt. Col. Jack Bleasdale, and flew off for New Britain. Four hours
later, under a blindingly sunny sky, the faster Liberators were the first to
reach Rabaul. Anti-aircraft batteries erupted and screens of Zeros buzzed
as the B-24s selected their targets, dropped their bombs from 8,000 feet,
and turned to hightail it home.

When the 64th's B-17 formation arrived over Simpson Harbour less
than ten minutes later, legions of Japanese fighter planes awaited them.
Five of the six Fortresses managed to scope their targets and drop their
payloads as the Zekes attacked from all angles. The last anyone saw of the
sixth aircraft, the *San Antonio Rose*, it was trailing smoke from the left outboard engine, losing altitude, and racing east toward a far-off cloud bank
with between 15 and 20 Zekes swarming after it like a ravage of gnats. It
never sent out a radio message.

Later that afternoon, back at Port Moresby, everyone waited anxiously
until it became apparent that the *San Antonio Rose* and Gen. Walker were
not returning. Eleven of the 12 bombers had made it home to Jackson
Airfield with only minor damage, their crews suffering barely more than
scratches. The mission's combined After-Action reports claimed ten vessels bombed to varying degrees, and seven Zeros destroyed. This techni-

cally constituted a success, but all knew better. The enemy convoy had hardly been nicked, and the Southwest Pacific Theater's bomber commander was missing.[*]

When Kenney discovered that Walker had disobeyed not one but two direct orders, he was livid. Yet his anger was tempered by anxiety, and he ordered a vast grid search in the hope of locating his bomber commander, or at least the wreckage of his plane. In a fitting if depressing coda, four of the search planes sent out after the *San Antonio Rose* never returned, and nothing connected to the aircraft was ever discovered.

It was War Department policy not to declare a missing Airman killed in action until he had been lost for 13 months. But Kenney knew better. The general, who had been prepared to punish Walker's insubordination with an official reprimand, instead heeded the sage advice that would later be uttered by the Marine Corps' revered Gen. Lewis "Chesty" Puller: "There is only a hairline's difference between a Navy Cross and a general court-martial." He put Walker up for the Medal of Honor. MacArthur approved Kenney's recommendation, and two months later President Roosevelt presented the nation's highest wartime honor posthumously to Walker's two surviving sons.[†]

Up at Port Moresby, the death of such a popular general overcame

---

[*] Years later, researchers combing through Imperial Japanese Navy war records confirmed Gen. Kenney's prescience. The convoy Kenney had ordered "taken out" with a dawn attack had in fact sailed from Simpson Harbour two hours before Walker's formation reached Rabaul.

[†] According to the magazine *Air Power*, one of those sons, Douglas Walker, has for years conducted what has thus far been a fruitless search for his father's missing bomber. The ongoing search has attracted the assistance of a diverse group of experts, including a Japanese diplomat, the daughter of a 5th Air Force pilot who has had previous success in locating crash sites, and an Australian geologist who has done 35 years of fieldwork in Papua New Guinea. The geologist has created a reconstruction of the flight path of the *San Antonio Rose* that suggests Gen. Walker's bomber went down in a mountainous area of extremely rugged terrain, which to date has proved too costly and time-consuming to search.

any lingering anger felt by the members of Maj. Benn's 63rd Squadron. That night Jay entered a somber single sentence in his diary: "Today we lost a good officer, and a better man."

Two days later, in retaliation for Walker's raid on Rabaul, the Japanese blasted Port Moresby with a bombing run carried out by an armada of 104 aircraft. It was, his subordinates reported to Kenney, an all-out attack.

17

PUSHING NORTH

THE COMING OF THE NEW YEAR SAW THE CORPSES OF NEARLY 20,000 JAP-
anese soldiers rotting in the fetid jungles surrounding Guadalcanal's
Henderson Field. This, combined with the Allies' advances through the
nearby islands of Tulagi, Gavutu, and Tanambogo, prompted Imperial
General Headquarters to finally declare Guadalcanal and the lower Solomons a lost cause.[*]

In Rabaul's Simpson Harbour and Bougainville's Tonolei Harbour—
quickly establishing itself as Japan's second most important holding in
the South Seas Force sector—a rescue convoy began assembling to evacuate any troops that had escaped the meat-grinding combat. The ships

---

[*] At home in Japan these retreats were portrayed in the press as long-planned realign-
ments of Japanese forces.

would also deliver a fresh battalion of infantry to cover the retreat. But American recon flights detecting the nearly two dozen enemy vessels lining the wharves at both anchorages misinterpreted the movement as the beginning of another run down The Slot to reinforce Guadalcanal.

Three months earlier Adm. Nimitz had placed Adm. Halsey in charge of all combat forces in the South Pacific Theater, which included the Solomons, on the reliable assumption that if any man was capable of reversing the Japanese momentum, it was "Bull" Halsey. Now, when the erroneous intelligence about the enemy shipping reached Halsey, he ordered his own resupply convoy, screened by a cruiser task force, to steam west to Guadalcanal.

At 60, Adm. Halsey was the self-proclaimed scion of "seafarers and adventurers, big, violent men, impatient with the law, and prone to strong drink and strong language." He sailed determinedly in their wake. A stateside headline writer ·had nicknamed Halsey "Bull," and newsmen the world over picked up the sobriquet. Though he disliked the epithet—"I got that name from some drunken newspaper correspondent who punched the letter 'u' instead of 'i' writing Bill"—he tolerated it, and among his admirers he certainly lived up to the snorting connotation.

When he was presented with his new South Pacific command, for instance, Halsey's first recorded reaction was, "Jesus Christ and General Jackson! This is the hottest potato they ever handed me!" And when word spread throughout the South Pacific that Halsey had been appointed the theater's new commander, a young Marine officer on Guadalcanal summed up the effect on morale. "One minute we were too limp to crawl out of our foxholes," he said. "The next we were running around, waving the dispatch, and whooping like kids."

Halsey had already borne much of the Allied cause on his shoulders, from the first flickering hours when, less than two months after Pearl Harbor, his raids on the enemy-held Marshall Islands and Gilbert Islands constituted America's initial offensive assaults of the war. He solidified his stature twelve weeks later, in April 1942, with his daring transport of

Col. Doolittle's Mitchell bombers to within hailing distance of Tokyo. The raid had been, as one war correspondent wrote, a dose of vitamin B-25 for a nation still staggering under the trauma of the Japanese surprise attack on Pearl.

Unfortunately for the Allied cause, ordering the task force to Guadalcanal in January 1943 was one of the few errors Halsey committed during his first months on the job. For two days the exposed American vessels were stalked and attacked by Japanese torpedo aircraft, which ultimately sank the cruiser USS *Chicago*. At this Halsey reversed course and instructed the limping convoy to turn back and reconfigure out of enemy aircraft range in the Coral Sea. This gave what was left of the Japanese 17th Army on Guadalcanal the time and space to withdraw to the island's western coastline.

From there, on the first night of February, the emaciated enemy soldiers began clambering onto 20 fast destroyers lying off the beaches. Within a week, with the fresh battalion acting as a rear guard, the remaining 10,000 Japanese troops who had fought for the island were in retreat. It took the Americans two days to realize that the territory was now theirs. On February 9, the Allied commanding officer on the ground at Guadalcanal, Gen. Alexander Patch, declared the island secured, and the Marines were relieved by Army infantrymen.

ALTHOUGH GEN. PATCH MAY HAVE BEEN TAKEN ABACK BY THE SWIFTNESS of the Japanese evacuation of Guadalcanal, Allied war planners had sensed its inevitability for several weeks, as nearly simultaneously the Japanese had also withdrawn most of their forces from Buna and distributed them among their holdings at Lae and Salamaua.

It was obvious that the enemy was cutting its losses at Buna in order to strengthen its hand in northern New Guinea. Yet however tactically sound the moves, in a metaphorical sense the dual retreats constituted the first cracks in the Japanese military's hitherto impregnable reputation. The evacuations of Guadalcanal and Buna meant surrendering territory

for which the Empire had sacrificed many lives. It was left to an English-
man commenting on similar Allied advances half a world away in North
Africa to frame what Americans back home felt on receiving the news
about the victories in the Pacific, particularly the triumph on the "Bloody
'Canal." "Now is not the end," said Winston Churchill. "It is not even the
beginning of the end. But it is, perhaps, the end of the beginning."

Churchill's turn of phrase was apt. In late 1941, only weeks into the
war, the Navy's Adm. King had briefed President Roosevelt and Secretary of the Navy Frank Knox on his strategy for triumph in the Pacific.
He acknowledged that the Dutch forces in what is now Indonesia had
been routed; and despite England's hold on the Asian subcontinent, for
all intents and purposes the British, too, would be of no help in the Pacific Theater, having committed nearly all of their resources to battling
Germany. Stalin was now an improbable ally of the United States after
Hitler's offensive into the Soviet Union, but the Russians would continue
to devote all of their efforts to defeating Germany. That left the United
States, and to a small extent, Australia and New Zealand, to counter the
Japanese. King concluded that the path to Japan itself and ultimate victory in the Pacific Theater was straightforward: "An assault into the Solo-
mon Islands, New Guinea, and the Bismarck Archipelago."

This would begin with a two-pronged strategy that the Joint Chiefs
were soon to dub Operation Cartwheel. Now, with Guadalcanal retaken,
the strategic and tactical road King had laid out came into sharper focus
at Gen. MacArthur's headquarters. The Supreme Commander well understood that geography was destiny, and even a cursory glance at a map
made it obvious that the Solomons were stepping-stones leading to New
Britain and the viper's nest surrounding Rabaul.

So while Halsey's Marines island-hopped northward through the
Solomons, MacArthur would begin a remorseless advance along northern New Guinea's 1,600-mile coastline. Both campaigns would serve
the dual purpose of not only reversing the Imperial Command's vaunted

Southern Strategy, but also diverting to the Southwest Theater precious enemy ships, planes, and men who would have otherwise been available to reinforce the Empire's defense of the Central Pacific Theater against Nimitz's navy.

In theory, Operation Cartwheel would leave the Allies poised to achieve their penultimate and ultimate goals—the recapture of the Philippines and, from there, an assault on the Japanese homeland. And in some quarters it was beginning to seem as if the major obstacle standing in the way of this endgame was not Rabaul after all, but the island of Bougainville, at 350 square miles the largest in the Solomons chain.

Bougainville rises a mere 150 miles south of New Britain, and if the Allies could establish airbases on the island, this was more than close enough for Kenney's fighter planes to provide screening escorts to shield his bombers as they pounded Rabaul into irrelevance so that American ground troops could eventually bypass this Japanese stronghold entirely. Halsey was already considering the idea, although MacArthur proved hesitant. His Bomber Command had expended so much blood and treasure on missions over Rabaul that the notion of letting it sit, unconquered, stuck in his craw. He even gave thought to commencing simultaneous assaults against Rabaul and Bougainville. But before committing to any strategy, the Army and Navy commanders would have to resolve their own intramural rivalry.

MacArthur had never forgiven Admirals King and Nimitz and the perceived "Navy cabal" for depriving him of the unified authority he was certain he deserved as Supreme Commander of the entire Pacific Theater. The general vociferously and publicly dismissed the reliance on U.S. sea power for conducting the war as a panacea and argued instead that the defense of Australia and all subsequent offensive campaigns required an amphibious army supported by a concentration of land-based bombers under his command. He already had his air forces, and in Gen. Kenney a capable officer to command them. Now all he needed were boots on

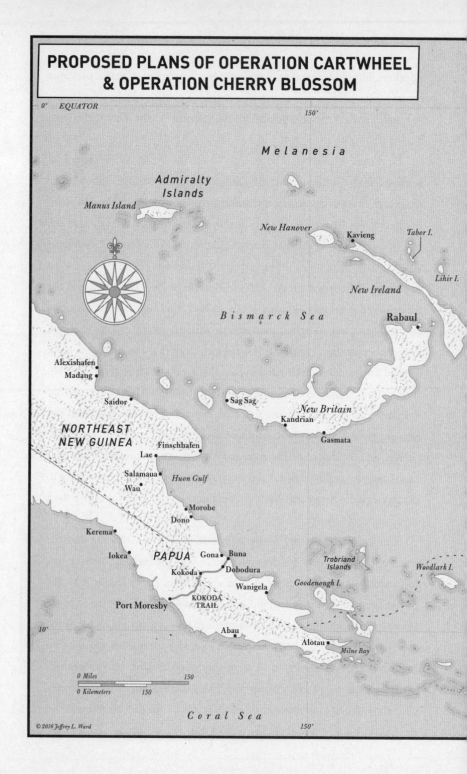

PROPOSED PLANS OF OPERATION CARTWHEEL & OPERATION CHERRY BLOSSOM

0°   EQUATOR   150°

M e l a n e s i a

Admiralty Islands

Manus Island

New Hanover

Kavieng

Tabor I.

Lihir I.

New Ireland

B i s m a r c k   S e a

Rabaul

Alexishafen
Madang

Saidor

• Sag Sag

New Britain

Kandrian

NORTHEAST NEW GUINEA

Finschhafen

Lae

Gasmata

Salamaua

Huon Gulf

Wau

Morobe

Dono

Kerema

PAPUA   Gona • Buna

Iokea

Kokoda   • Dobodura

Trobriand Islands

Woodlark I.

Wanigela

Goodenough I.

KOKODA TRAIL

Port Moresby

Abau

Alotau

Milne Bay

10°

0 Miles   150
0 Kilometers   150

C o r a l   S e a   150°

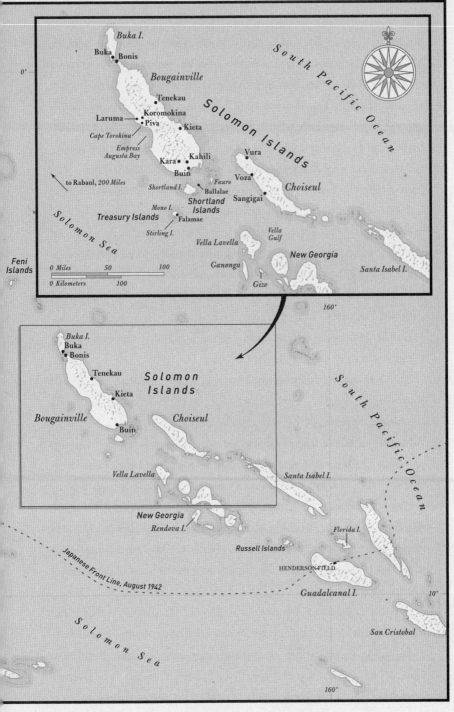

Buka I.
Buka • Bonis
Bougainville
Tenekau
Koromokina
Laruma — • Piva • Kieta
Cape Torokina
Empress
Augusta Bay
Kara • Kahili
Buin
Shortland I.
Fauro
Ballalae
Shortland
Islands
Mono I.
Treasury Islands
Falamae
Stirling I.

Vura
Voza
Sangigai
Choiseul

Vella
Gulf
Vella Lavella
New Georgia
Ganonga
Santa Isabel I.
Gizo

0°
South Pacific Ocean
Solomon Islands
to Rabaul, 200 Miles
Solomon Sea
Feni Islands
160°

0 Miles   50   100
0 Kilometers   100

Buka I.
Buka
Bonis
Tenekau
Solomon Islands
Kieta
Bougainville   Choiseul
Buin
Vella Lavella   Santa Isabel I.
New Georgia
Rendova I.
Florida I.
Russell Islands
HENDERSON FIELD
Japanese Front Line, August 1942
Guadalcanal I.
Solomon Sea
San Cristobal
South Pacific Ocean
10°
160°

the ground, and to that end he even advocated for the abolishment of the Marine Corps, postulating that its troops could better serve his army—a viewpoint not forgotten, nor forgiven, by veteran leathernecks to this day.

In turn, Navy brass allowed it to be known that they considered the general an unhinged megalomaniac with a corncob pipe. They remembered how as early as July 1942, MacArthur had scoffed at the idea of the Guadalcanal landings and how he had instead demanded that Adm. Nimitz cede him two carrier task groups for a daftly conceived invasion of Rabaul. Admiral King in particular wondered if MacArthur had learned nothing from his Philippines debacle and if he still failed to comprehend the horrors of jungle warfare against an entrenched and ideologically rabid enemy. In fact, King objected so vehemently to MacArthur's Rabaul invasion plan that Gen. Marshall had the MacArthur-Nimitz boundary of authority "adjusted" by one degree of longitude, about 60 miles, in order to transfer supervision of the entire Solomon Islands chain and not just Guadalcanal to Nimitz and Halsey.

Such bureaucratic maneuvers, however, could not make the issue of Rabaul disappear. Even as Halsey's troops swept up the Solomon Islands toward the ultimate goal of Bougainville, any campaign against New Britain relied on MacArthur fortifying the Allied facilities on New Guinea, particularly at Milne Bay and up the coast at Dobodura, near Buna. These bases would serve as a precursor to clearing the Japanese from the entirety of northern New Guinea. With New Guinea under Allied control, this would in theory put either MacArthur's soldiers or Halsey's Marines in position to land on New Britain's southern coast, from where they would hack their way across the island and into the heart of the enemy's Rabaul citadel.

Halsey considered this option premature. He suggested that if his landing forces could secure even a portion of Bougainville on which to carve out an airbase while MacArthur cleared the Japanese from New Guinea, New Britain would be encircled in such a manner as to forestall a needless fight for Rabaul, certain to cost thousands of American lives.

Halsey reasoned that with the enemy forces on Rabaul made irrelevant, Operation Cartwheel could be kick-started from Bougainville instead of from New Britain, further hastening MacArthur's northern offensive.

The one strategy everyone agreed on was that any push north was contingent upon clearing the Japanese out of New Guinea and the Solomons. And as those bases were reliant on Rabaul for men and matériel, even as the last of the bloody fighting had continued on Guadalcanal, Kenney's bombers had begun to step up their near-nightly runs on Rabaul.* So anxious were the Allies to incapacitate the fortifications at Rabaul that nearly any tactic, however harebrained, was considered. One such idea was a plot to bomb Mount Tavurvur in hopes that the detonation would trigger a massive eruption in the active volcano or, failing that, perhaps shudder open a new volcano.

The man chosen to carry out this plan was Capt. Carl Hustad, one of the 43rd Bomb Group's most experienced pilots. One day in January 1943, as the rest of his squadron's bombers were loaded with regular ordnance for a mission over Rabaul, Hustad's Fortress was armed with two 2,000-pound bombs specifically constructed with delayed fuses for the purpose of exploding the volcano.

The operation began as planned. Hustad held his B-17 back while the planes preceding him attacked the town and shipping in Simpson Harbour. Hustad then swooped in behind the formation and, circling what he believed to be Mount Tavurvur, released his blockbusters. Nothing happened. Not only were the bombs, per the 43rd's combat diary, "not seen to explode," but it was later speculated that Hustad had mistakenly hit a dormant crater two miles northwest of Mount Tavurvur.

It was also around this time that some innovative bomber crews from the 43rd began dropping rolls of toilet paper and empty beer bottles

---

* Following Gen. Walker's disappearance and presumed death—Walker was officially classified as "missing in action" for three months—Kenney had suspended all daylight raids over Rabaul.

along with their lethal ordnance. There was a belief that the unspooling toilet-paper sheets might disrupt enemy searchlights. As for the empty bottles, that was just a way to blow off steam, and no higher-ups seemed to object. An ingenious Airman whose name is lost to the mists of time had discovered that as the bottles hurtled toward the earth they emitted a shrieking whistle eerily similar to that of a falling bomb. If they could not kill the enemy on the ground, maybe scaring them to death was the next best thing. Many of the beer bottles were the Iron City brand, rumored to have been shipped from the company's Pittsburgh brewery with enough formaldehyde to stun a mule. At the very least, as Jay noted in his diary not long after the failed volcano mission, "the chemicals in the Iron City had a better shot at exploding that volcano."

By February 1943, Rabaul was, in the laconic words of the 43rd Bomb Group's official history, "really catching hell." Captured Japanese documents reiterated that the raids were indeed having their desired effect. "[The American] attacks are furious," read one such report. "Tonight's bombing was so terrific I did not feel as if I was alive." "The position of the command section was completely destroyed by aerial bombing," read another. "Company Commander Yamasaki and Master Sergeant Toda are missing. They were probably killed."

These assaults were not without setbacks. Three days after Gen. Walker's Fortress disappeared, the notorious "Brooklyn Bombardier" Meyer Levin died attempting to retrieve a life raft for floundering crewmates after his damaged Fortress ditched into the Pacific. A year earlier Levin had made headlines back in the States when he was credited with sinking an enemy battle cruiser as a member of the famous Capt. Colin Kelly's bomber crew, which attacked a Japanese task force near the Philippines just days after Pearl Harbor. During that action Kelly's aircraft became the first American B-17 to be shot down in combat, and Kelly was celebrated posthumously as one of America's earliest World War II heroes.

Now, Levin, a master sergeant, joined his old captain on the death roll. Days after Levin's death it was revealed that he had not even been assigned to his final flight, but had volunteered to go aloft because of his expertise at identifying Japanese surface ships.*

Then, in perhaps the most pernicious blow to date for Ken's Men, in late January, Bill Benn's aircraft failed to return from a daylight reconnaissance mission.

---

* Conflicting versions of Meyer Levin's WWII actions persist to this day. Subsequent to Kelly's mission, for which Kelly was awarded the Distinguished Service Cross for "extraordinary heroism and selfless bravery" for sacrificing his own life to save his crew, Airmen who flew with Levin claimed that he was resentful of that portrayal. One bombardier from Levin's 11th Bomb Group said that Levin told him that the bombs Kelly's plane dropped hit no enemy vessels, much less a cruiser, and that Kelly had panicked when a fire broke out in the cockpit. Levin, his crewmate reported, maintained that Kelly bailed out through the wrong hatch, leaving his copilot to man the controls while the rest of the crew jumped to safety, and was killed by his own plane's horizontal stabilizer. Levin allegedly kept a diary portraying this event, and vowed to make it public. No diary was ever discovered. More bafflingly, following Levin's death a story circulated that the only reason he made his final flight was not as a volunteer to identify enemy shipping, but that he needed one more combat mission to earn a promotion.

18

A FINE REUNION

THE EARLY WEEKS OF 1943 WERE A PERIOD OF ATROCIOUS LOSSES FOR Jay's 43rd Bomb Group. Flights of Japanese bombers continued to pound Port Moresby, and near-daily accidents plagued not only the 43rd, but every American bomb group throughout the theater. With the loss of aircraft and their crews piling up, Gen. Kenney decided to pull Maj. Benn from combat missions. He was planning on promoting Benn to an executive role in the Bomb Group and did not want to risk losing him. It was a dicey move. Benn, as Kenney himself noted, "had sunk or damaged more Jap shipping in the past month than all of the rest of the Air Force put together."

Kenney was also aware that Benn was viewed by the other fliers as the general's pet pilot. This was of course true. But in order to offset this notion, Kenney had gone out of his way in public to avoid displaying any hint of preferential treatment, even to the point of asking MacArthur to step in for him and pin the medal to Benn's tunic when the major was awarded a decoration for valor. So when Kenney decided to put Benn in for a promotion to lieutenant colonel in order to smooth the transition for him to take over as CO of the 43rd, he did it by the book.

Unfortunately, that book was a bureaucratic morass into which even the most expeditious promotion requests could disappear for months. And Benn, never one to shy from the sky, refused to sit around waiting for the paperwork to make its way up through channels. He may have been barred from combat missions, but that didn't mean he couldn't get into the air. To that end he began commandeering any available plane and its crew in order to scout locations on the other side of the Owen Stanleys that might make sites for future Allied airstrips.

So it was that on the morning of January 18, Benn slid into the left-hand seat of a B-25 Mitchell and filed a flight plan that would take him up New Guinea's northern coast. Coastwatchers and Airmen returning from missions that morning reported heavy thunderstorms crashing over the mountains, but no one could believe a flier as experienced as Benn could be taken out by mere weather. Yet that was exactly what happened. A subsequent investigation surmised that Benn's aircraft, possibly flying with one or more failed engines, had attempted to follow a headwater valley through an uncharted pass in the mountains. His likely plan was to clear the range and power-glide back into Port Moresby. But he misjudged the elevation of the pass by a little over 150 yards and slammed into the face of a sheer cliff.

When news of the fatal accident reached Gen. Kenney, he felt as if he had lost a son. He was not the only grieving Airman. Ken McCullar was devastated. Two weeks later McCullar was joined in mourning by Jay, whose good friend Maj. Thomas Charles was lost with his entire B-17 crew during a run over New Britain. It was not long before the two pilots' sadness turned to an anger that began to agitate and flow, like water coming to a boil. So they hatched a scheme to make an unofficial bombing raid to vent their rage. McCullar and Jay took off in *Black Jack* on a solo run to "strafe the hell out of Rabaul," with McCullar's crew all volunteering.

They made it back to Port Moresby safely, with *Black Jack* suffering no more than a few shrapnel holes pocking the fuselage. However, as word of their off-the-books flight spread, some of the other Americans on the base were put off by the stunt. These included friends of the colonel whom McCullar had beaten up in the officers club. This group pressed the 43rd's commanding officer to file court-martial charges against McCullar and Jay. But by this point in the war McCullar's combat exploits were approaching legendary status throughout the Southwest Pacific Theater, and his reputation was enough to allow him and Jay to escape punishment. The unsigned court-martial papers were buried deep in a filing cabinet.

For Jay, who had already been dismissed from one Bomb Group for his cavalier attitude, the incident was just another day in the war. As he told a relative, "I never took the pressure from the higher-ups very seriously. It wasn't so much outright disobedience as it was just trying to do what we thought was the right thing. Ken McCullar was just like me when it came to that. I suppose that's why we got on so well."

THE POUNDING MISSIONS OVER RABAUL AND THE NEAR-CONSTANT RUNS on the remaining enemy garrisons on the north coast of Papua New Guinea—Madang, Wewak, and Lae in particular—continued to take a devastating toll on the American bomber fleet. By mid-February the 22nd Bomb Group, Jay's old outfit, was down to 28 of the 51 Marauders with which it had arrived in Australia nearly a year earlier. And six months of hard wear and tear had left approximately 20 of the 43rd Bomb Group's 55 Fortresses undergoing constant depot repair. Of the remaining 35 deemed fit for combat, five had finally been set aside and outfitted with special cameras for daily reconnaissance and search-and-rescue missions.

General Kenney was able to spot-rest some of his fatigued flight crews with the trickle of fresh Airmen arriving from the States, and had even managed to wangle a few replacement aircraft out of "Hap" Arnold. Washington's focus, however, remained on Europe, and Kenney was told he would have to continue to make do with the number of planes assigned to the theater when he'd arrived seven months earlier.

By this time Jay had managed a transfer from the Group's intelligence staff to its 65th Squadron as the unit's Operations Officer. Yet it continued to irritate him that he remained a flier without an official plane. The good news was that although he had never been officially checked out as a lead pilot, the combination of disease, personnel depletion, and what von Clausewitz termed "the friction of war" gave Jay the opportunity to fly with an assortment of crews from the 65th. During one mission, he was filling in for a pilot down with malaria when his Fortress sank an 8,000-ton cargo ship by means of his mentor McCullar's skip-bombing technique. After circling the flaming ship to ensure that it was indeed scuttled, Jay was just about to rejoin his formation when he spotted a lone Zero below him on his port side. He rolled his bomber over and went into a dive. "I caught him by surprise," he later wrote in his diary. "He was heading back into Rabaul and didn't expect a B-17 to peel down and go after him. He looked around just as I hit him."

Not only was Jay awarded an Air Medal for sinking the Japanese vessel, he was also pioneering a new flying technique for heavy bombers. As far as anyone at the time knew, never before had a bomber pilot employed dogfight acrobatics against an enemy fighter. Jay was fashioning a completely unorthodox method of flying, and not everyone was impressed. Some pilots sneered at the showboating and whispered that Jay was really just masking the fact that he wasn't a good enough aviator to fly by the regulation manual. There were also plenty of crewmen who wanted nothing to do with flying with a commander who went out of his way looking for trouble. Most felt that the best thing about flying a B-17 mission was having flown one. Bombing runs were perilous enough as it was.

Jay was aware of the reputation he was gaining, but it was not in his nature to pass on an opportunity to engage with a bogey, to take chances that other pilots would not take. He could not blame any Airmen who did not want to go up with him, and deep down he did not want to fly with any man who refused to crew with him. But after all those years he had fulfilled his dream of piloting a B-17 whenever the opportunity arose, and nothing short of being grounded was going to stand in his way. It was a good time for fate to intervene.

Only a few days after scuttling the Japanese cargo vessel, Jay was approached by a navigator and a bombardier from the Group's reconnaissance squadron. Their B-17 had been tabbed for a recon run over northern New Guinea to scout out a new airstrip the Japanese were rumored to be building on the tip of the Huon Peninsula at Finschhafen. But their pilot was missing in action. They asked if Jay was available. Jay was vaguely familiar with the navigator, a captain named Charles "Rocky" Stone. But it was the bombardier, only recently arrived at Port Moresby, who had been the impetus behind the invitation. It was his old friend from Langley, Joe Sarnoski.

Joe was now a master sergeant, and had grown a lot of hard bark since his days of putting on shows for the brass hats back in Virginia. Clad in his bomber jacket with his thick Airman's goggles perched atop his snug sheepskin-and-leather trooper hat, he bore more than a passing resemblance to the Hollywood tough guy George Raft. His footwear, however, gave him away. Whereas the leather of Jay's boots was scuffed and dull with the legitimacy of experience, Joe's were a smooth and shiny black.

That night the two old friends dined together in the mess tent and caught up. Joe had married his girlfriend Marie just before his unit had shipped out almost a year earlier, and the bombardier's recounting of his ocean crossing on the SS *Argentina*, particularly the fear every man felt of being stalked by German U-boats, left Jay not a little guilty about any complaints he'd voiced concerning his own voyage from San Francisco to Hawaii. When the *Argentina* had berthed in Sydney after a brief call at Perth, Joe said he had never been so happy to feel earth beneath his feet—even if it meant he had alighted in a combat zone where bombs from above, and not torpedoes from below, would be soon trying to kill him.

He and his 403rd Squadron, the first of the 43rd Bomb Group's four units to reach Australia, had initially made camp in the oval of the Randwick Racecourse outside Sydney, which was still hosting meets for the horse-mad Australians. He described to Jay how they had been put to work as ticket vendors and ushers by the track's operators. He was still amazed at how the Aussie jockeys ran their horses "in the wrong direction."

When the bulk of the Bomb Group joined Joe's squadron a month or so later, Joe found out how fortunate he'd been to have shipped out ahead of the rest. It turned out that only days before the 63rd, 64th, and 65th squadrons were scheduled to depart from New York on the *Normandie*, the French liner had capsized and burned to the keel in the harbor with most of the Group's equipment on board, including vital spare aircraft parts. The Group's Airmen were then rerouted to Boston to make the crossing on Britain's *Queen Mary*, which had also been converted into a troop transport. When the 43rd had finally assembled in Sydney, passed their flight checks, and deployed to various Australian airbases for combat assignments, Joe had been left behind to serve as a roving bombing instructor. Since then he'd remained stuck far from the front lines.

Joe wasn't so much angry about this as resigned. He said he understood his contribution to the greater war effort. He was good at his job and he knew it, and if something he imparted to one of his students resulted in even one more enemy ship resting at the bottom of the sea or one more ammunition dump blown sky-high, he could feel proud. Still, Jay could sense his frustration, and Joe finally admitted that the longer the war went on, the more not flying into combat ate at him. As he'd written to his sister Jennie just a few weeks earlier, "My main job here is instructing, but I do hope that I will do some bombing. I would like to sink at least five enemy ships. I have told my squadron commander that if I don't, I'm going to be ashamed to go back to the States."

In the meanwhile, scores of bombardiers, usually in groups of five to 10, had passed through Joe's advanced training courses on dusty outback bases with names like Daly Waters, Charleyville, and Torrens Creek. There was no little irony in the fact that even while training his students, Joe could not get into the air. The daily eight-hour classes were strictly "ground courses only." Eventually, Joe began pleading with his superiors for an assignment with a forward unit. His CO had finally relented just a few days ago, and had given him permission to transfer to the Mareeba Airbase up the Queensland coast from Townsville. Now, he told Jay, he was free to latch on to any mission in need of a bombardier.

Jay listened closely as Joe unwound his travelogue and spoke from the heart about wanting, needing, to feel he was contributing to the war effort from the air, and not from a classroom. He grinned at Joe's liberal use of Aussie slang—friends, flashlights, and trains had suddenly become *cobbers*, *torches*, and *trams*—which struck Jay as tonally off when spoken in Joe's thick Carbondale accent. He had not realized how much he had missed his old friend, nor how much they had in common. Here, in this strange place fighting this strange enemy, Jay realized that he and Joe were more than just comrades in arms. They were closer to brothers, in the sense that each could almost divine what the other was going to say, what the other was thinking, before the words were even spoken.

Nor was a dark irony lost on Jay. Bill Benn was gone. His pal Tom Charles was gone. So many were gone. But Joe Sarnoski, one of the best bombardiers in the Army Air Force, was back and asking him to pilot a recon mission. Of course he would accept. His mother used to say something about a door closing and a window opening, but he had never taken it this literally.

The flight over Finschhafen went off without a hitch. And the next day Jay pulled Joe and Rocky Stone aside with an idea. What if, he asked, they set out to recruit and train their own crew?

PART

III

Only those who will risk going too far can
possibly find out how far one can go.
—T. S. Eliot

LEFT: Jay Zeamer Jr. at three years old, soon after Jay Sr. and Marjorie Zeamer had moved from Carlisle, Pennsylvania, to Orange, New Jersey. *Courtesy of the Zeamer Family.* RIGHT: The former Eagle Scout Jay Zeamer as a student at Culver Military Academy in Indiana in 1935, when he was 17 years old. *Courtesy of Culver Academies.*

Jay Zeamer Jr. (left), his younger brother, Jere, and (in between) sisters Anne and Isabel and their mother, Marjorie Herman Zeamer. *Courtesy of the Zeamer Family.*

Joe Sarnoski (third from left) and his 15 brothers and sisters at the family homestead in Pennsylvania. *Courtesy of the Sarnoski Family.*

Being a member of the Buddy Howe band provided Joe (far left) with an opportunity to indulge his love of music and help support the Sarnoski family, aided by his accordion. *Courtesy of the Sarnoski Family.*

Anne, Isabel, Jere, and Jay Zeamer Jr. soon before
Jay left home to attend the Massachusetts Institute
of Technology. *Courtesy of the Zeamer Family.*

Langley Field in Virginia in 1941, where Jay
Zeamer Jr. and Joe Sarnoski first met, the following
year. *Courtesy of the Air Force Historical Research Agency.*

LEFT: Joe Sarnoski and fellow Airmen at Langley Field during training days in the early 1940s. *Courtesy of the Sarnoski Family.* RIGHT: Jay made a last visit to the Zeamer family home in New Jersey before shipping out to the Pacific Theater. *Courtesy of the Zeamer Family.*

Marie Maddox and Joe Sarnoski married early in 1942, shortly before the bombardier was deployed to Australia.

Courtesy of the Sarnoski Family.

Joe Sarnoski was one of thousands of American military personnel shipped to Australia on the SS *Argentina*, eluding Japanese submarines as the ship made the perilous journey across two oceans. *Courtesy of Susan Lanson.*

Joe Sarnoski as a bombardier with the 43rd Bomb Group stationed in Port Moresby, where he was reunited with Jay Zeamer Jr.

Courtesy of the Sarnoski Family.

An aerial view of the airfields at Port Moresby in New Guinea, the most important Allied base in the Southwest Pacific. *Courtesy of the National Archives.*

The Japanese and the Allies used leaflets as a form of psychological warfare. During the first year of the war, leaflets dropped by Japanese aircraft sought to persuade the remaining beleaguered defenders to surrender. *Courtesy of the National Museum of the U.S. Air Force.*

LEFT: General Douglas MacArthur commanded Allied forces in the Southwest Pacific and occasionally clashed with U.S. Navy brass in his quest for authority over both their ships and the Marine Corps. *Courtesy of the National Archives.* RIGHT: Soon after the hard-charging General George C. Kenney took over the 5th Air Force, his "Ken's Men" began to turn the tide of the war. *Courtesy of the National Archives.*

Admirals Ernest King and Chester Nimitz, flanked by fellow senior officers, were the naval commanders who oversaw U.S. operations in the Pacific Theater. *Courtesy of the National Archives.*

The B-26 Marauder was a fast-flying plane whose powerful engines made take-offs and landings a dicey proposition. *Courtesy of the U.S. Air Force Museum.*

During the first year of the war, Japanese bombers and fighter planes, seen here over Bataan, ruled the skies. *Courtesy of the U.S. Air Force Museum.*

The Boeing Corporation took a huge risk by building and introducing, in 1935, the first B-17 bomber. The Flying Fortress turned out to be a powerful weapon in the Allied arsenal.

Courtesy of the U.S. Air Force Museum.

In April 1942, Colonel Jimmy Doolittle and his crews prepare to take off from the USS *Hornet* to launch their daring raid on Tokyo. *Courtesy of the U.S. Air Force Museum.*

Allied bombs rain down on Rabaul, the Japanese stronghold that defied defeat throughout the war. *Courtesy of the U.S. Air Force Museum.*

The pilot Paul Irvin "Pappy" Gunn, shown here before the war broke out, was a master innovator and mechanical genius who spearheaded new strafing techniques. *Courtesy of the National Archives.*

General Kenneth Walker was a vociferous advocate for daylight bombing runs. After his plane went missing, he received a posthumous Medal of Honor. *Courtesy of the National Archives.*

Major William Benn, a daredevil pilot and a favorite of General George Kenney's, helped to develop the technique known as "skip bombing" enemy ships. *Courtesy of Alfred Hagen.*

The dynamic Captain Kenneth McCullar, one of the most popular and effective bomber pilots in the 5th Air Force, taught Jay Zeamer to maneuver his Flying Fortress like a fighter plane. *Courtesy of the National Archives.*

Admiral Isoroku Yamamoto, the man behind the Japanese attack on Pearl Harbor, became a target for U.S. fighter planes in April 1943. *Courtesy of the National Archives.*

Admiral William Halsey galvanized the Allied war effort with his aggressive leadership of Navy forces in the South Pacific. *Courtesy of the National Archives.*

Colonel Merian C. Cooper (left). *Courtesy of the National Archives.*

The Zero was the deadliest weapon in the Japanese air arsenal. Dozens swarmed Old 666 during the mission over Bougainville. *Courtesy of Jim Landsdale/Donald W. Thorpe Collection.*

Captain Jay Zeamer Jr. and his original "Eager Beavers," in front of Old 666. Kneeling (left to right): William Vaughan, George Kendrick, Johnnie Able, and Herbert "Pudge" Pugh. Standing (left to right): Bud Thues, Zeamer, Hank Dyminski, and Joe Sarnoski. *Courtesy of Jim Rembisz.*

Resurrected from the Port Moresby graveyard, the plane dubbed Old 666 was rebuilt by the Eager Beavers.

Courtesy of World War II Magazine.

One of the photographs taken by George Kendrick as Old 666 flew over Buka Island on the morning of June 16, 1943.

Courtesy of Jim Rembisz.

LEFT: Thanks to the Old 666 mission, Marine Corps units were able to land on Bougainville and eventually occupy the island, securing the Solomon Islands chain. *Courtesy of the U.S. Marine Corps Library.* RIGHT: A gaunt Jay Zeamer Jr. spent well over a year in American hospitals recovering from the wounds he suffered. *Courtesy of* World War II Magazine.

Marie Sarnoski, with her parents to her right, receives her husband's post-humous Medal of Honor from Brig. General Caleb Haynes. To Haynes's left are Joe's mother, Josephine; a niece, Marion Dukerich; and two of Joe's sisters, Helen Sarnoski and Nellie Dukerich. *Courtesy of the Sarnoski Family.*

Boothbay Harbor honored its local hero on Jay Zeamer Day on June 16, 1993, the 50th anniversary of the Bougainville mission. *Courtesy of Boothbay Register.*

"He knowingly gave his life for that which we hold most dear": Members of the Sarnoski family—Joe's mother and 12 siblings—gather at a memorial dedicated to Joe in Carbondale, Pennsylvania. *Courtesy of the Sarnoski Family.*

19

"A MOTLEY COLLECTION
OF OUTCASTS"

RECONNAISSANCE. THE WORD HAD TAKEN ON A MAGICAL AURA FOR JAY
Zeamer since his reunion flight with Joe Sarnoski. And if he and Joe were
now on a mission to recruit their own flight crew, there was no more fertile
hunting ground than among the men who had volunteered for multiple
recon runs. Even routine reconnaissance work during World War II was
considered the most dangerous assignment a flier could draw. This was
doubly true in the Pacific Theater, with its hellacious storms and vast
stretches of uncharted ocean. Bill Benn's death was evidence enough of
this, and a man had to possess a certain kind of lone-wolf mentality to
actually want to be sent aloft with no protective company. Jay had fought
hard to participate in the large bombing formations that flew over Rabaul
and northern New Guinea, or to be a member of the American squadrons searching for Japanese ships attempting to sneak down The Slot.

But there was something about the notion of solo scouting missions over enemy territory that excited him even more. It may have been his renegade spirit, or perhaps the pull of his idol Eddie Rickenbacker, who famously roamed deep behind German lines during World War I seeking targets for Allied artillerymen.

Reconnaissance. It had never been for the faint of heart.

Rickenbacker's exploits during the last war had been only the latest and most logical version of the age-old military practice of commanders seizing the high ground. Sometimes lost in Sun Tzu's oft-cited counsel in *The Art of War* to always occupy the sunny side of the mountain is that the ancient Chinese military theorist wanted his troops on the mountain in the first place. Invading and defending armies had striven to fight from the heights ever since, but it took two millennia before a pair of French brothers conceived of scouting and mapping enemy positions from even higher ground—the sky.

When Joseph-Michel and Jacques-Étienne Montgolfier first began experimenting with the idea of hot-air balloon flight in the 1780s they thought it was the smoke, and not the heated air, that lifted their egg-shaped silk-and-cotton contraptions off the ground. They soon learned better, and within a decade the Montgolfiers' invention had been incorporated into the army of the First French Republic in the form of a new Aerostatic Corps whose balloons were used as observation posts during several battles of the French revolutionary wars, including the 1795 Siege of Mainz.

The mechanics of balloon flight became more sophisticated in the nineteenth century, and in 1861 President Abraham Lincoln urged his generals to incorporate a Balloon Corps into the Union Army. The invention of compact hydrogen gas generators made these uninflated balloons easier to transport around the front lines, and the Union aeronauts who piloted them worked with the Army's topographic engineers to create the most accurate maps to date of potential battlefield sites. The Balloon Corps' functions expanded during the First Battle of Bull Run, where its aeronauts were tasked as artillery spotters, using signal flags to flash the position of Confederate cannons to their counterparts in the Army of the Potomac. Thereafter Union Army balloons often took flight with a tethered telegraph line to relay instant analytical locations of enemy troop movements and encampments. The South's attempts to match this innovation were hampered, and finally discontinued, owing to its lack of matériel—not only had the Union embargo created a dearth of available gas to get the Confederacy's balloons off the ground, but sewing together silk dressmaking material into giant balloons was deemed too inefficient.

As the Civil War dragged on the Union's interest in its air wing flagged, but not before several balloons and their generators were loaded onto a converted coal barge, towed down the Potomac River, and flown aloft to observe Confederate troops digging fortifications to defend Richmond. It has been argued that this coal barge, the USS *George Washington Parke Custis*,* constituted the world's first aircraft carrier.

By the onset of World War I aerial reconnaissance was still considered primarily a means to discover where the enemy was hiding his big guns. Some forward-thinking officers on both sides of the Western Front recognized the opportunity that the new science of aviation provided for battlefield commanders to gain valuable situational awareness—tactical intelligence—as well as photographic information regarding the enemy's strength, logistics, and capabilities: strategic intelligence. A French pilot in 1914 provided essential scouting information that resulted in the Allies' victory in the First Battle of the Marne, but for the most part the prevailing military theory regarding flight kept to its original objective of guiding artillery fire.

The end of World War I ushered in an age of war-weariness that blunted almost all innovation in military aviation, including reconnaissance. The French did send a few covert photo flights beyond the Rhine

* The barge was named after the step-grandson of George Washington, who also happened to be the father-in-law of Robert E. Lee.

upon Hitler's emergence. And English scientists quietly refined defogging devices for wide- and long-lens cameras whose mechanisms would not freeze and whose film would not crack at upper altitudes. But for the most part aviation reconnaissance became a forgotten luxury. In the United States, the Army Air Corps devoted almost no equipment, personnel, or resources to the art of aerial spying. After Pearl Harbor, this shortsighted policy came back to haunt the service.

In the Southwest Pacific Theater, for instance, Gen. MacArthur and Gen. Kenney had long made do with only the five retrofitted F-4s belonging to Maj. "Pop" Polifka's 8th Reconnaissance, which had acquired the nickname the "Eight Ballers." But however much Polifka squawked about the lack of spare parts keeping his planes on the ground, it did him no good. Moreover, when Polifka or one of his pilots did manage to get an F-4 aloft, they discovered that flying alone over seemingly endless stretches of ocean through the region's terrifying storm fronts on blind tactical forays in search of Japanese naval vessels only increased the odds of a blown engine, a shorted-out fuel pump, a cracked canopy, a malfunctioning fuel or hydraulics line, faulty exhaust stacks . . . the list went on and on.

Nor could pilot error be discounted. On one recon foray over northern New Guinea, Polifka, one of the most experienced fliers in-theater, accidentally shut off his oxygen supply at high altitude and passed out. He woke up 43 minutes later flying upside down at 3,000 feet through a valley with towering mountains on either side of his plane. He righted the aircraft and made it back to Port Moresby only to be gibed at for the excellent series of photographs he had taken detailing cloud formations that his activated undercarriage cameras shot every 45 seconds for the duration of his incapacitation.

However vigilant a reconnaissance pilot might be, fate, chance, and luck played an equally important part in any mission. It was a scout bomber crew blown off course that first spotted the Japanese construction of Guadalcanal's Henderson Field. And in the run-up to the Battle of

Midway, a Japanese reconnaissance pilot's inexplicable failure to immediately report his sighting of the American Pacific Fleet—and an American recon flier's nearly simultaneous alert that he had located the Combined Imperial Fleet—resulted in the time delay between strikes and counterstrikes that proved critical to the decisive outcome.

In these recon Airmen, Jay recognized shards of himself, as if looking into a broken mirror. For their part, the men who flew reconnaissance missions were drawn to both Jay's aggressive piloting and the play of his wits. It was only natural that, together with Joe and the navigator Rocky Stone with whom they had reconned Finschhafen, Jay began to invite certain Airmen with whom he felt such simpatico back to his tent "to shoot the breeze and hatch schemes to outsmart the Jap."

Jay rarely raised his voice during these bull sessions—"he always spoke as if he were quietly reading an essay in a classroom," wrote an American war correspondent who sat in on some of the informal gatherings. Paramount in the lessons Jay strove to impart was his belief that teamwork among a flight crew could trump any obstacle. Quaint as that notion may have seemed even at the time, the group whom Jay had begun referring to as his "skeleton crew" lapped up his Tom Swift philosophy. Given his growing combat record, he was looked upon as the "Old Man" of the outfit. He was twenty-four years old.

Like Jay, several of his new acolytes, notably the copilot Lt. Hank Dyminski, had seen combat since arriving in the Southwest Pacific. But there was one man among the group whose experiences trumped even Jay's. The radio operator William "Willy" Vaughan was a shy 22-year-old with a jaw like a curbstone and a cool, penetrating gaze set off by a pair of eyebrows the size of fruit bats. Vaughan was a sphinx without a riddle during Jay's informal chin-wags, preferring to sit quietly in a corner and listen and observe. His reticence belied the fact that he had been in-theater since the outbreak of the war and had over 200 hours of flight time under his belt.

Like both Jay and Joe, Vaughan had grown up with a passion for airplanes. As a teenager he was a fixture around the flying fields of his home-town: Youngstown, Ohio. Neighbors recalled the young Willy constantly pestering the local pilots for a ride, and remembered him taking a quiet pleasure in discovering the mechanical aspects of any aircraft. Vaughan was a consummate tinkerer, something that Jay noticed straight off. The M.I.T. engineer who had rebuilt his own jalopy in high school could not help admiring the way Vaughan always seemed to be fooling with one gadget or another, usually an old radio, taking it apart and putting it back together just to learn how it worked.

Vaughan had enlisted in the Air Corps three weeks before the attack on Pearl Harbor and had seen action at Corregidor, Java, and Singapore. He had also been a member of the flight crew that evacuated President Manuel Quezon from Manila to Australia just before the Japanese captured the Philippines capital. Unlike MacArthur, Quezon had not been too proud to jump onto an old Flying Fortress to flee the Imperial Army's advance.

But buried in the radioman's combat history there was another, more compelling story that caught Jay's attention. The giveaway was the angry scar that ran down the right side of Willy Vaughan's neck.

Six months earlier Vaughan had been part of the advance air ech-elon flown in to assist the American and Australian infantry defending against the Japanese landings at Milne Bay. During the height of the fight-ing Vaughan's bomber squadron had put down to refuel at a primitive forward airstrip and come under heavy shelling. Before they could hand-pump enough aviation fuel into their tanks they were ambushed by a force of 500 Japanese soldiers and Imperial Marines. The American fliers de-tached their .30- and .50-caliber machine guns from their gun mounts, holstered their sidearms, and set up a defensive perimeter. They held off the assault for more than 10 hours. Finally, with both sides running out of ammunition, the fight devolved into hand-to-hand combat.

Vaughan had already shot close to a dozen Japanese—the last two with the final bullets from his .45-caliber—when an enemy soldier charged at him. He ducked to avoid a bayonet thrust to his face, and the blade sliced his neck. He swiveled and killed his attacker with his jungle knife. He also knifed to death an Imperial Marine just as Australian reinforcements arrived and drove the Japanese back into the bush.

After the episode, Vaughan was promoted to technical sergeant and awarded a Silver Star for his actions. Jay was in awe of the quiet radio operator's sand. He did not anticipate many knife fights at 20,000 feet, but if on the off chance one occurred, he wanted Willy Vaughan by his side.

Another rough character drawn to Jay's inner circle was the suave, mustachioed George Kendrick, also a technical sergeant. Kendrick had been a champion swimmer back in his home state, California, and since deploying to Port Moresby as a waist gunner he had also become one of the 43rd's new bomber recon outfit's most decorated camera operators, always volunteering his services when one of Maj. Polifka's Eight Ballers came calling. Jay came to think of him as "the screwball of the crew," yet Kendrick was as hard as a sandbag and considered himself something of a cowboy.

The B-17s beginning to emerge from Boeing's manufacturing plants had staggered waist-gun windows, but in the spring of 1943 the stations in the 43rd Bomb Group's Fortresses were still positioned directly across from each other. The standard procedure was to assign two gunners to the waist windows, and in the heat of aerial combat this often resulted in the men banging heads, shoulders, and elbows, and even tripping over each other's feet. As a waist gunner, George Kendrick preferred to work alone, manning both machine guns on either side of the fuselage. "He said didn't want to be bumping asses with another guy back there, and he wanted all the guns he could get," Jay wrote of Kendrick. "He told me, 'These are my guns and I'm going to shoot them all.'"

The swashbuckling Kendrick could barely move about the airbase without being trailed, as if by a puppy, by Sgt. Johnnie Able, a 19-year-old flight engineer. Able's most striking feature was his large eyes, their sable pupils floating in a pale-blue field, which lent him an aspect of perpetual astonishment. His father had fought in World War I, and as a youngster

Johnnie had been a voracious reader of war stories. He was only five months out of high school and working as a farmhand in South Carolina when the Japanese struck Pearl Harbor. Ten days later he enlisted in the Army Air Corps. Able's innate mechanical talents had proved a double-edged sword. On the one hand, they had earned him two promotions by the time Kendrick began bringing him around to Jay's informal gatherings, making him one of the youngest sergeants in the outfit. But they had also left him grounded on a maintenance crew, as his facility with aircraft engines was too valuable a talent to risk losing to a flight crew.

Able was somewhat bitter about this and made no secret of his longing to go up on missions. Jay could certainly empathize when Johnnie wondered if someday Jay might have the time and patience to teach him the rudiments of piloting a bomber. Although not so precocious as Willy Vaughan, who harassed his hometown flyboys for rides, Able as a child had liked nothing better than whiling away hours on end watching the Army Air Service pilots practicing their touch-and-gos on the grass strip at Myrtle Beach. Jay and Joe recognized that if they ever secured their own Fortress, they would need a keen eye manning the top turret's twin .50-caliber machine guns. Johnnie Able had entered the service a crack shot, and continued to practice almost every day at Port Moresby. When he said that he would love to be a member of Jay's burgeoning crew, Jay socked his request away in the back of his mind.

It was Joe who found their unlikely tail gunner. Back at Langley he'd hit it off with a fellow sergeant named Herbert Pugh, who also came from Pennsylvania and wore his coal-black pompadour slicked so high off his forehead it resembled a ski jump. The men in Pugh's outfit had given him the ironic nickname "Pudge" because he was close to six feet tall with a body that resembled a slab of marble with four limbs and a head. Pugh had a passion for exercise and during the Bomb Group's physical fitness competitions he invariably ran the fastest and farthest, jumped the highest, and racked up the most sit-ups, push-ups, and pull-ups. But it was more than their shared athleticism that united Joe Sarnoski and Pudge Pugh.

Pugh hailed from the aptly named Steelton, a working-class city on the banks of the Susquehanna River dominated by the imposing red-brick walls and metal sawtooth roofs of the furnaces, mills, and machine shops of the Bethlehem Steel Company and its subsidiary, the Bethlehem Shipbuilding Corporation. What Joe's hometown, Carbondale, was to coal, Steelton was to the forges, foundries, and smelters of America's steel industry, then the symbol of the nation's industrial might. For a good 50 years European immigrants like Pugh's Welsh forebears had flocked to the hard men's jobs in the honeycomb of shipyards, coke ovens, and brickyards that formed the backbone of Steelton. As the son of Polish immigrants, Joe felt a connection to a working-class fellow like Pugh, not least because Pugh had also been raised as a devout Catholic, and the two often attended Mass together.

A year earlier, when the first of the 43rd's units had arrived in Australia, the two had gone their separate ways as Pugh traveled to Port Moresby via Mareeba and Milne Bay while Joe shuttled about the Australian interior teaching his course. Pugh had not been assigned to a specific crew but he had flown as a tail gunner in a succession of Fortresses—an unappealing job, to put it mildly. Depictions of American bombers in movies made during World War II such as *Flying Fortress*, *Air Force*, and *Thirty Seconds Over Tokyo* show rather roomy interiors. The truth was much less grand. The inside of a Fortress in particular was in essence a thin, cramped, low-ceilinged airborne pipe, with sharp-edged projections—landing gear, piss pipes, gun mounts—at every turn. Even stable and on the ground the plane was a bruised head, elbow, or knee waiting to happen. Once in flight, buffeted by turbulence or violently swerving to avoid enemy fire, a Fortress became a mantrap. And the tail gunner's compartment was one of the tightest on the aircraft.

After squeezing through the claustrophobic ventral tunnel in order to reach their stations, gunners like Pudge Pugh were forced to assume an uncomfortable kneeling position for hours on end while supported by a kind of modified bicycle seat. No man prone to airsickness made a good tail gunner, as the rear of the plane so often "wallowed" and "mushed" like a dizzying carnival ride. To add to the misery, the tail was also the coldest section of the airplane. Although almost all American bombers were manufactured with rudimentary heating ducts emanating from the flight deck, the B-17 was not a pressurized aircraft, and being in a Fortress at altitude from the waist guns aft was like flying in cold storage. Tail gunners were constantly squinting through windows fogged thick with ice while fending off frostbite.

Piled atop these indignities was the fact that the tail gunner's station was also the least armored section of the plane. The laws of aerodynamics precluded packing too much weight into the tail of a fully loaded Flying Fortress, and it is probable that Pugh—like most Airmen based in New Guinea—had heard the story of the tail gunner who persuaded a friend in supply to surreptitiously issue him extra flak vests so he could build an armored "nest" in his station. The gunner did not realize that his cozy coop would shift the plane's center of gravity. He also failed to inform the rest of the crew. On its next mission the unbalanced bomber stalled and crashed on takeoff, killing all aboard.

Despite these horror stories, it took little convincing for Pugh to sign on to Jay's and Joe's new venture once he reconnected with his old bombardier pal from the Keystone state. For a man with a build like his, squirming into the cramped tail section of a B-17 may have felt like toothpaste being squeezed back into the tube. But it was not often that an Airman in a combat zone was offered the opportunity to be a part of a team building its own ethos—even if other pilots considered that team no more than a "motley collection of outcasts."

"[Zeamer] recruited a crew of renegades and screwoffs," wrote one of the 43rd's squadron commanders who had known Jay since Langley. "They were the worst—men nobody else wanted. But they gravitated toward one another and made a hell of a team."

20

BLOOD ON THE
BISMARCK SEA

IT WAS TIME ONCE AGAIN TO MAKE THE AMERICANS PAY.

In early March 1943, the Imperial Command was staggered by the defeats on Guadalcanal and at Buna. The Japanese decided to stanch the bleeding by reinforcing their base at Lae. Less than 200 miles over the Owen Stanleys from Port Moresby, Lae was a natural site from which to launch a counteroffensive on the Allied airfields there. But first they would need to resupply Lae. It had worked before.

Two months earlier a dozen Imperial Navy ships had traversed the Bismarck Sea to deliver about 4,000 troops to Lae—this was the convoy that Gen. Walker's attack had barely missed on his ill-fated mission over Simpson Harbour. That reinforcement was for the most part a success—one enemy troop transport was eventually damaged by American bombers, but most of its soldiers and cargo had been recovered and disembarked. For the Allies, there were lessons to be learned.

During that operation Australian intelligence officers charged with plotting the course of Japanese shipping had received information from their coastwatchers about an increase in the number of aircraft at three enemy bases—Wewak, Madang, and Salamaua—along the convoy's route. Now, less than a month later, the coastwatchers were reporting similar buildups. Nearly simultaneously, U.S. Navy code breakers informed MacArthur and Kenney that a major Japanese operation appeared to be scheduled for New Guinea in late February or early March. When Allied reconnaissance flights confirmed an inordinate amount of merchant vessels capable of transporting troops and supplies amassed in Simpson Harbour, it was obvious that something was afoot.

The American signals officers had still not broken the entire Japanese code system, so they had no idea of the size of the convoy about to depart from Rabaul. But decrypted message fragments seemed to rule out Wewak or Madang as a destination, a strong indication that Lae was the landing spot for what the Allies increasingly suspected was a large force of infantry. They took this as a sure sign of another overland offensive on Port Moresby. And in fact on the last day of February a fleet of six Japanese troop transports carrying 7,000 soldiers and accompanied by two merchantmen laden with cargo set sail from Simpson Harbour beneath an aerial escort of 100 or so Imperial Army and Imperial Navy Zeros. They were screened by multiple warships, including three cruisers and eight destroyers.

Kenney ordered an array of search flights into the air over the waters surrounding New Britain, but a gale-force tropical storm swept through the area that day, grounding the Zeros though still providing initial cover for the flotilla. On the afternoon of March 1, however, a B-24 Liberator flying a zigzag recon patrol called a "creeping line search" spotted the procession of vessels rounding New Britain's Cape Gloucester. The ships, the bomber's pilot reported, were riding low in the water and spread over 15 miles. The next morning an Allied armada of 129 bombers and 207 fighter planes took flight.

They lifted off from Port Moresby, from Milne Bay, and from Dobodura, spearheaded by 27 Flying Fortresses from Jay's 43rd Bomb Group. While a small formation of Australian bombers was diverted to Lae to distract the enemy fliers there, the main force of Allied aircraft intercepted the convoy steaming into the Vitiaz Strait, the lead ships within sight of New Guinea's coast and some 100 miles from their destination. It was a slaughter.

So laden with men and supplies were the vessels that they were capable of making only around seven knots. For 72 hours Allied aircraft pounded the convoy, attacking in waves—the 43rd's B-17s in the vanguard, followed by B-24s from the 90th Bomb Group, A-20 Havocs, and even a few old Australian Beaufighters armed with torpedoes. Finally, the coup de grâce was administered by a formation of Pappy Gunn's low-altitude cargo busters, the B-25 Mitchells specifically modified with the tail-gun turrets grafted onto their noses. One of the American pilots compared the scene to sinking "toy boats in a bathtub. One minute a ship would be sitting as pretty as could be, and in the next the top would lift off in a cloud of debris and smoke." He added that the carnage "went on until every ship was sunk or burning, and the sea was littered for miles with every conceivable sort of wreckage."

For the most part, American and Australian P-39s and P-40s managed to keep the hosts of Zeros screened from the Allied bombers during the battle. But on the second day, after the fighters withdrew to refuel, a Fortress from the 43rd piloted by Lt. Woody Moore was engulfed by at least 10 Zekes and shot to pieces. Just as Moore ordered his crew to bail out, one of the Zeros rammed his B-17, severing its tail from the fuselage. The subsequent carnage was witnessed by several nearby Fortress crews. As one of the outfit's pilots recorded in the 43rd's Combat Diary: "We had no fighter protection today. Lt. Moore's plane was set on fire by attacking Zeros and it plunged into the sea. Seven of the crew were seen to bail out, one man slipped through his harness as the chute opened. The others were strafed by Zeros as they floated helplessly down."

Later that afternoon, after another Japanese destroyer was crippled and its crew forced to abandon ship, the 43rd's revenge was swift and savage. As the Combat Diary continued, "The other B-17s went down to 50 feet strafing the Japs who were in life boats, rafts, and floating around in life jackets. Everyone in the Group would have given much to have been in on the strafing after what had happened to Lt. Moore and his men."

For as long as their fuel and ammunition held out, American bombers continued to buzz the floundering survivors. They also gleefully reported the floating survivors being devoured by thick schools of sharks as "the sea ran red." As another pilot noted, "We could see big clusters of men struggling in the water and the sleek brown sharks striking at them."

The feral response to the execution of Moore and his crew continued into the next day as enemy infantrymen who had abandoned the smoldering merchant cargo ships continued to litter the sea. Clad in full jungle uniforms, clinging to any debris that floated, they were "blown to bloody rags" by the Fortresses' blistering nose and ball turret guns. All told, the Americans expended 100,000 machine-gun rounds on the floaters. In a last indignity, on the final night of the battle five American PT boats steamed out of New Guinea to finish off any survivors they could find. Despite reports of Australian Airmen being "sickened" by their counterparts' no-quarter reaction, the 43rd Bomb Group was awarded a Presidential Citation Unit for its outstanding performance during what came to be known as the Battle of the Bismarck Sea. A marker had been set— against the "heathen" Japanese, too much was never enough.

By the end of the three-day battle all six troop transports and both cargo ships had been sent to the bottom of the sea, as were four of the eight destroyers. The surviving Tin Cans had managed to land just over 1,000 troops at Lae, but the effort proved futile; they were the last contingent to ever reinforce the Japanese base. Allied aircraft had dropped 253 1,000-pound bombs and 261 500-pounders during the relentless attacks, including 37 500-pound skip bombs, 27 of which hit their targets, an astonishing kill ratio.

The Japanese death toll was mightily exaggerated by MacArthur and Kenney, but it was true that at least 3,000 Japanese sailors and soldiers perished. In addition, Kenney claimed at least 60 enemy planes shot down, with another 25 "probables." This constituted about two thirds of all aircraft stationed at Rabaul. A postwar analysis deemed this figure highly inflated, but no one disputed the Allies' relatively light losses. Including the air operations over Lae, the final tally was 13 Allied Airmen dead, 12 wounded, and six planes lost. The crews of two of the lost planes were recovered after crash landings.

Midway had indeed been a profound setback, but the Japanese considered the furious onslaught during the Battle of the Bismarck Sea as the most decisive air-sea debacle they had suffered to date. When Emperor Hirohito learned of the disaster he demanded to know why his naval staff had not diverted the ships' course and landed the troops elsewhere on New Guinea. He also ordered a shake-up of the Imperial Naval Command. And as one of Adm. Yamamoto's chagrined aides noted, the convoy's destruction "opened the way" for the Allied advance into the Philippines.

The American press virtually ignored the massacre of the floating Japanese and celebrated the victory as it had none before. General Kenney, who two months earlier had been on the cover of *Time* magazine, now appeared on the cover of *Life*, standing erect as a ship's mast before a huge B-17 propeller, his protruding bottom lip hinting at a smug smile. *The New York Times* hailed the battle as "one of the greatest triumphs of the war" and ran several follow-up articles chronicling the step-by-step lead-up to the engagement. And MacArthur's description of "one of the most complete and annihilating combats of all time"—along with his own inflated body count—was flashed by wire services to newspapers around the world.

More important, the smashing victory allowed MacArthur to seriously begin contemplating the first stages of Operation Cartwheel, with the landings on Bougainville Island as the plan's first key acquisition.

With the conquest of North Africa currently faltering, Washington may have considered the war in the Pacific the minor leagues. But MacArthur, Nimitz, Kenney, Halsey, and the rest had different ideas.

For after a solid 15 months of unabashed success, Japan's great Southern Offensive was about to turn defensive.

THE BATTLE OF THE BISMARCK SEA ALSO MARKED ANOTHER MILESTONE of sorts, serving as what Jay called Joe Sarnoski's "baptism of fire." Jay had been selected to fill in for a sick pilot during the second day of the attack, and it was pure serendipity that the B-17 to which he was assigned also needed a bombardier. Joe had flown on several recon missions by this point but had yet to drop any ordnance. Naturally, Jay arranged for Joe to man the Greenhouse when the 65th Squadron went aloft late in the afternoon to pursue what was left of the Japanese convoy.

The rain had picked up, and Joe could hardly see through the Plexiglas canopy when his bombs put the finishing touch on a limping troop transport—all he could make out were the pillars of black smoke swirling nearly three miles high from the sinking vessel. From that day on Jay and Joe finagled to fly together whenever possible. This was not too difficult, as the usual combination of deaths, injuries, illness, and transfers continued to diminish the 43rd's aircrews.

From that moment on the two became, in Jay's words, "close enough to feel that we were born to fly together."

It was a connection that would soon prove invaluable.

21

THE FLIGHT OF
THE GEISHAS

WHILE JAY'S BURGEONING REPUTATION AS A B-17 COMBAT PILOT FLOUR-
ished, he continued to straddle the line between glory and insubordination. That dichotomy was encapsulated one day in late March, when he
was ordered on a bombing mission over New Guinea's north coast.

Navy code breakers had relayed an urgent message to Port Moresby
about a fleet of Japanese "Betty" bombers that had just arrived at Wewak,
a port town some 500 miles from Port Moresby. The intercepted decryp-
tions indicated that they had been ordered to strike Jackson Airfield the
next morning. The 65th Squadron, with Jay and Joe flying together in a
borrowed Fortress, was instructed to take the enemy bombers out that
night before they could get off the ground again. The squad's B-17s were
loaded with 100-, 200-, and 300-pound fragmentation bombs, which, at
Gen. Kenney's suggestion, were wrapped in thick concertina wire, whose

shards, upon detonation seconds before contact with the ground, could obliterate a plane and cut a man in half.

At the operations meeting prior to the mission the American Airmen were shown reconnaissance photos of the enemy airstrip on Wewak that ran parallel to the shoreline. The pilots were told make their runs at between 6,000 and 7,000 feet, at seven-minute intervals. This elevation left the Fortresses extremely vulnerable to ground fire, but the Operations Officer stressed that there were to be no strafing runs because the Wewak complex was too heavily defended by anti-aircraft batteries. The thinking was that if a plane and its crew were going to be lost over Wewak, they were going to be lost blasting the hell out of the Japanese Bettys and not unnecessarily exposing themselves to ground fire.

Jay's aircraft was on point when the squadron reached its target. He lowered the nose and, with a maneuver bomber pilots called "running downhill," swooped in parallel to the enemy runway. Joe, now a battle-tested bombardier, scored several direct hits on the parked Japanese bombers. The innovative frag bombs exploded at revetment height and sparked a chain reaction of bluish-orange fires from detonating gasoline tanks whose heat Jay and his aircrew could almost feel. With bombs away and the bays closed it was almost as if the Fortress had found a new gear, and Jay pulled away at a tremendous clip, the needles on the plane's altimeter nearly bobbing into the *Do Not Exceed* limit. Seasoned pilots knew that the first bomber on a night raid ran the least risk from anti-aircraft fire; the enemy crews were more often than not "caught with their heads up their revetments." But inevitably, as Jay noted, "For the following planes, all hell breaks loose."

With his run complete, Jay circled out over the Bismarck Sea and awaited the approach of the second bomber in the formation. Before the plane even reached the airstrip, fulgent fingers of white light lit up the night sky. The enemy's crisscrossing arc lamps were interspersed with pinkish-orange tracer rounds that reminded Jay of the Fourth of July fireworks displays arcing over Boothbay Harbor. Ignoring his orders, he dropped his Fortress to 1,000 feet, fell in a little ahead of the attacking B-17, and escorted it in with a strafing run, his forward and belly gunners raking the searchlight batteries with their machine guns. He noticed what looked like cubes of frozen moonlight reflecting off the sea as he vectored back out over the water, once again preparing to provide the same cover for the next bomber, and the next, and the next, until each had released its payload.

On the flight home Jay tallied his "kills." In addition to Joe's scores, his machine gunners counted three batteries of searchlights completely destroyed, and two others severely damaged. With so many anti-aircraft lamps disabled, every bomber from the 65th returned safely from the run. Still, Jay had disobeyed a direct order, and there was hell to pay back at Port Moresby. What seemed to irritate his superiors the most was his insouciance; when confronted with the infraction Jay merely shrugged it off. He believed it was the end, not the means, that counted. The mission had been a success, the Bettys destroyed. He did not see the problem.

The Group's Operations Officers viewed the incident through a harsher lens. Jay was ordered confined to his quarters pending a disciplinary hearing. It was only the presence of an Associated Press correspondent visiting Port Moresby that saved him. The reporter got wind of the story and in his dispatch quoted several of the 65th's pilots crediting Jay's inventive intuition with the success of the mission and their safe return. A congressman on a fact-finding tour of Australia read the article and began making his own inquiries. With the political pressure building, Jay was released from his quarters and he and his entire crew were awarded the Silver Star.

With his second Silver Star stowed away in his barracks bag, Jay now had more leverage than ever to ensure that his "skeleton crew" would fill the slots whenever there was an opening on a mission he piloted. Rocky Stone had been transferred back to the States, and Joe had established himself as Jay's regular bombardier, and it was not unusual to find Pudge Pugh manning the tail gun, or the young Johnnie Able pulling double duty at the navigator's table and up in the top turret, or Willy Vaughan operating the radios.

Once, albeit quite by accident, Jay found himself on a bombing run over Rabaul with his entire cast of misfits aboard. The flight began as a simple "grocery run." One of Jay's primary concerns since his appointment as the 65th Squadron's Operations Officer had been the men's health and morale. The sanitary conditions at the Port Moreby base were atrocious—running water, for example, was an occasional luxury. The engineer in Jay discovered that he could at least stem, if not eradicate, the ubiquitous jungle rot by constructing a makeshift shower room from a large canvas spread hanging between poles that caught the rain and funneled it into 50-gallon drums with holes punched or shot through the bottoms. Still, a variety of stomach ailments, particularly dysentery, continued to run rampant through camp, and there was not much he could do about that.

The steady intake of horrible rations, however, was another matter. A man could stomach only so many green bananas and fricasseed cassowaries, and the squad was sick of rancid hardtack, mealy potatoes, and the "shit on a shingle" served at every mess and memorably described by one Airman as a "pinkish-looking meat in some sort of gravy poured over a single slice of five-day-old bread." One day the squadron pooled its cash and asked Jay to use the money to procure some decent food. He would have to skirt formal requisition channels to do it, but he had an idea. After all, he reasoned, it was Napoleon himself who had noted that "insubordination may be only the evidence of a strong mind."

Jay had retained a connection with the quartermaster at his former base at Townsville, and through him he managed to purchase a cache of fresh beef, mutton, and vegetables from local farmers. Now it was just a question of delivering his haul. At the time the Americans were recycling stripped-down B-17s no longer fit for combat to ferry equipment and men to and from Australia and the New Guinea bases, and Jay arranged for one of these planes to transport the food. In order to avoid the red tape such a semi-legal shipment entailed, he also filed a flight plan stating that the bomber's mission was a refueling stop at Port Moresby en route to a raid on Rabaul. It was just "bad luck," he wrote, that the 43rd Bomb Group's Operations Officers chose that particular aircraft to inspect when it landed at Jackson Field.

His superiors confiscated the groceries. Jay suspected someone from one of the other squadrons, or perhaps even from the 90th Bomb Group, had ratted him out. But that was the least of his worries. By reporting that the bomber was on its way to Rabaul, he had deliberately "misrepresented" a flight plan, a serious offense. He now faced either a court-martial or the prospect of piloting the unarmed Fortress on its stated purpose. As it happened, there was a bombing mission over Rabaul scheduled for that night. No one from the 65th wanted anything to do with going up in an airplane lacking guns and armor plating, so Jay turned to his skeleton crew. Yet even they balked at flying such a dilapidated old crate on a combat mission. Finally they relented, on one condition—Jay had to agree to carry an extra 2,000 pounds of fragmentation and incendiary bombs that they could toss out by hand when Joe salvoed his regular ordnance. The bombing run went off without a hitch and the grocery plane and its crew returned to Port Moresby unscathed—and Jay unprosecuted. Naturally, no one from the 65th Squadron ever saw the meat and vegetables again. But in a surprising development, Jay's devil-may-care attitude toward authority seemed to be rubbing off on at least one member of his crew.

Not long after the botched grocery run, Jay and Joe were again tapped to join a formation prepping for a night mission on Rabaul in yet another borrowed aircraft. But the brass had special plans for their plane. Specifically, they were tasked with bombing the city's Royal Pacific Hotel, an elegant prewar Georgian building on the edge of the city's Chinatown. Most of the structures that still stood at Rabaul, from churches to libraries to private homes, had been commandeered as barracks for Imperial troops, but intercepted intelligence reports indicated that the Royal Pacific's penthouse had been set aside as a "special purpose house" where esteemed Japanese officers, including generals and admirals, were thought to be entertaining comfort women. And not just the usual sex slaves from conquered territories. These were high-end geishas imported directly from the homeland.

During the preflight operations meeting Jay noticed that Joe was unusually quiet. And after the session broke up the bombardier spent the afternoon in the intelligence hut studying reconnaissance photos of Rabaul's town center and the surrounding area. Jay assumed Joe was merely charting their flight path for the run on the hotel. As a bomber neared its target, it was standard operating procedure for the pilot to take his flight headings from the bombardier via the pilot's direction indicator, or PDI, located in the Greenhouse. When the aircraft reached its preordained initial point, or IP, the pilot would "slave" the plane's autopilot over to the bombardier's control for the run itself. Once the ordnance was away, the pilot would take back control of the ship. Jay assumed the ever-meticulous Joe was merely studying how to best avoid the heaviest of the ack-ack batteries.

It was just past midnight when Jay's Fortress approached Rabaul. He did not think much of it when Joe directed him well west of the targeted hotel. Again, Jay assumed that his cautious bombardier was picking his way around the most dangerous of the anti-aircraft gunners. The plane was far from the town center when Jay was shocked to hear Joe's voice over the interphone shouting, "Bombs away!" Joe had "pickled his rocks" and turned the valve to close the bomb bay doors before Jay saw the bomb-release light flick on in the cockpit and took back the controls, still wondering what had just happened. As he banked toward home he glanced over his shoulder and caught sight of a tremendous series of explosions. The sky over above the target remained a fiery red until they cleared the horizon. Tons of bombs, torpedoes, and artillery shells were stored at various sites around the town, and Joe had just hit one of the enemy's largest ammunition dumps.

At the debriefing back at Port Moresby, the Group Operations Officers were incensed that Jay and his crew had ignored their orders. In fact, they were so angry that as punishment they ordered Jay's Fortress back into the air that night, with the Royal Pacific's "special purpose" penthouse again as its target. Again Joe spent the afternoon studying photographs. Hours later, as they approached Rabaul through a heavy cloud cover, Jay ceded control to his bombardier. This time Joe banked them even farther away from the hotel. Jay had no idea that Joe had used his control valve to open the bomb bay doors, had set the bomb rack on the "select" position, had flipped on the bomb switches, and had fixed the settings until he again heard the telltale "Bombs away."

Once again a tremendous fire flared. Joe had bombed a Japanese fuel dump. For the second time the debriefing officers were not amused, and in the Group's official After-Action reports they refused to credit Jay, Joe, or the crew with destroying either the ammunition depot or the fuel dump.

"But they gave up on us and did not assign us for another attempt," Jay wrote to Joe's younger sister Victoria. "Joe went up to his tent, did his rosaries, and went to bed happy. We had not bombed innocent geisha girls!"

WHEN JAY AND JOE COULD NOT MANAGE TO GET THEIR SKELETON CREW into the air, they made certain to keep up their training on land. Each man was told that it was his responsibility to "belt" his own ammunition, with one twist. Machine guns on most B-17s were generally armed with a sequence of two armor-piercing bullets followed by two incendiaries followed by a flare bullet, or tracer. Jay preferred that in his guns, every other bullet be a tracer. Though tracers were the least accurate shells, they shot through the sky like a meteor shower. This, Jay insisted, provided a not-so-subtle reminder to any bogeys that his gunners were aware of their presence.

The crew spent mornings honing their aim by firing at logs floating off shore in the harbor. Then Joe would take the men aside and time each one as they stripped and reassembled their .50-caliber machine guns blindfolded. If they took over one minute, he made them do it again. The pilot and his bombardier drilled into the crew precisely where they were to assume their ditching positions in the forward bulkhead in the event of a land or water crash until it became second nature. If it ever came to that, they knew, there would be no time to think. The men joked that with their arms folded over their shoulders and clasping their scapulae, they looked like vampire bats tucking their heads beneath their wings to sleep. They even simulated emergency bail-out procedures by having the crew leap from the open bomb bay doors or waist windows of a parked aircraft. It was George "Cowboy" Kendrick who wryly suggested that he'd prefer to remain in one piece until the plane crashed as opposed to being cut in two by either of the bomber's twin rudders. Jay and Joe made him practice his jumping anyway.

Gradually Jay recognized that his team was meshing in ways he had only imagined during those bull sessions back in January. In turn his men, Joe in particular, were also becoming comfortable enough with their captain to occasionally push his buttons. A typical B-17 was packed with radio equipment including a command radio for short-range communication with ground stations and other aircraft within hailing distance and a radio compass for navigation. A few Fortresses were even equipped with the new liaison radios for longer-range communication. It was said that when the weather was right—not often in the Southwest Pacific—a pilot could transmit across 3,000 miles with one of the liaisons, though Jay had never seen it done. But of all the communication gear, it was the plane's interphone system that got the most use. The interphones allowed all crew members to speak to one another. Some crews were Chatty Cathys, but one of Jay's hard-and-fast rules was that there was to be minimal palaver— and no cursing whatsoever—over the interphone during a mission. Joe, however, liked to tease his flight commander by lifting the receiver to his lips and softly singing the words of popular American songs—"Come along with me, Lucille, in my merry Oldsmobile." Sometimes Joe sang in

Polish, leaving Jay to constantly wonder if his bombardier was using profanities he could not understand. It was a sign of Jay's respect and admiration for Joe that he didn't end these spontaneous concerts by switching to the "call" position on his jackbox to override Joe's broadcasts. He even allowed himself a chuckle at the groans from the other crewmen when Joe broke into song. He knew when to allow his men to blow off some steam.

All in all, the camaraderie that Jay's crew developed served them well during missions in "borrowed" aircraft. But it could not solve Jay's biggest problem: he still needed his own plane.

22

OLD 666

IT WAS GEORGE KENDRICK'S IDEA.

One rainy March morning Jay accompanied the waist gunner out to the rump end of Jackson Field to inspect the hulk of a spavined Flying Fortress languishing in the base's "boneyard." Kendrick had last seen the bomber three months earlier back in Australia, where Karl Polifka's Eight Ballers from the 8th Reconnaissance Squadron had been in the process of refurbishing it with camera-mapping equipment for a photo run over Rabaul. Sometime between then and now the plane had been permanently grounded, not even considered airworthy enough to serve as a supply ferry between Australia and New Guinea. How it came to rest on Port Moresby's scrap heap was anyone's guess.

The Fortress was still equipped with its three K-17 trimetrogon time-lapse cameras, but most of its salvageable equipment had been cannibalized by the base's maintenance crews. The aircraft also carried a cursed reputation. Although it was less than a year old, it had been so thoroughly shot up on so many occasions that it was considered a jinxed plane—a "Hangar Queen" in the vernacular. Adding insult to injury, it had even been shredded by bullets when a crew had taken it up on a photo-reconnaissance mission over Rabaul only to discover at the target that the intelligence shop had loaded the cameras with the wrong type of film.

One incident in particular had secured for the aircraft a kind of black-comic notoriety, however. This had occurred five months earlier, when the Fortress was tabbed to take part in a bombing run over Lae. It was 30 miles out from the target when one of its life rafts accidentally de-ployed at 15,000 feet, The expanding neoprene ripped off the bomber's radio antenna and became wrapped around the port elevator hinged to the tailplane. The pilot took the plane down to below 10,000 feet, where the top turret gunner deflated the raft with his guns. But then the flaccid synthetic rubber threaded itself through the elevator's flanged lightening holes, and the mission had to be scrubbed—the only occasion, ironically, when the plane had not taken enemy fire.

The aircraft may have resembled nothing so much as the rotting skel-eton of an immense raptor, but to Jay it was the most beautiful plane he had ever laid eyes on. That afternoon he sought and received permission from the Bomb Group's CO, Lt. Col. John Roberts, to attempt to restore it, and had the bomber towed to a quiet corner of the 65th's Squadron's flight-line area. Then, just as he had with his jalopy back at Culver Acad-emy, he began to "Zeamerize" it. "We did what the kids back in my day did with an old car," he wrote in his diary. "Stripped it down, souped it up, and made a hot rod out of it."

The B-17 was one of the early E models, and the name *Lucy* had been stenciled in bright yellow cursive across its nose by a previous crew. Al-most all Allied bombers were given nicknames during World War II. Most were indicative of their destructive intent—*Hell From Heaven, Short Bier,*

Tojo's Jinx. But it was not unusual for a homesick pilot to honor a wife, a daughter, a mom, or even the gal who got away by emblazoning her name across his aircraft. The inspiration for *Lucy* is lost to the mists of time, and Jay had the crew paint over the name. In a small surprise, he did not overpaint the U.S. Army Air Force "meatball" insignia—a white star with a large red dot in the center—that was being phased out for resembling too closely the Japanese Rising Sun.

The only identification that remained on the bullet-riddled airframe was the plane's serial number printed in white across the tail fin: B-17E 41-2666. To Jay and his new crew, the aircraft simply became "Old 666." It is not recorded whether or not they were conversant with the biblical connotation of the number.

The resurrection of Old 666 began the next day. Maintenance personnel were even more scarce at Port Moresby than back in Australia, and for months American flight crews throughout the theater had performed most repairs themselves. Jay's men were no different. Half of them, he wrote, "had been born with a wrench in their hand." They were also wary of the sticky fingers of the rival ground crews who were based at Jackson Field, and decided they needed no help from outsiders. Jay and other Airmen had personally witnessed crew chiefs descend on crippled bombers that had crash-landed and strip them of any and all usable parts before the dust even settled.

Johnnie Able's expertise came in handy when they replaced the bomber's dilapidated engines with four working Wright Cyclones salvaged from other junked planes lying fallow behind the busy runway. They also managed to scavenge a set of serviceable tires. Jay ordered his men to discard much of the plane's heavier internal fittings. Ammo chutes, excess cartridge belt holsters, and even the aircraft's two piss pipes were chucked. If anyone felt the need to urinate during a mission, the camera hatch in the bomber's deck would have to do.

By the time the crew finished "Zeamerizing" the bird, in the interest of pure speed the aircraft had shed 2,000 pounds of equipment. Jay, naturally, had other plans for that missing ton.

Up in the nose, he ordered the two factory-installed .30-caliber machine guns on either side of the bombardier's Plexiglas-enclosed Greenhouse switched out for a brace of swivel-mounted M2 Browning .50-cals. The navigator's compartment had a single .30-caliber gun, which he also replaced with two .50-cals. These weapons would allow the bombardier and the navigator to jump from one firing station to another depending on what a dogfight called for. Their firepower also bookended the two machine guns Pudge Pugh would man in the tail. Jay knew from experience that you could never have enough .50-caliber machine guns.

By 1943 the 84-pound, belt-fed "Ma Deuce"—the reference is to its M2 designation—had become the workhorse of the U.S. Army. Developed in the waning days of World War I by the American firearms designer John Browning and refined throughout the 1930s, the .50-cal was deadly effective against a vast range of targets, from infantry to lightly armed vehicles and ships, and was even used as an anti-aircraft weapon against low-flying planes. The gun could be easily affixed to and detached from all manner of land-based vehicles, seagoing vessels, and, of course, fighter planes and bombers. And it packed a wallop.

The machine gun fired up to 800 armor-piercing rounds per minute, its finger-sized bullets traveling at nearly 3,000 feet per second. As the speed of sound is a little over 1,100 feet per second, a .50-cal's human target would literally never hear what hit him. The M2 had an effective range of 6,000 feet and a maximum range of four miles: Japanese Zeros may have been able to outrun a comparatively lumbering B-17, but Jay planned on making damned certain they would never be able to outgun his plane.

To that end he also upgraded the radio operator's single-gun position just aft of the 12-inch catwalk that spanned the bomb bay. Some pilots had removed the guns from their commo stations when a rash of inexpe-

rienced radiomen shot up the tails of their own planes in the heat of dog-
fights. But Willy Vaughan's bayonet scar, and the story behind it, proved
that he knew what to do with a weapon in his hand. Jay installed a pair of
synchronized .50-calibers in Vaughan's compartment that would allow
him to fire both upward and backward. Jay also scrounged yet another
set of .50s to complement the normal allotment of one per side in the
bomber's midsection.

George Kendrick, naturally, claimed all four of these waist weapons as
his own, and also volunteered to operate the twin .50s installed over the
manhole-sized opening Jay had cut through the bottom of the aircraft's
thin fuselage just forward of the tail wheel. Combined with the ball turret gunner's two .50-cals, these would give Old 666's underside nearly
double a B-17's usual firepower on strafing runs and, more important, increase its ability to fend off bogeys attacking from below. He also ordered
the three horizon-to-horizon time-lapse trimetrogons mounted over the
new hole in the bomber's belly on either side of the aircraft's standard
camera, and put Kendrick in charge of them, too.

The .50-caliber machine gun's major flaws were that it was prone
to jamming—many an Airman's hands sustained major burns in clearing
crinkled ammunition belts—and, if not operated correctly, to burning out
from sustained firing. Combat scenes depicted in scores of Hollywood
movies showed Airmen continuously firing their weapons, when in fact
if they did so for longer than six or seven seconds they risked melting
the guns' air-cooled barrels. This fact was drilled into all recruits in boot
camp with a simple saying: short bursts harvest more meat per bullet. In
the heat of battle, however, it was easy to forget protocol and blast away at
an enemy blasting back at you.

To compensate for the inevitability of at least some of their guns
jamming or melting down, Kendrick and Vaughan suggested that they
clear space above the catwalk for another brace of .50s to be cached for
emergencies. Jay agreed and not only brought the extra guns on board
but also instructed the men that at the first sign of trouble they were to

immediately jettison any malfunctioning weapons and replace them with the backups. In the same spirit, Jay ordered all ammo cans dumped overboard once they were empty. Yet he still wasn't satisfied. He required one more weaponry innovation, and he knew just the man to make it happen.

Technical Sgt. Forrest Dillman had been a late addition to the crew. Old 666 needed a ball turret gunner, and Johnnie Able had suggested his friend Dillman as a candidate. The gimlet-eyed Dillman, Able told Jay, was one of the best he'd ever seen with a machine gun, at least George Kendrick's equal as a weapons specialist. Dillman was from McCook, Nebraska, a former frontier railroad depot rising in the Republican River valley barely a stone's throw from the Kansas border. McCook was a traditional Old West boomtown, and its sons—the scions of Indian-fighters and Civil War veterans—took pride in the town's fighting tradition. Dillman had volunteered for training as a belly gunner because he thought it offered the quickest route into combat.

At first he considered it the biggest mistake of his life. The USAAF's month-long aerial gunner course in which he had enrolled included three weeks of classroom topics such as Armaments and Ordnance, Mathematical Theories, Turret Operations, and Recognizing Friend and Foe. Dillman, fairly certain that he could tell an American from a Japanese, was bored to tears. It was only during the course's final week that potential gunners finally got to fire real weapons, first from stationary positions at fixed targets, then at moving targets, and finally from moving positions at moving targets. This was where Dillman shone, and he graduated near the top of his class.

Another reason Able had suggested Dillman was that he had completed three semesters at the University of Denver, and Able thought Jay might appreciate having another college man on the team. This naturally raised the question of how intelligent any man could truly be who volunteered as a belly gunner.

Of the 276,000 warplanes that rolled off American assembly lines between December 7, 1941, and September 2, 1945, 40,000 would be lost overseas, including 23,000 in combat. (Another 14,000 crashed or were disabled in the continental United States.) This meant an average of 70 American planes lost for every day of hostilities. Allied war planners took some solace in knowing that for every American plane downed, the Japanese were losing six, but there was not an Airman flying in combat unaware of the long odds he faced each time he lifted off on a mission. And manning the ball turret of a Flying Fortress was a particularly nasty piece of business. It took a certain mind-set to be willing to crawl into a tiny glass sphere and hang exposed from the underside of a bomber as flak burst in every direction and enemy fighter planes buzzed you like angry hornets.

The thin Plexiglas that encased a ball turret gunner's station would barely stop a .22-caliber bullet, much less a Japanese Zero's 7.7 machine-gun round. And while the overall mortality rate for B-17 crews in 1943 stood at 30 percent, it rose to a harrowing 60 percent for ball turret gunners. In a cruel irony, the one thing a belly gunner rarely had to fret over was being wounded—the position had the lowest wound rate on the aircraft. Manning the ball turret was quite literally a life-or-death proposition, and most men pressed into the job eased themselves into the bubble as if there might be snakes inside.

The turret itself was not much larger than a good-sized beach ball, and as a rule only men under five feet four inches were eligible for the job. The station remained empty during takeoff. Once in flight, the belly gunner would rotate the bubble electronically until its twin .50-cals faced straight down, and then lower himself onto a fixed cast-armor plate about the size of a child's swing. That was his seat. Crouched in the fetal position, his legs hanging in midair by dangling footrests, he snapped on his safety strap and closed and locked the hatch above him. It was so cramped that many gunners didn't bother to wear parachutes. Yet even without a parachute there was not enough room to reach back and cock the two machine guns, whose barrels extended through the turret on either side of the gunner. Instead, he operated a loading cable running through the fuselage that was attached to the cocking handles by pulleys.

The two advantages a ball turret gunner had were speed and maneuverability. The electric motor driving the two hydraulic transmissions that rotated his sphere could turn 360 degrees in just over a second, offering a panoramic shot at any enemy aircraft attacking from below, behind, or the front. Given the tendency for a wildly swiveling gunner to lose perspective in his relationship to his own plane during a dogfight, his machine guns were equipped with automatic cutoffs that prevented them from firing when they were aimed forward at the aircraft's propellers.

Following a bombing mission or a photo run the belly gunner was expected to remain on station until his plane was completely clear of antiaircraft batteries and bogeys. At this point in the war, with Japanese airbases strung like pearls along the north coast of New Guinea, this meant until his plane had crossed the Owen Stanleys and was on approach to Port Moresby. Missions could last for up to 10 hours, and because these journeys were so adrenaline-sapping, all belly gunners were issued an industrial-strength Hershey bar to maintain energy. But it was so cold in the turret that if the gunner forgot to store the candy against his flesh inside his boilersuit he was left with a frozen, jawbreaking hunk of chocolate. In a final indignity, when a member of a B-17's crew needed to use the aircraft's aft piss pipe, he was first supposed to warn the belly gunner to rotate his bubble to face forward lest the urine ice up his sight line. Unfortunately, many crewmen forgot. Since Jay had removed Old 666's pipes, this didn't apply to Forrest Dillman.

Before Sgt. Dillman could begin to contemplate the risks that lay before him, Jay handed his newest crewman one final task. He wanted his own gun. It was common knowledge among Airmen at Port Moresby that Zero pilots had long since discovered that a B-17's most vulnerable point was the nose. Jay had personally seen enemy fliers race out ahead of his aircraft to turn to meet him head-on, and the Zekes that had taken out Gen. Walker's bomber had inflicted their mortal damage through repeated frontal attacks. Jay vowed that whatever had happened to the bombardier, navigator, and top turret gunner manning the forward weapons on Walker's plane—jammed guns? killed or incapacitated early on? melted their barrels in panic?—would not happen on Old 666. If it came to that, he would go out blasting. This was where Forrest Dillman came in.

Like Willy Vaughan, Dillman was blessed with an innate ability to grasp the workings of almost anything mechanical. He puzzled over Jay's request for a day or so before hitting on the idea of mounting a fixed .50-caliber on the cheek of the nose deck below and forward of the cockpit. This bore-sighted gun—its sights aligned with its barrel, which in turn aligned with a row of rivets on the plane's nose—would be charged to fire by the bombardier below and activated from a button mounted on Jay's control wheel. Jay loved the idea. No other B-17 carried what he took to calling his "Snozzola Gun."

By the time every weapon was installed, Old 666 bristled like an angry porcupine, the six-foot barrels of the 17 machine guns—with two to spare—protruding from the fuselage like deadly quills. The modifications took the term "Flying Fortress" to the extreme, and Jay's B-17 was now the most heavily armed bomber in the USAAF. The Bible warns that at the time of the Apocalypse, "If anyone has insight, let him calculate the number of the beast, for it is man's number. His number is 666."

As far as Jay and his crew were concerned, the Japanese were about to discover the number of the beast. Unfortunately, the tone and tenor of the entries in Jay's combat diary took a more somber turn when, days after Dillman installed his personal nose gun, he learned that Ken McCullar and ten members of his crew had been killed on a predawn takeoff.

23

THE OUTLAWS

KEN McCULLAR WAS MORE POPULAR AND RESPECTED THAN EVER AT THE time of his death. He had recently been promoted to major and placed in command of the 43rd Group's 64th Squadron. *Black Jack*, a bullet magnet, had only just been retired, which is why McCullar occupied the left-hand seat of a Fortress named *Blues in the Nite* as it taxied to the downwind end of Jackson Field shortly after midnight on April 11, 1943.

McCullar and his crew had been tasked with acting as the weather and observation ship for his squadron's bombing run over Rabaul. As was customary, he was lifting off an hour before the bulk of the formation. *Blues in the Nite* was midway down the runway when personnel in the flight control tower saw a tongue of flame shoot from its right inboard engine and lick at the right wheel assembly. The spark lasted no more than an instant, and the B-17 continued liftoff. It was several hundred feet into the air when it swiveled into a tight chandelle, stalled, nosed over, and dropped like a 36-ton stone.

The crash was followed almost instantaneously by a huge explosion as a full complement of 2,400 gallons of fuel burst into a towering fireball. This in turn set off the aircraft's bomb load. There was not much left of either metal or flesh for the medics and meat-wagon volunteers to gather as they picked through the charred debris.

The shards of *Blues in the Nite* had barely been bulldozed into a hole by the side of the runway before a somber ritual was under way back in the tent city where McCullar's crew had bunked. It was the Italian poet Petrarch who observed that placing a body in the ground after a good death does honor to the deceased's entire life, but in a combat zone with few formal funerals, the best a compatriot could do was to open a fallen comrade's footlocker, lift his stashed bottle of liquor, and toast his memory. As a bottle was being passed on this particular occasion someone noted that McCullar's squadron had recently established a record for the number of bombing runs in a single month, having successfully completed 104 sorties in March.

When word of the crash reached Brisbane, Gen. Kenney was again devastated. First Bill Benn, now Ken McCullar. What were the odds that two men who had survived so many harrowing combat missions would both perish in accidents? Kenney was told that a mangled animal corpse, either a wallaby or a tree kangaroo, had been discovered on the runway at daybreak. It was assumed that McCullar's plane hit the animal, whose carcass then ruptured the aircraft's hydraulic system and set alight the thick, flammable fluid.

In his service obituary McCullar was credited with sinking five Japanese vessels with skip bombs, and his death reverberated out from Port Moresby like the downbeat of an ax. Jay was hit particularly hard by the loss of the bold friend who flew with a panther's grace and whom he would later call "the greatest fighting flier I ever knew."

Yet the war went on, the only constant, and Jay was left to console himself with a cautionary lament as old as flight itself, memorized by American Airmen since boot camp: There are old pilots, and there are bold pilots, but there are no old, bold pilots.

IN RESPONSE TO McCULLAR'S FATAL CRASH AND THE SUBSEQUENT PLUM-
met in morale, Gen. Kenney began relieving as many flight crews from the 43rd Bomb Group as he dared spare. Some of these Airmen had been stationed at Port Moresby for over six months and it showed, in both their physical appearance and their mental acuity. There was one problem. So few newly trained B-17 crews were arriving from the States that several B-24 Liberator crews had to be temporarily assigned to fly the 43rd's Fortresses.

With the replacements came a smattering of new maintenance personnel, and Jay warned his crew to be on alert. Word had spread throughout the base about the scrounging oddballs rebuilding their own plane, and as Jay expected some of the new crew chiefs began lurking about the 65th's flight line hoping to snatch the occasional working part from Old 666 for use in their own bombers. Jay was so wary that he had his men take round-the-clock shifts guarding their Fortress. Then, just when he felt that Old 666 was nearly ready to make its first flight test, Jay picked up a rumor that someone at Bomb Group Headquarters was considering assigning *his* airplane to a pilot and flight crew who had just arrived at Port Moresby from Australia.

To forestall any hijacking Jay and his crew began sleeping on their plane while letting everyone know that their guns were, in the lingo, cocked and locked. As a fellow bomber pilot wrote of Jay and his men, "They told everyone to stay the hell away from that damn airplane. Everyone was talking about [Zeamer] and his renegades and their loaded fifty-calibers." Their reputation as outlaws spread rapidly, as did the suspicion that they would indeed use those guns if a trespassing crew approached.

A round of bureaucratic wrangling ensued that reached all the way to Bomber Command. In the end the new crew was assigned another aircraft, and Jay and his men continued their restoration project in peace. As the reclamation of Old 666 proceeded, Jay and the crew discovered that living together on the aircraft intensified their sense of mission. The Fortress became their second home, and while Joe Sarnoski continued overseeing their physical training, Jay's constant lectures and pep talks instilled in the crew an overriding confidence in precisely what their aircraft was capable of.

Blown engines? Jay liked to recount the story of Lt. Harry Brandon, who over a year earlier had been among the five pilots to stage the first B-17 run over Rabaul. A Zero's cannon shell had exploded the right inboard engine of Brandon's Fortress at the same time as the right outboard engine inexplicably died. Yet Brandon kept the plane aloft for several hours on just his two left engines until the right outboard could be restarted. Jay also recalled how he had personally flown with another pilot who had remained aloft, albeit tenuously, with only one working engine.

One of every Airman's greatest fears was that his plane would fall into an uncontrolled spin. But Jay taught his crew that even spins are not necessarily fatal. He used Paul Lindsey's experience as proof. Early in the war Lindsey was piloting his shot-up Fortress home from an attack on shipping off the Philippines when he ducked into a thunderstorm over the Java Sea to evade pursuing bogeys. The convective energy threw Lindsey's plane into a vortical dive so frightening that his copilot and navigator panicked and jumped at 7,000 feet. But Lindsey continued to wrestle the yoke, and after another 3,000 feet of free fall he was able to stabilize the ship and fly it home. The crewmen who bailed were never heard from again.

This story often prompted Jay to reiterate his belief that despite all their jump training, bailing out was always the last resort. He stressed that no matter how hopeless a situation might seem, he preferred to ride a sturdy bomber down for a crash landing. It was safer, he felt, than jumping, and he made certain that each of his crewmen knew his crash station should their aircraft be forced to either crash-land or ditch into open sea.

He even wrote up a checklist of what each man was expected to carry for postcrash survival—flares, flashlight, medical kit, sidearms—and he would pull surprise inspections to ensure that these items were stored properly in the aircraft.

Most aircrews stationed in the Southwest Pacific had heard apocryphal tales of men staying alive by sticking together after a crash. But Jay had actually witnessed this. Less than a year earlier two B-26 Marauders from his former Group had gotten lost in severe weather over the north coast of New Guinea. With the engines running on fumes, the crew of one ship bailed while the crew of the other remained with their plane as its pilot belly-flopped into a jungle clearing at 100 miles per hour. No one from the second crew was seriously injured, and within a month all nine men had found their way back to Port Moresby as a group. As for the crew who had jumped, only half of them were ever heard from again, and at that it had taken the separated, emaciated survivors close to six months to trickle back into the airbase one by one.

Jay was a natural storyteller, and his instructional yarns, always delivered in a professorial, low-key fashion, could not fail to leave a lasting impression. His credibility as an officer who would ensure the survival of his crew was enhanced by the fact that the rigors of living in a combat zone seemed to agree with him. Not only were the exhausted flight crews of the 43rd in the air nearly constantly on missions, but Port Moresby had suffered more than 100 aerial attacks since the war began. The whole base would shake with the rolling concussions of the Japanese carpet bombing— even men who had never actually been in Africa compared it to the footfalls of a charging rhino. After being stationed at Port Moresby for only a few months a frightening number of Allied Airmen began to have the gaunt if not ghostly countenance of dead men walking. It was not unusual to see entire flight crews with bags like heavy satchels of flesh under their eyes.

Jay was not immune to the physical rigors and demands of the Southwest Pacific, and had indeed lost a dangerous amount of weight. Yet one visiting reporter, struck by the vibrancy of Jay's blue-gray eyes, noted that despite Jay's near-skeletal appearance he somehow managed to retain the mien of "a cultured gentleman with bedroom eyes." Photographs from the time suggest that Jay's facial features had matured, making him a dead ringer for the matinee idol Lew Ayres. And to take the analogy a step further, like an actor inhabiting a new role, he was not afraid to stretch the limits of his craft. As he later told a friend, "Some people thought I took too many chances. But I didn't regard them as chances. I simply found from experience that a Flying Fortress was a pretty indestructible thing, and that there were ways to pull through some seemingly desperate situations."

That April, Jay informed his squadron commander, a brash major from Texas named Harry Hawthorne, that Old 666 was finally ready for a combat-ready flight test. With a fresh coat of neutral gray camouflage paint reflecting the dawn rays of the sun, the refurbished Fortress lifted off from Jackson Airfield and soared into the sky above Papua Bay. Despite its added armament, enough weight had been jettisoned to make it the most agile B-17 in-theater. To prove this, Jay could not resist showing off its maneuverability, at one point cutting the throttles and nearly standing the plane on one wing to demonstrate how he could turn inside an attacking bogey by pulling back "for all I was worth" and meeting the Zero head-on.

"The airplane was faster than any other in the squadron, and could pivot on a wing tip," he wrote. "This was important because my method, when jumped by fighters, was to jump them first by turning hard into them and forcing them to pull up so they couldn't shoot at us but we could get under their belly with our .50-caliber guns."

Old 666 passed its shakedown cruise with ease, and Jay, Joe, and what a fellow pilot referred to as their "outlaws" wasted no time getting into the game. The next morning the crew arrived outside the Operations Hut, volunteering for any "lousy mission" no other flight crews wanted. At first they were ignored, but they repeated the routine until it became as regular as the Angelus. Their persistence paid off. Since Jay had never

discarded Old 666's time-lapse cameras, he and his crew were finally assigned a succession of daylight reconnaissance flights without a fighter escort. With each successful flight their stock rose within the Bomb Group,
and they became known as the crew to call when photos were needed of
virtually any enemy installation. Because of their zeal they also acquired a
nickname: "Eager Beavers."

"You couldn't keep them on the ground," wrote the flight commander
Walt Krell. "It was the damnedest thing."

Most American bombers at the time flew with camera configurations
of some sort either fastened to their bays or mounted on their top turret
or belly turret. In a neat bit of mechanical ingenuity, the filming devices of
turret cameras were activated whenever the machine gun fired. It was one
sure way to verify a flamed bogey. But the trimetrogons with their long-
focus optics—one vertical and two oblique—were the preferred lenses
for high-altitude reconnaissance missions. The K-17s mounted in Jay's
bomber took high-resolution nine-by-nine-inch "trimet strip" images,
which could penetrate as deep as 30 feet below the surface of the sea.

With George Kendrick operating the cameras (as well as the waist
and undercarriage gun when they got into trouble), Old 666 successfully
photo-mapped the Admiralty Islands and the north coast of New Britain,
and once returned from New Ireland with evidence of a new Japanese
airbase being constructed on the outskirts of Kavieng. Old 666 was initially so active that its crew took pride in the fact that, unlike most of the
bombers in-theater, it was never on the ground long enough to acquire
the traditional nose art.

Eighteen months into the war the Pacific Theater remained a chaotic
area scattered over thousands of square miles. The enormous span of the
war zone combined with the dearth of personnel to make enforcing Army
Air Force rules and regulations nearly futile. In Europe, for instance, the
Eager Beavers would certainly have been prosecuted for insubordination
if not mutiny for their stunt of sleeping on Old 666 with loaded guns. But
the Southwest Pacific was a different reality. Most COs on the front lines

were willing to look the other way, even past an "outlaw crew" led by a captain who had yet to earn his pilot's wings, as long the Airmen were willing not only to volunteer for risky missions at a moment's notice, but to complete them with alacrity and competence. Moreover, it wasn't as if the brass further up the chain of command were beyond bending, or even breaking, the conventional rules of warfare. Perhaps no example of this was starker than the decision to assassinate the man who had planned and coordinated the attack on Pearl Harbor, Adm. Isoroku Yamamoto.

IT WAS THE UNITED STATES, AT THE DIRECTION OF PRESIDENT ABRAHAM Lincoln during the Civil War, which became the first government to formulate a military code of conduct forbidding the assassination of enemy combatants, referring to such acts as "relapses into barbarism." John Wilkes Booth notwithstanding, a half century later Lincoln's tenets had been codified into international law, which affirmed that soldiers may be killed only provided that they are not "individually singled out." Yet the U.S. Army's World War II field manual, citing Article 23(b) of the Fourth Hague Peace Conference of 1907—to which the United States was a signatory—appeared to reject this accepted international doctrine by stating that forbidding attempts to target and snuff out a specific life during wartime "does not preclude attacks on individual soldiers or officers of the enemy whether in the zone of hostilities, occupied territory, or elsewhere."

Such was the confusing mélange of moral choices facing Adm. Chester Nimitz when, on the morning of April 14, 1943, Navy signals officers in Pearl Harbor handed him a top secret report detailing an upcoming "morale-boosting" inspection tour that Adm. Yamamoto planned to make through the upper Solomon Islands. Yamamoto was known for his punctuality, and the decrypted communiqué in Nimitz's possession rather amazingly listed his itinerary down to the minute. The Americans now knew that the admiral, whose prominence in Japan was second only to that of the emperor, would be landing four days hence at precisely 0800 hours on the tiny island of Ballale, an arrowhead-shaped speck some 14 miles south of Bougainville.

Nimitz deferred any decisions about what to do with the information to Washington, where Secretary of the Navy Frank Knox consulted with a group of religious leaders about the morality of assassinating a specific enemy commander. The churchmen gave the attack their blessing, and Nimitz handed the assignment, dubbed "Operation Vengeance," to his South Pacific Theater commander, Bull Halsey, with the message, "Good Luck and Good Hunting." Four days later, on Palm Sunday, April 18, 1943—coincidentally, the first anniversary of Doolittle's raid—seventeen P-38s fitted with extra wing tanks launched from Henderson Field at dawn. Two hours later they intercepted Yamamoto's squadron of two Mitsubishi bombers and six Zero escorts near the southern coast of Bougainville. Yamamoto's flight formation was heading for the airfield at Buin on the southern tip of that island—not for Ballale as the code breakers had reported. This was of little consequence.

Eight of the American fighters engaged the Zekes. The rest sped after the olive-painted Bettys, now diving for a spinney of treetops. The American squad leader, Maj. John Mitchell, had not expected two bombers. Which one carried Yamamoto? Mitchell took no chances: machine-gun and cannon fire sent one Betty flaming into the jungle canopy; the other, also hit and trailing black smoke, pancaked into the sea. The next morning Japanese troops hacked through the undergrowth and recovered the remains of Yamamoto. The admiral's body, clad in a pressed green khaki uniform and brand-new Airmen's boots, was still strapped into its seat, unblemished except for two tidy holes, encrusted with blood, left by the bullet that passed through his jaw and exited his temple. He was still gripping his ceremonial samurai sword, a gift from his deceased older brother.

As the historian Samuel Eliot Morison would later record, Yamamoto's death resulted in "wild if restricted elation" among the Allies. The killing was also something of a vindication for American airpower. A mere 16 months after Japan had rocked the United States at Pearl Harbor, the vaunted Empire of the Rising Sun was now showing hints of strategic as well as tactical vulnerability. From the Allies' point of view, this made the invasion and capture of Bougainville all the more urgent.

24

NO POSITION IS SAFE

IN LATE APRIL, AFTER SEVERAL RECON FLIGHTS, JAY FLEW OLD 666 ON ITS first bombing mission. It was the lead plane in formation during a raid over Simpson Harbour, taking out the tops of trees and, one crewman recalled with not a little alarm, "brushing the town's housetops" on its approach. A week later, on a daylight patrol over the Solomon Sea, Jay made a skip-bombing run on a Japanese cruiser, with Joe releasing his ordnance when Jay took the plane down to just 50 feet off the deck. The crewmen saw several explosions but could not fully assess the damage before they were swarmed by Zeros. Jay managed to lose the bogeys by escaping through what looked like an upside-down ocean of low-hanging clouds.

It was not uncommon for the 43rd's B-17 pilots to encourage their copilots to take control of an aircraft on the return trip from a long mission. This enabled the junior officers to gain the experience to qualify for the left-hand seat. Jay, remembering his "boredom" while he was co-piloting Marauders for the 22nd Bomb Group, took the practice a step further. Once beyond the range of any trailing enemy fighters, he invited any crewman who showed an interest into the cockpit to receive personal instruction. This usually occurred with Jay and his crew flying borrowed Fortresses—including one named *Blitz Buggy* and another dubbed *The Old Man*—as the 43rd was loath to risk the loss of Old 666's valuable trimetrogan cameras on routine bombing runs.

Although a few of the flight crew showed an affinity for piloting, none proved a more willing and adept student than Johnnie Able. So evident were his skills that Jay would often slip into the right-hand seat while co-pilot Hank Dyminski napped on the catwalk and allow Able to fly the plane almost all the way to the Owen Stanleys. Having a crewman take the controls, however, was not always an option. One night during a bombing run over Madang, flak from anti-aircraft fire tore 60 holes in their bomber's left wing, exploded the stabilizer, and knocked out the central oxygen system. Jay brought the plane home with no injuries to his crew in large part because the pilot in formation beside him turned on his running lights to draw away some of the ack-ack. Back at Port Moresby the Eager Beavers worked overnight side by side with maintenance personnel repairing the stabilizer, replacing the oxygen bottles, and patching the shrapnel damage with flattened tin cans. By the next morning Jay was back in the Operations Hut looking for work.

It was during these initial missions that Jay perfected his technique for countering the frontal attacks that Zeros had used on Allied bombers since the onset of the war. As the faster enemy fighters overtook his plane and lined up on either side in preparation for a head-on run, Jay waited patiently until they rolled into their turns. That was his cue to throw the aircraft directly into their paths on his own collision course—"jumping them first."

The astonished enemy pilots were forced to break off their flight patterns and sail past on either side of the American bomber. This exposed the Japanese fighters to successive .50-caliber fire as the bombardier's and navigator's machine guns handed them off to Johnnie Able in the top turret and Willy Vaughan in the radio compartment, who in turn passed the targets to George Kendrick on the waist guns until, finally, they flew into Pudge Pugh's tail gun sights. If an alert Zero pilot chose to flee beneath the Fortress, Forrest Dillman's twin .50s and Kendrick's extra guns mounted on the underside of the fuselage were waiting for him. It almost wasn't fair.

Jay and his crew took their toll on the enemy in punishing bombing runs and flaming Zeros, but his "eccentricities" were still never far from the surface. During another night raid on Rabaul, for instance, Jay was tasked by the Bomb Group's psy-ops officer with circling back over the town after making his bombing run and dropping propaganda pamphlets citing the recent Japanese defeats, particularly on the Bismarck Sea, and calling for the enemy to surrender. This was a rather daffy idea, and it is doubtful anyone expected anything to come of it. Yet never one to leave a stone unthrown, Jay told the crew, "I'll go down low enough so you can throw the whole bundle on their heads—tossing one pamphlet at a time won't hurt anyone." There is a common axiom: "Whoever is calm and sensible in the midst of combat is insane." If such be the case, Jay's crew welcomed their skipper's idiosyncrasies as long as he got them home in one piece.

Soon after Yamamoto's death, with the entire Army Air Force seemingly reinvigorated, the Eager Beavers took part in a raid on the distant harbor of Kavieng in New Ireland. Twenty-one B-17s from the 43rd and nine B-24s from the 90th Bomb Group surprised the enemy at dawn and sank two Japanese cruisers and a destroyer, further degrading the Imperial Navy's ability to resupply its bases on New Guinea. The raid elicited an unusual congratulatory message to Kenney from MacArthur, who wrote that he considered the Kavieng mission "a real honey." Shortly thereafter, perhaps in anticipation of a visit to the front lines by MacArthur, Kenney issued a terse General Order to the 43rd stating, "Beards must go." As the Group's official history records, "Tears mingled with the falling foliage."

IN MAY 1943 NEW B-24 LIBERATORS OF THE 90TH BOMB GROUP ARRIVED in-theater from Hawaii, ensuring that no Japanese position in the Southwest Pacific was safe. Rabaul and the bases on the north coast of New Guinea remained constant targets, and American bombers were now venturing as far afield as the Dutch East Indies to pound enemy airfields, fortifications, and rail lines. At the same time, the deep, distant thrum of heavy aircraft pistons was a constant presence over the shipping lanes of the Solomon, Bismarck, and Coral Seas.

The presence of the Liberator crews also instigated a good-natured feud with the men of the 43rd. It was well known that Gen. Kenney's long-range plans included turning much of the 43rd Bomb Group's duties over to Liberator crews. This did not sit well with the Fortress fliers, and when one B-24 crew mistook a string of rocks for a Japanese convoy and attacked, the 43rd's Airmen were merciless in their mockery. Offering to make peace, the officers from the 90th invited their counterparts from the 43rd to a dinner at their camp seven miles away, near the newly completed Durand airstrip. The main lure for the B-17 Airmen was a fresh shipment of Australian beer.

That night, traveling up the road to the 90th's officers club, the Fortress fliers noticed an outhouse festooned with a sign that read, "Headquarters, 43rd Bomb Group." No one mentioned this over the strained conversation at dinner, but the next morning a mysterious B-17 appeared in the skies above the camp and set the shitter ablaze with .50-caliber incendiary bullets. When news of the incident reached Kenney, he passed word through back channels to both Bomb Group COs that he would not tolerate any more intramural live fire.

This did not stop the officers of 90th from erecting a sign outside their camp proclaiming themselves "The Best Damn Heavy Bomb Group in the World." They were playing off a throwaway line that Kenney had uttered at a press conference when asked about the Liberator's greater speed. It was true: the B-24 was faster than the B-17, and could fly farther with the same payload to boot. But the official logs told quite a different tale. Since arriving in-theater, the 90th had an appalling combat record, with half of its crews either shot down or missing, including the loss of 11 Liberators and 84 men in the Group's first six weeks of operations.

It was no secret that Kenney held a soft spot for the 43rd Bomb Group, his deceased protégé Bill Benn's old 63rd Squadron in particular. They were, after all, known as Ken's Men,* and the general recognized that the Airmen of the 43rd were not amused by the newcomers' insolence. He warned them to let it go, citing their losses as well as invoking the spirit of camaraderie. The Fortress officers were not so forgiving, and retaliation was swift in the form of a Jeep raid on the 90th's camp. Airmen from the 43rd splattered the offending sign and "bombed" the camp's huts and tents with old lightbulbs filled with red paint. Each Group continued to steal or trash the signs outside the other's camp until Kenney once again, this time in an official reprimand, warned the commanders to tone down the antics.

But it was in the air that bragging rights mattered most, and with the 43rd's low-altitude skip-bombing techniques having been accepted as standard attack procedure, there really was no contest. The Flying Fortresses of the 43rd were hitting airbases and sending Japanese vessels to the bottom of the sea at a rate the Imperial Navy considered alarming, and a perusal of the Group's official Combat Diary from the spring of 1943 reads like a laundry list of sunken destroyers and troop transports. Em-

---

* Although Gen. Kenney notes in his memoirs how honored he was when the members of the 43rd Bomb Group, on Benn's suggestion, began calling themselves "Kensmen" (as Kenney spelled it), some argue that the nickname was actually an homage to the late Capt. Ken McCullar, the Group's most illustrious Airman, or even an appreciation of Gen. Ken Walker, killed over Rabaul. There is a consensus that the nickname probably applies to all three.

blematic of the outfit's proficiency was the frequent use of one phrase in particular that began to appear with more regularity in the Combat Diary: "Target obliterated, area plastered."

Still, it wasn't enough. In late March, during a military conference held on New Caledonia, the Army and Navy had finally found common ground on at least one aspect of the war—that airpower alone would never be enough break the Japanese grip on the Southwest Pacific. Yet sending infantry divisions into Japanese-held New Guinea was not promising. The coastline terrain north of the Owen Stanley Range was a tangled mass of vast mangrove swamps through which prewar Australian engineers had despaired of building any roads, much less a railroad line. Any movement of men through this morass would have to be along dirt footpaths, most barely more than a yard wide, with their equipment and supplies carried by pack animals. Frequent violent downpours dissolved these trails into calf-deep mud with a gluey consistency that would halt even the most willing mule. The same storms would turn the numerous streams and brooks running out of the mountains into raging, impassable torrents. And there was no use waiting for the end of the so-called "rainy" season, which the Aussie infantrymen referred to simply as "The Wet." As one American Airman noted, "It rains daily for nine months and then the monsoon starts."

Back in Brisbane, George Kenney was already at work on a solution to this problem with the help of one of his oldest and most trusted friends, Col. Merian C. Cooper. Cooper was to adventure what the Ancient Mariner was to storytelling, and Kenney trusted implicitly in Cooper's "ability to come up with more ideas in an hour than most people get in a month." Their friendship extended back over two decades, to 1917, when they had both enlisted as cadets in the Army's nascent Air Service. Cooper, a Naval Academy dropout, was fresh from chasing Pancho Villa through Mexico with the Georgia National Guard, and Kenney had immediately been taken by the stout, dark-eyed raconteur with an ever-present pipe stem clamped between his teeth.

When America entered World War I, the two young officers were deployed to Europe together. Cooper's bomber was shot down on the wrong side of the Rhine soon afterward, and he spent the remainder of the conflict in a German POW camp. Upon his release he and a cadre of American volunteer pilots formed the Kosciuszko's Squadron to fly for the Polish air force in its war against the Soviets. Somewhere over the shifting Polish-Soviet border his plane was again brought down and he was captured by sword-wielding Cossacks. If anything, nine months in Russian captivity only enhanced Cooper's wanderlust, and after escaping from his prison camp and making it to Latvia he returned to the States and plunged headlong into the new motion picture industry.

The silent-movie adventure documentaries he directed took him from the plateaus of northern Persia to the jungles of Thailand, and he filmed his classic feature *The Four Feathers* among the actual warring tribes of the Sudan. In 1933, he introduced the world to *King Kong*, which he produced, codirected, and acted in. (Cooper is one of the pilots who mortally wound the giant ape as he clings to the top of the Empire State Building.) Between making movies he found time to become one of the founding board members of Pan American Airways as well as run several film studios.

Cooper reenlisted following Pearl Harbor and spent the early months of the war in India, Burma, and China, where he served as chief of staff to Gen. Claire Chennault's roguish Flying Tigers squadron. When Kenney learned that his old friend had been shipped home from Yunnan Province in order to recover from a severe bout of dysentery, he immediately requested his presence in Australia. "Coop," Kenney wrote, "could visualize and plan a military operation with the best of them." This is precisely what he did when Kenney brought him to Port Moresby. Kenney and Cooper recognized that any Allied gains on the ground would require not only close air support, but more than a soupçon of stealth. By this point in the war the Japanese airbase farther up the north coast of New Guinea at Wewak had eclipsed Lae in strategic importance. Wewak, however, lay beyond the effective range of American fighter planes. Kenney was loath to risk losses to his bomber fleet with unescorted runs over this new stronghold guarding Rabaul's western flank; the only solution was to build an airfield closer to Wewak.

To that end Cooper was instrumental in hiring several hundred Papuans to begin cutting and clearing an airstrip and erecting a Potemkin village of grass huts in a clearing southwest of Madang. He knew this would raise enough dust to attract the attention of Japanese reconnaissance flights. The plan was to make the Japanese believe the Americans were building an airbase there while, in actuality, construction had begun on a base being hacked out of the jungle farther to the northwest. The ruse worked to perfection, and by mid-June the enemy was bombing the sham strip daily. The misdirection allowed the other, secret airstrip to be built, and in time it would prove vital to MacArthur's successful offensive across northern and western New Guinea.

It was possible to conceal diffuse ground assaults on an island the size of New Guinea. A smaller island such as Adm. Halsey's key target, Bougainville, however, presented quite a quandary. Any fake airstrip would be quickly discovered on an island about half the size of the state of Maryland, although other forms of subterfuge prior to an invasion might certainly be put into play. In order to throw the Japanese off the scent of a Bougainville invasion, for example, Adm. Nimitz and Adm. Halsey hatched a plan to land a division of New Zealand troops at the same time on the beaches of the nearby Treasury Islands, southwest of Bougainville. This landing would be shortly followed by infiltrating the island of Choiseul, a spit of land in the Solomons chain to Bougainville's southeast. While the Japanese were trying to discern exactly what the Allies were up to, the admirals hoped, Halsey's main landing force would sweep onto Bougainville.

To steam an invasion force of slow and thin-skinned troop transports—"straw-bottomed scows" to the weary and sarcastic leathernecks they carried—Allied war planners would need more than mere surprise, however. They would need information. Despite the pounding the enemy was taking from American bombers across an area extending from the southern Solomon Islands to northern New Guinea, Imperial construction battalions were constantly building new bases and reinforcing old ones across the theater. But where, and to what extent? MacArthur, Halsey, and Kenney needed to know what number and what type of aircraft the Japanese could throw up against the great wheeling motion of a landing by Marines on Bougainville.

So it was that toward the end of May word filtered down from the 43rd's headquarters that operations would soon call for volunteers to make one of the most dangerous reconnaissance flights yet—a photomapping mission over Bougainville Island.

When those rumors reached Jay, he sensed an opportunity.

25

NEW ADDITIONS

ALLIED INTELLIGENCE ESTIMATES OF THE NUMBER OF TROOPS JAPAN could pour into the defense of Bougainville varied wildly, ranging from 45,000 to 65,000. But with U.S. Marines steadfastly inching up the Solomons chain, MacArthur and Halsey suspected that Imperial General Headquarters was rushing as many reinforcements as possible onto the big island to either repel an invasion or, if the U.S. Marines managed to cling to the beaches, stage a counteroffensive.

The airfield complex at the southern tip of Bougainville near the coastal village of Buin, the same field that Adm. Yamamoto's plane had been making for on the day of his death, had been built up into an important staging area during the battle for Guadalcanal. At the north end of the island, across a narrow saltwater passage on the islet of Buka, a grass airstrip originally fashioned by the Royal Australian Air Force had been extended to nearly 2,500 feet with a mixture of crushed coral and asphalt. Japanese construction crews had also dug tunnels for underground fuel tanks on Buka, installed a power plant, and ringed the airdrome with anti-aircraft batteries.

This was the Empire's soft southern underbelly, and Halsey's stepping-stone invasions of New Georgia, Vella Lavella, and, finally, Bougainville—dubbed Operation Cherry Blossom—were meant to tear a hole in it. If the Allies could establish bases on Bougainville, they would for the first time in the war have acquired airfields from which single-engine fighters could reach Rabaul. The decision by the Joint Chiefs of Staff to formally adopt Halsey's strategy of bypassing and isolating Rabaul was still two months away, but as of June 1943, Bougainville clearly remained the key to Operation Cartwheel.

American intelligence knew that at least one Japanese Air Group had been deployed to the Buin airfield in the south of the island, and Halsey informed Nimitz that he needed confirmation of the enemy's strength on Bougainville's western coast. The few maps he had of the area contained numerous unexplored regions, and he had to know if the terrain was firm enough to support his landing forces and their vehicles. More important, he wanted the precise locations of the coral reefs lacing Empress Augusta Bay should his landing craft need to traverse those waters. At the moment Halsey was still weighing his options for invading Bougainville. With the Japanese having constructed airbases in the north, east, and south ends of the island—where, near Buin, an anchorage at Tonolei Harbour was also in place—Marines landing on the southern beaches could be rushing into the teeth of an entrenched defensive force. An end run around this bulwark to Bougainville's Cape Torokina in the west was looking more and more like an ideal way to establish an Allied presence.

Empress Augusta Bay near the cape was a somewhat protected harbor, perhaps not as ideal as Tonolei, but passable. But what made the site particularly inviting for a landing was the tangle of nearly impassable mountain ranges and jungle that ringed the plain abutting the beachhead. This would make mounting a counterattack difficult, particularly considering that the American invasion force would be small for the operation, consisting of fewer than 40,000 Marines and soldiers. But before making any decision, Halsey needed to know where those reefs were; he could not have his landing craft hung up and exposed.

Prior to the war, Bougainville had been administered by the Australian government, and following the Japanese landings there two intrepid coastwatchers remained behind. One, a former cattle rancher, had concealed himself in the northern jungles. The other had established a secret camp atop a forested hill near the south end of the island. Their terse, coded radio reports were relayed across a circuitous route from Port Moresby to Townsville to Pearl Harbor before arriving in Brisbane, and their warnings of enemy bombing formations passing overhead had been integral in alerting the Americans from Fletcher's task force on the Coral Sea to Halsey's Marines on Guadalcanal about incoming enemy aircraft. But even if the coastwatchers had been able to make their way to Bougainville's western coast, the Allies could not rely on these brave men to supply them with the precise locations of the Empress Augusta Bay's submerged reefs. Moreover, the invasion planners required more than just ordinary photographs.

The cartographers from the Army Corps of Engineers charged with developing the charts and tactical maps that would guide any landing force would have to see beneath the bay's surface. This was a matter of some urgency as summer approached, because the Bougainville landings were already scheduled for mid-autumn. The Eight Ballers from the 8th Reconnaissance Squad had made several attempts to photo-map the island in a borrowed bomber, but a combination of bad weather and malfunctioning equipment had resulted in blank strips of film. Now Gen. Kenney and his Bomber Command decided to send a plane of their own. As Bougainville was 600 miles from Port Moresby, it would have to be a

Flying Fortress equipped with trimetrogon cameras as well as supplementary fuel tanks.

The mission would need to be flown on a day with no cloud cover and, given the distance, without a fighter escort. Even the P-38s out of Guadalcanal fitted with extra fuel tanks that had intercepted Adm. Yamamoto near Buin had reached the end of their tether on that mission. Further, in order for the trimetrogon's photo images to be properly aligned, the pilot of the recon aircraft would have to keep his plane on a steady course with pinpoint precision, his compass needle glued to the glass no matter the circumstances. If he dipped his wing even a single degree, the ground focal point on his cameras would shift over a mile, rendering the photos useless.

In all, such a pattern was a flight crew's nightmare. Owing to any and all of these variables, the mission was deemed too perilous to officially order anyone to take it on. It would have to be completed by volunteers.

When Jay learned of this he gathered the Eager Beavers and laid out the situation. He emphasized the journey's hazards—a 1,200-mile round-trip over large uncharted stretches of the Solomon Sea, with no fighter escort or mutual support from the guns of fellow bombers. No one knew what kind of defenses the Japanese had stood up in western Bougainville, and they could very well be flying into a wasp's nest of anti-aircraft batteries in perfect weather without the option of ducking into a cloud or even taking evasive action. He stressed that between the enemy strips carved out of Bougainville and nearby Buka and New Georgia, as well as the Japanese bases in northern New Guinea, Old 666's flight path would take it perilously close to half a dozen hostile airdromes. He guessed that the odds of returning alive were about one in 10. There was a brief silence when he finished his pitch. Then the entire crew stepped forward.

Moments later, Jay strode into the 43rd's Operations Hut searching for his old squadron commander, Harry Hawthorne, who since overseeing Old 666's trial run had been promoted to colonel and succeeded Lt. Col.

Roberts as the Group's commanding officer. Jay found Hawthorne con-
ferring with another of the 43rd's former COs, Col. Roger Ramey. Ramey
was waiting for his promotion to brigadier general to come through so he
could be appointed head of the 5th Air Force's Bomber Command. The
two officers were, ironically, writing the notice that would call for volunteers for the Bougainville recon mission. It was about to be tacked up on
the hut's bulletin board.

If the presence of such a senior officer intimidated Jay, he did not
show it. He told Hawthorne and Ramey that Old 666 was the plane for
the job. His crew was outside waiting to sign up. All he asked was that no
one interfere with his preparation and game plan for the mission. Ramey
and Hawthorne agreed.

JAY'S SUPERIORS WERE NOT SURPRISED WHEN HE VOLUNTEERED TO PHO-
tograph Bougainville's reefs and whatever Japanese fortifications might
exist. By now his unorthodox techniques had lent him and his flight
crew a reputation as men who rarely did anything "by the book," and it
didn't get much further from the book than a 1,200-mile round-trip run
over enemy territory in a lone bomber. Similarly, neither the brass nor
Jay would be concerned when, during the second week of June, two of
Old 666's regular crewmen—the copilot Hank Dyminski and the navigator Emile "Bud" Thues—contracted malaria and were confined to sick
bay. There were plenty of good men on the airbase with whom to replace
them. Jay was familiar with one copilot in particular, a respected young
second lieutenant from Arizona named John Britton. Britton was known
by his initials, J. T., and once Jay read his service jacket, he suspected he
would fit right in with the Eager Beavers.

Before the war Britton had attended the University of California-
Davis for two years; there, he'd starred on the school's boxing team while
earning beer money hustling the locals at a nearby pool hall. Congress
had enacted the Draft Bill in 1940, and like any good pool shark weighing

the odds, Britton enlisted in the Air Cadets rather than take the chance that he'd be humping a ruck and a rifle through some godforsaken North African desert or South Pacific jungle.

After making it through boot camp and graduating from Advanced Flight School, Britton began his USAAF career copiloting B-18 Bolos on anti-submarine patrols off the coast of the Hawaiian Islands. Since being transferred into the 43rd he'd been training on Flying Fortresses in Australia and at Port Moresby. His record showed that he took to the heavy bomber with the ease and familiarity of an old hand, exhibiting particular proficiency for skip-bombing attacks on Japanese shipping. By the time Jay approached him about stepping in for the ailing Hank Dyminski, Britton had made over two dozen missions in the right-hand seat. These included several during the Battle of the Bismarck Sea. Jay's request that Britton join the Bougainville mission was barely out of his mouth before the copilot signed on.

It was Joe Sarnoski who discovered their new navigator. Joe was an officer now, having been promoted from sergeant to second lieutenant—a "shavetail" in the parlance. The field commission had been the idea of a group of pilots, including Jay, who had banded together and petitioned 5th Air Force headquarters to promote any bombardiers who had graduated from the Bombsight Maintenance Course. The argument behind the campaign was based on the fact that these bombardiers were flight officers in all but name, and deserved the formal recognition. General Kenney agreed, and by the time Joe sought out First Lt. Ruby Johnston and asked him to join the Bougainville recon run as flight navigator, it was an officer-to-officer request.

During his time hitching rides as a freelance bombardier with no assigned plane, Joe had flown several missions with Johnston, and he admired the navigator's savvy and cool head. Johnston may not have been much to look at, packing a mere 140 pounds on his 5-foot-nine frame, but Joe knew that his bantam appearance belied a man with some sand. Johnston came from Pensacola, Florida, where, like J. T. Britton, he had spent a couple of years at a university before enlisting in the Army Air Force. This was also one of the reasons Joe had thought to recruit Johnston—the Pennsylvania farm boy had never lost his childhood respect for college men. But it was the navigator's combat history that jumped off the page.

Several months back Johnston had been the regular navigator on a B-17 called *Tugboat Annie*—the pilot, Lt. Harris Lien, was apparently a fan of the 1933 movie of that name. During a run over Simpson Harbour in heavy weather *Tugboat Annie* had taken murderous flak and machine-gun fire that damaged its wings, holed the tail section, and flamed out one engine. Lieutenant Lien thought he could coax the plane home until, somewhere over the Solomon Sea, a second engine began to sputter and cough. The crew jettisoned the guns and ammunition to lighten the load, leaving the skipper a choice. He could head into the teeth of the worsening storm on two engines with a shot-up tail and wings, or attempt to fly around the most flagrant thunderheads and pray that his fuel held out. He chose the latter. He chose wrong.

Johnston reckoned they were somewhere off the north coast of New Guinea, near Buna—where the pitched battle was still raging between American and Australian infantry trying to dislodge the town's Japanese occupiers—when the needles on the fuel gauges touched empty. *Tugboat Annie*'s radio operator transmitted a final S.O.S. and everyone but Lt. Lien crawled into the forward bulkhead to assume crash positions. Lien vectored the plane toward the sea holding it as level as he could, spotted the calmest waters he could find, and ditched it near shore.

As *Tugboat Annie* filled with seawater the crew successfully deployed the two life rafts and sculled through the darkness toward land. A few hours later they reached a beach north of Buna, where they spent the rest of the night hiding the rafts beneath mounds of palm frond scrub. At dawn they began to walk south through the jungle, intending to make for the Allied base at Milne Bay some 200 miles away. But within 48 hours their food and water reserves had run out, and by the fourth day two members of the crew had developed such painful blisters on their feet that they could no longer walk. Ruby Johnston volunteered to remain with the injured men while the rest pushed on.

That afternoon their luck turned when the forward party stumbled into a circle of Papuan huts. Most Americans had picked up rudimentary words and phrases in the native Motuan language such as "friend," "please help," and (most imperatively) "reward." The villagers agreed to fetch Johnston and the two stragglers with makeshift stretchers. By nightfall all the survivors were together again.

With the aid of the Papuans, *Tugboat Annie*'s survivors continued their trek, jumping from coastal village to coastal village by night in outrigger canoes. Finally, they made contact with a coastwatcher, who managed to summon a small Australian launch to pick them up. That night the Airmen gorged on heaps of canned bully beef and marmalade during the sail south to another coastal town under Allied control. From there they boarded an American liberty ship returning from delivering supplies to Buna and were transported on a two-and-a-half-day journey to Milne Bay. They had barely stepped onto the pier when Japanese dive-bombers breached the horizon. They scrambled to slit trenches and watched slackjawed as the cargo vessel from which they had just disembarked was sent to the bottom of the bay. An eight-day sail on yet another liberty ship finally returned them to Port Moresby, and Ruby Johnston was back in the air within a week.

When Jay met with Johnston and listened to his tale, the final match was made. To Old 666's skipper, the pool-hustling copilot and the survivalist navigator seemed the perfect duo to complement his knife-fighting radio operator, his gun-crazy photographer, his muscle-bound tail gunner, his wannabe-pilot top turret gunner, his contortionist belly gunner, and the best damn bombardier in the Southwest Pacific Theater of War.

Preparations for the flight were well under way when Jay learned that Joe might not be flying with them after all.

• • •

AT THE SAME TIME JAY WAS VETTING J. T. BRITTON AND RUBY JOHNSTON,
Joe was astounded to receive orders transferring him back to the States.
After 15 months in-theater, including dozens of combat missions, he was
scheduled to depart from Port Moresby in less than three weeks for a
stateside assignment training recruits. His days as the Old 666 bombardier were literally numbered. Now he was faced with a decision. With
Old 666's bomb bay scheduled to be outfitted with spare fuel tanks, the
plane would be hauling no ordnance on the Bougainville mission. This
obviated the need for a bombardier. Yet even as he packed up his trunk
and barracks bags—and received from his fellow crew members the de ri-
gueur going-home present of a garishly decorated piss pipe—Joe refused
to bow out. In a quiet moment he pulled Jay aside and told him that if the
mission could be scheduled before his departure date in the last week of
June, there was no way he was going to miss it.

Joe felt that Old 666's vulnerable nose section should be protected
on such a perilous recon run by a gunner who knew the plane best. He
also recognized that given the precision with which Jay would have to
pilot this particular mission, it would never hurt to have an extra pair
of eyes in the navigator's compartment to help Ruby Johnston monitor
the bomber's drift, speed, and altitude as well as man the vertical camera
switches located in the nose that activated George Kendrick's trimetrogons. Finally, he felt, the introduction of two new crewmen—Johnston
and Britton—no matter what experience they had, only heightened the
need for his presence. As his fellow Pennsylvanian Pudge Pugh put it in
a letter, "Joe never shirked his duties and never did he even hint or suggest that anybody take his place if there was any one job that was a little
tougher than another."

Men fighting beside one another have throughout history developed
an esprit de corps that runs wide and deep, and Joe was no different. He
had gone through so much with his brothers in arms; how could he cut
and run from this final mission? The fact was, he could not. Further tip-
ping the scales was his relationship with Jay. Over the months the bond

between them had grown stronger. They were no longer amiable captain and bombardier; they were, in Jay's words, "best friends."

An insight into Joe's mind-set might be taken from a long poem he sent home to his younger sister Agnes not long before the Bougainville photo run. Entitled "We Swoop at Dawn" and written by a pilot from Jay's old 22nd Bomb Group, the poem had been copied and passed around to Airmen in-theater, many of whom flew with it stuffed into a pocket of their boilersuits. It includes the stanzas:

No matter how many missions a man may fly,
He never gets over being afraid to die.
It's a funny feeling, hard to explain,
You tighten all up from your toes to your brain
Your stomach's all empty, and your face feels drawn.
When you hear the old cry, "WE SWOOP AT DAWN."

But the men who went out into the morning cold
Thought not of medals and heroes bold.
Most likely they thought of their girls and their homes
And the hell they'd give those yellow gnomes
For causing the war, the pain, and the strife,
And for taking away the best years of their life.

The poem went on for 18 more stanzas and included the line "We'll all go to town and get drunk as a skunk." Joe, fearing that the image of a staggering American Airman might upset the deeply religious Agnes, hastened to scrawl in the margin of the letter next to the stanza, "This line was only a dream."

It was amid this conflicting rush of emotions that Joe made his decision to fly a final mission. The only question that remained was which would arrive first, the day of the Bougainville mapping run or his scheduled departure date.

26

"HELL, NO!"

JUNE 1943 WAS ONE OF THE WETTEST MONTHS ON RECORD IN THE SOUTH-
west Pacific. As the days and weeks progressed, Old 666's mapping
mission was postponed time after time as a succession of tropical storms
settled over Bougainville, making photography impossible. Even when
it wasn't raining, Navy meteorologists could not forecast a day when
the island would be free enough of cloud cover to allow the trimetrogon
cameras to snap usable photos. To reduce their restlessness, Jay and his
crew honed their expertise by flying a slew of disparate reconnaissance
flights in borrowed bombers.

They photographed Japanese installations on the Admiralty Islands west of Rabaul, and days later they flew a recon run over New
Britain just east of Simpson Harbour. Before and after these solo missions they also took part in several of the 43rd's regularly scheduled

bombing runs. It was during one of these, against a convoy carrying supplies to the Japanese-held island of New Georgia, that Jay and his crew had its closest shave yet.

Coastwatchers had spotted and alerted the Americans to the presence of the enemy ships steaming for New Georgia, and Jay's 65th Squadron was tabbed to find and destroy them. It took the squad close to six hours to locate the vessels, which were sailing without air cover, and the job initially looked like another milk run. During one of the squadron's skip-bombing attacks, however, the guns from a flanking Japanese destroyer homed in on Jay's bomber and the enemy fire tore up the fuselage and disabled the radios. What appeared to be the worst damage was incurred when a shell blasted, just above the landing gear, a hole that one war correspondent later described as "large enough to jump through." But a piece of shrapnel had also nicked the fuel line, and on the way home, as the plane drew near the north coast of New Guinea, Jay realized that he was running dangerously low on fuel.

The Owen Stanleys were his first hurdle, and Ruby Johnston plotted a course by dead reckoning through a gap in the mountains. The Fortress, flying on fumes, slid down the south side of the range and approached Port Moresby. It was now dark, and Jackson Airfield was blanketed by fog so thick that that Jay could not even see his own wing lights, much less the flickering smudge pots lining the airstrip. With the bomber's damaged radios emitting nothing but whiny static, he could not even inform the control tower of his predicament. He vectored the ship out over the Gulf of Papua and checked his altitude by firing tracers and dropping flares over the water. This allowed him to set his altimeter for 1,500 feet—200 feet higher than the tallest foothills surrounding the airstrip. He then turned the aircraft around to feel his way back toward what he hoped was the runway. The engines began to sputter as they burned the last drops of fuel, and Jay prepared to make an emergency water landing on instruments when he suddenly felt an increase in turbulence. He knew this meant that they had had crossed the coastline, precluding any option for a ditch into the gulf. If they crashed now, it would be into hard earth.

The only choice now was Jackson Field or a crash landing, and Jay's first and second passes searching for the airstrip were like flying into a black hole. On his third approach, someone on the ground recognized the sound of a bomber juddering above looking for a place to put down. Within seconds every searchlight on the base was turned on to guide him in, although Jay could make out only a "faint, blurry glow." Finally, with the needle on the fuel gauge bouncing below "E," Johnnie Able in the top turret spotted the faint glimmer of the two rows of runway lights through the mist.

Jay descended to study the lights. He knew that if they glowed "fat" it meant he was coming at the strip at an oblique angle. If the lights were more elongated and narrow, the bomber was lined up on course. Jay took in the parallel rows of hazy smudge pots, sucked in a deep breath, and pushed the throttle forward. The wheels touched the runway before he could see the ground. Later, he discovered how lucky they had been— three aircraft attempting similar blind landings in his wake had all crashed and burned.

The Eager Beavers spent the next several days working with maintenance crews to repair the damage to the plane until, on June 15, Army meteorologists informed Jay that the weather to the northeast over Bougainville was about to break. They were scheduled for takeoff at four a.m. the next day. Jay and the Eager Beavers hustled out to Old 666 to go through their preflight preparations.

Willy Vaughan double-checked his reconstructed radios, while Ruby Johnston nervously folded and refolded his charts and maps for what seemed like the thousandth time. J. T. Britton and Johnnie Able joined Jay as he circled the aircraft inspecting the engines, tires, and patched-up fuselage and fuel lines. Back in the waist gunner's station George Kendrick fiddled with his cameras, cleaning the lenses and loading the film he had drawn from the 8th Photo Reconnaissance Squadron's refrigerator. Finally, Jay had all men assume battle stations and fire off a short burst from each gun. Their checklist complete, Jay urged the crew to rest up in preparation for the long flight. No one, however, could sleep that night. Joe and Pudge Pugh visited the unit's chaplain to receive Communion, while Jay paced his tent, too jumpy to even study his maps. His reputation as a renegade pilot was well earned, but even the renegade could not keep tomorrow's mission from tugging on the loose ends of his imagination. Only two weeks earlier one of the 64th Squadron's Fortresses, piloted by his friend Ernie Naumann, had been sent up alone to photograph New Britain. It never returned. No one knew for sure what had happened, but it didn't take much of a leap to make an educated guess.

Jay was still awake when his phone rang at 10 p.m. It was an officer from 5th Bomber Group Operations Command; Jay did not catch his name. In a thin, clipped voice, the stranger issued an order. Naval Intelligence had received word of increased activity at the Japanese airdrome on the small island of Buka, separated from Bougainville's north coast by a deep and fast-flowing tidal channel perhaps 600 feet wide called Buka Passage. Before photo-mapping the west coast of Bougainville, Jay was to swing Old 666 north over the passage and reconnoiter the Buka airfield.

From a strategic point of view, the request made perfect sense. When the invasion of Bougainville commenced, the Japanese defenses would consist of aircraft from both islands. Intelligence reports from previous missions flown by the 13th Air Force out of Guadalcanal indicated that no more than a dozen or so Zeros were stationed on Buka. That information had been confirmed by the Australian coastwatcher hiding in the northern jungles of Bougainville with a clear view of the Buka airdrome. But both of those dispatches were weeks old. Who knew what changes the Japanese had made under the cover of bad weather? Jay certainly recognized the need for updated intel on Buka. Still, this new proposal sat in his stomach like a broken bottle. Detouring north would add almost an extra hour to his Bougainville mission, and for a single plane, spending so much time in the air over enemy-occupied territory was tantamount to a suicide run.

In the next moment a million thoughts raced through Jay's mind. He and the new navigator, Ruby Johnston, had already roughed out the Bougainville calculations. They reckoned that if Old 666 were to maintain a constant airspeed of around 200 miles per hour in accordance with the needs of the trimetrogon cameras, it would require 22 minutes to photograph the 127 miles of the island's west coast along Empress Augusta Bay. Over that time it would be necessary to keep Old 666 on a straight and level beeline at 25,000 feet to ensure the proper percentage of overlap with each photo frame that George Kendrick snapped. American bomber pilots knew that Japanese ack-ack gunners were often inaccurate in the early stages of bombing runs, whether conducted at night or by day. But 22 minutes of level flight would be more than enough time for even the most inept gunners to fix their sights on a lone aircraft. As the west coast of Bougainville was a blank slate to Allied intelligence, Jay could only hope that the Japanese had not yet installed any anti-aircraft batteries there.

But ground fire was a secondary concern. A slow-moving target like Old 666 flying steady and straight would certainly attract its fair share of enemy fighter planes. And Jay would have no leeway to take evasive action if he wanted to get those photos. When he was intercepted by Zeros—as Jay was sure he would be—he would just have to pray that a few of the Zekes strayed directly into his gunners' paths. During the entire mapping run the lone bomber would be a big, fat target. And now Group Operations wanted to widen that bull's-eye by adding a Buka recon? Why not just radio the Japanese their course and arrival time?

Jay lifted the phone back to his ear. "Hell, no!" he barked at the Operations Officer. Even if Buka was as lightly defended as reported, he said, it would be "sheer foolishness" to alert the Japanese prior to the main goal of photo-mapping Bougainville. "I'm only doing the one mission and I'm not letting anyone fool with that."

He then cut the conversation off before the officer could ask again, surprising himself by the violence with which he slammed down the receiver.

Jay was so riled by the request that sleep was now out of the question. His emotions ricocheted like live ammo; it was another one of those moments when the service to which he had sworn allegiance seemed irrelevant, even cracked. If the Bougainville mission was so important, why would anyone think to compromise it by ordering an extraneous recon over Buka? He was tired, and he was angry. He had no way of knowing, much less understanding, that these sensations probably stemmed from some form of battle fatigue.

There was little precedent for the physical punishment borne by men in combat in 1943 under the harsh conditions of the Southwest Pacific, where the neuropsychiatric disorder rate for American soldiers was the highest of any theater in the war. As a subsequent report from the U.S. Army Center of Military History notes, "Men on both sides collapsed, exhausted from the debilitating tropical heat and humidity; soldiers shook violently from malarial chills or from drenching in tropical downpours. Others simply went mad."

Jay had flown more than 45 combat missions and lost hundreds of comrades and friends. He certainly qualified for the "changes in personality" that the 43rd Bomb Group's own flight surgeon noted in men with far fewer missions in their ratings jackets. Whatever the cause of his foul mood, he was still brooding over the telephone call when he forced himself to crawl into his bunk. But after a few moments of fitful tossing he rose, grabbed his gear, and headed over to the deserted mess tent for coffee. There he met the Eager Beavers as they trickled in over the next several hours.

Jay knew that once a pilot began exhibiting any signs of stress, the edginess familiar to all Airmen as the "pucker factor" became contagious among his flight crew. So as each of his men joined him in the mess tent he tried to mask his anger at the last-minute phone request—to "shake it off," as he put it—and greet them with a few optimistic jokes or quips.

This hail-fellow facade continued through the preflight briefing in the Operations Room. Finally, as the Eager Beavers filed out of the meeting under a bright "bomber's moon," they went through the morbid ritual of handing over their wallets and any other valuables to the intelligence officers standing by the truck that would deliver them to Old 666. By 3:30 a.m. they had pulled their own chocks from beneath the aircraft's wheels and boarded the plane in the silence typical of men preparing for a flight that might be their last.

There were no other planes prepping for takeoff that morning, and the new day greeted the crew with the melodic yowls of the wild jungle. New Guinea's eerie "singing dogs" competed against the distinctive drums of red-cheeked palm cockatoos beating their sticks against dead boughs. Moments later the cacophony was drowned out by the sound of Old 666's 48 cold motor cylinders coughing to life. Jay was taxiing the Fortress from its hardstand toward the runway at a walking pace when he nearly collided with a Jeep swerving in front of his nose. The driver waved frantically, and a courier jumped from the vehicle. Jay idled the bomber as the man ran to the belly hatch and passed a piece of paper to George Kendrick. Kendrick hurried past the flight engineer Johnnie Able monitoring his panel of gauges and up to Jay on the flight deck.

The cockpit was dark, and Jay squinted hard at the message. It was an order to jump Buka Passage and make the recon run over the airdrome on Buka before turning south to photograph Bougainville. Someone was trying to make it official. It appeared to be signed by Col. Ramey, the same officer who had assured him full autonomy to run this mission as he saw fit.

Jay doubted the colonel had ever even seen this order, much less signed it. But he said nothing. He nodded toward the officer on the tarmac, pointed Old 666 toward the downwind end of the runway, and awaited the flash of the green flares signaling that he was good for takeoff.

27

BUKA

JAY REVVED THE FOUR RADIAL ENGINES TO FULL, FEELING THEIR FAMIL-
iar vibrations as they worked up to speed. He released the brakes and the
bomber lunged forward, the dust from the takeoff coating the fronds of
the nipa palms with a fine powder. Johnnie Able called out the speed at
intervals as the big plane lumbered down the runway before Jay horsed
the ship into the air and banked toward an unnamed pass through the
Owen Stanleys that topped out at 7,000 feet.

Despite the forecast for clear skies over Bougainville, the New Guinea
mountains were shrouded in their customary mist. No matter how many
times a pilot negotiated those heights, feeling his way through the peaks
by instrument, it remained a nerve-racking experience. It was as if the
mountains were not quite there and yet everywhere at the same time,
hidden within wisps of brown haze. The Americans stationed at Port

Moresby, like men in combat from time immemorial, countered their ex-
istential dread of the dark and unknown with black humor. The best joke
was that meteorologists had discovered a new type of cloud hovering over
the Owen Stanleys, and had designated it cumulogranite. It was a much
funnier line back on the ground.

Once Old 666 broke through the clouds every man in the ship exhaled,
and Jay took the occasion to pass around what he had come to consider
Col. Ramey's "alleged" order. After each crewman had read it—Forrest
Dillman even crawled back into the tail to hand it to Pudge Pugh—Jay announced over the command intercom that he had no intention of comply-
ing. Their mission was Bougainville, and Bougainville alone.

Jay set the Fortress on a north-by-northeast heading. It struck him,
not for the first time, how difficult it was targeting even familiar islands
over dark stretches of the featureless Pacific Ocean, what the poet Robinson Jeffers called the "unsleeping Eye of the earth." Jay and his crew
had never before set course for Bougainville, and over such alien seas the
water below took on the semblance of a great, gray sinuous muscle, swell-
ing and contracting with the rhythms of the planet. Every one of his crew
recognized the importance of this mission to the next step in the Southwest Pacific campaign, perhaps even to the entire war, yet flying over so
great an expanse made them feel lonely and small.

An hour into the flight Jay turned over the controls to J. T. Britton
and ducked down out of the cockpit for a final meeting with Ruby Johnston. He knew the navigator was expert at calibrating the intricate spheri-
cal trigonometric measurements from the array of flashing instruments
at his station. But those fragile instruments could fail in an instant during a sudden storm or in the erratic wind shears that swept across the
Solomon Sea. Jay and Johnston agreed that if worse came to worst, they
would shoot star sightings from the Astro Tracker Dome projecting from
the bomber's nose and if need be they would plot their course using ancient navigation techniques devised by the long-ago Phoenicians in their
square-rigged ships.

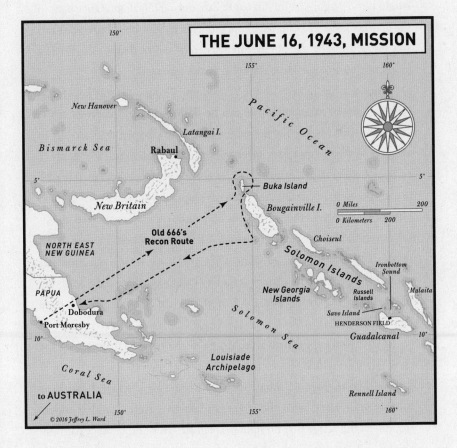

THE JUNE 16, 1943, MISSION

150°
155°
160°

New Hanover

Latangai I.

Pacific Ocean

B i s m a r c k S e a

Rabaul

5°   5°

Buka Island

New Britain

Bougainville I.

0 Miles   200

**Old 666's
Recon Route**

0 Kilometers   200

Choiseul

**NORTH EAST
NEW GUINEA**

Solomon Islands

*Ironbottom
Sound*

**New Georgia
Islands**

*Russell
Islands*

Malaita

PAPUA

Savo Island

Dobodura

HENDERSON FIELD

•**Port Moresby**

S o l o m o n S e a

Guadalcanal

10°   10°

C o r a l S e a

**Louisiade
Archipelago**

to **AUSTRALIA**

Rennell Island

150°
155°
160°

© 2016 Jeffrey L. Ward

As Johnston entered the names of the flight crew into his personnel folder—a duty so familiar that he had already memorized the serial
number of each man—Jay crawled back up onto the flight deck, pausing
for a moment to watch Joe up in the Greenhouse inspect and reinspect
the wires connected to the vertical camera switches. Jay knew that there
would be no singing, in English or Polish, during this flight. Once back in
the left-hand seat he ordered a final gun check. Seventeen heavy .50-cals
spit fire, shrouding the bomber in a sheen of smoke that for the briefest
moment glowed blue in the starlight, before trailing off.

Counting his flights with the 22nd Bomb Group, this was Jay's forty-
seventh combat mission. If one can be both bored and nervous at the
same time, this was the moment. Men tended to dampen their anxiety in
a variety of ways in that dark space between anticipation and the reality of
an approaching target. Some wrote letters home while others read books,
usually the pulp mysteries and westerns shipped from the States in bulk.
Others, particularly the navigators and radio operators, busied themselves recalibrating their instruments. A few even napped. It was hardest
on the ball turret and tail gunners. They knew best what was happening
behind and beneath the plane but had no clue as to what might be taking
place above or up front. Tonight Forrest Dillman and Pudge Pugh were
literally in the dark.

If Jay's own experiences were any guide, he guessed that a few of his
crew might be a little sick to the stomach right now. Not scared, merely
uneasy. The frightening moments would come later, when they began
to truly understand what the chances of survival were. Jay also understood well the adage that no military plan survives first contact with the
enemy, and now he saw that this could come sooner than expected. With
no bombs in the bay Old 666 was flying light, and the same spanking
tailwinds that had swept the clouds from Bougainville now pushed the
Fortress northeast like a paper airplane.

About three hours later a thin sliver of sun appeared in the east just as

Bougainville's coastline came into view, a parenthesis of land surrounded by glistening dark waters. Jay checked his instruments. One hundred fifty-five degrees east longitude. Ruby Johnston, on the button. Then he looked at his watch. Thirty minutes ahead of schedule.

Though he had been in-theater for more than a year, Jay had never lost his awe for the sublime daybreaks found only in the tropics. Bougainville was a mere 35 miles south of the equator, and he remembered a Boy Scout troop leader once explaining that the startling sunrises and sunsets near the equator were the result of the sun being perpendicular to the horizon, while at higher latitudes it rose and set at a more oblique angle. That may have been the science of the phenomenon, but it did not make the tableau any less spectacular. Back in the States, particularly in the northern clime of Boothbay Harbor, the sun seemed to saunter over the horizon like a balloon carried on a gentle updraft, the black night gradually receding before subtle streaks of reddish-orange. Here the dawn was so sudden that it arrived almost without warning. One moment the eastern vista was a ribbon of dark purple the color of a mussel shell. In the next instant the sky was ablaze at every compass point.

Jay had time to ponder the wonders of the glistening sunrise; it would still be another 30 to 45 minutes before the light would be strong enough to provide the proper exposure for the camera's infrared filters. This also meant that he now faced a hard choice. From the first day of boot camp it was drilled into every soldier that the Army is not a democracy, and Jay understood that as the ranking officer of a B-17 Flying Fortress, he was the ultimate arbiter; any decisions were his alone. Still, the Eager Beavers were more than a mere flight crew. They had become a team, and their captain had to take that into consideration. He reached for his interphone and laid out their options. He could turn Old 666 northwest and kill the extra time vectoring over the pale green waters of the Solomon Sea. Out of sight. Safe. Or he could set a course due north and arrive over Buka Passage just as the sun was high enough to photograph the Japanese airdrome on the islet. They would use their standard camera equipment to photograph Buka before turning back south toward Bougainville and setting the more complicated trimetrogons. He put the decision to the crew.

As Johnnie Able later explained, he spoke for every man when he said, "We thought so much of Captain Zeamer and had such trust in him and his ability that we didn't give a damn where we went, just so long as he wanted to go there. Anything okay by him was okay by us."

Or, as Jay heard the collective response from his crew that morning, "Oh, what the hell. Let's take their G.D. reconnaissance photos, we've done it before."

Then Jay announced that if any crewman wanted to don his cumbersome 30-pound flak suit, now was the time to do it. No one did.

THEY APPROACHED BUKA FROM THE NORTHEAST. AT 25,000 FEET THE sea-horse-shaped spit of sand looked like a dangling appendage of Bougainville, separated from the larger landmass by only the narrow passage of water. Streaks of pale sunlight illuminated the waves building over the serrated reefs and breaking on its white sand beaches.

Jay had been briefed on what to expect. He saw the airstrip running adjacent to the island's southeast coast, surrounded by a honeycomb of earthen revetments carved out of the jungle. From five miles above the rutted roads connecting the aircraft hidey-holes gave the impression of a large spider's web encircling the crushed-coral runway that stretched for almost half a mile. Then, with Old 666 nearly on top of the strip, a peculiar shiver ran up Jay's spine. Below him he counted more than 20 enemy fighters parked wingtip to wingtip, with what looked like perhaps another dozen protruding from their revetments. The risks of the mission suddenly increased exponentially. Questions flooded his mind. Why had he accepted those bogus orders? Had he made a deadly mistake? Why hadn't he trusted his first instinct?

Jay had no way of knowing that the planes he saw had arrived from

Rabaul only the previous evening, deploying to Buka in preparation for a strike on Halsey's vessels assembled at Guadalcanal. Nor did he know that their Japanese pilots belonged to one of the Imperial Navy's most decorated units, which included two aces with a combined total of nearly 30 "kills." Within seconds, Forrest Dillman's voice crackled over the interphone. They'd been spotted. Pilots on the ground were scrambling into their cockpits.

According to the log maintained by George Kendrick, it was precisely 8:30 when a string of 15 enemy aircraft began lifting off in flights of two and three to intercept Old 666. For a split second Jay considered turning and running, scrapping the Bougainville mission altogether. They'd gotten the photos of Buka; the mission would not be a complete washout. At the very least Halsey could be warned of the flights massing against his vessels. The Zekes might chase him for a bit. But from experience he knew that Japanese pilots did not like to press attacks over the open sea at too great a distance from their home airfields or carriers. He could lose them. He knew it.

But there were 37,000 Marines and GIs preparing for the Bougainville invasion. Jay pictured them in their landing craft on the day they would hit the beaches after being transported for days at sea, their stomachs queasy, their packs laden with enough "battle rattle" to drown a dolphin. Even in the unbearable heat they would be overwhelmed by the clammy-cold sweat that drenches every man the nearer he comes to combat. He imagined their LSTs hung up on the jagged reefs of Empress Augusta Bay. Thousands of Japanese soldiers and a battalion of construction workers had labored for weeks to complete their defense systems, to dig in on those beaches awaiting the inevitable American assault. The Marines and GIs would be ducks on a pond for the machine guns and mortar tubes ringing the invasion site.

In the smoky war rooms and corridors of power where risks were calculated on a far grander scale, those leathernecks and dogfaces were simple numbers to be sacrificed for a strategic and tactical goal. But for Jay they were men with mothers and fathers and wives and sweethearts back home. He could see in them the faces of Bill Benn and Ken McCullar and the scores of good men he had known, now dead. He gripped the yoke and torqued the bomber south. Bougainville lay before him like a green mirage in a sea of blue.

The Flying Fortress's four big engines churned the air at a steady 200 miles per hour as Jay set a southern course along the island's west coast. Back in the waist George Kendrick snapped photo after photo; down in the nose Joe assisted Ruby Johnston with monitoring the aircraft's drift, airspeed, and altitude. And up on the flight deck Jay and J. T. Britton watched as all cameras clicked like clockwork on the cockpit's intervalometer, the stopwatch-like device, set by speed, altitude, and interval, which triggered the cameras' lens shutters for time-lapse exposures. Every man recognized that it was only a matter of time before the Zeros from Buka caught up with them.

A minute that seemed an eternity passed before Pudge Pugh in the tail reported another fighter squadron lifting off, this time from Bougainville's Buin airdrome. He counted perhaps a dozen attackers. In a dogfight a lone B-17 could reasonably expect to hold its own against six enemy bogeys, maybe seven or eight on a good day. With all its extra guns, Jay was confident that Old 666 could even take on 9 or 10 in a pinch. But 20? With more likely to follow in their wake? Again the thought occurred: suicide.

28

"GIVE 'EM HELL!"

CHIEF WARRANT OFFICER YOSHIO OOKI OF THE 251ST IMPERIAL AIR Squadron scanned the cloudless sky. The searing equatorial sun appeared to float on the eastern horizon, a red dahlia with blossoms ablaze. Ooki could not believe his good fortune. The pilot of a lone Boeing had dared to intrude into the airspace over Buka. It was if he were asking to be sent flaming into the sea.

The drone of the American bomber miles above had caught everyone on the Japanese airbase by surprise this morning. And now, as the prop wash from the engines of Ooki's Zero raised a curtain of dust on the Buka airstrip, the big B-17 was already a mere speck in the sky far to the south. Within moments he and his squadron were in the air, nursing every ounce of speed from their humming engines. Ooki and his pilots knew from simple geometry that they would eventually reel in the bomber. Most of

them, at any rate. Just after takeoff one Zero's engines gave out and its
pilot was forced to ditch into the Solomon Sea.

As Ooki and the remainder of his group gained altitude, they could
not have failed to notice a mass of clouds far to the west. These were
certainly thick enough for the American aircraft to duck into and hide.
But the Boeing's pilot exhibited no inclination to make for the cover. The
aircraft did not dive; it did not bank. It did not even seem to be taking
advantage of all of its engine speed. It merely continued on a straight and
level southern heading. It was obviously taking photographs. Ooki estimated that they would overtake the plodding bomber within 30 minutes.

FAR BELOW JAY THE SLANT OF THE MORNING SUNLIGHT WAS CAUSING
Bougainville's stunted eucalyptus trees to dapple the flowering frangipani
thickets with long, misshapen shadows. In another half hour, he knew,
small clouds would be forming in the foothills climbing toward the rim
of the volcano Mount Bagana, which was spewing thin streams of gray
smoke into the sky. But for now visibility was clear, with just a shading of
ground haze that the infrared camera filters would cut through with ease.
Old 666 flew past the island's wasp waist at the 11-minute mark, right on
schedule. Jay was surprised, and relieved, not to hear the telltale echo of
anti-aircraft guns.

There was no wind to speak of, and Jay kept Old 666's heading
straight and true as George Kendrick focused his cameras on the ribs of
coral shimmering just below the bay's surface. After ten minutes Kendrick's voice broke the cockpit's droning hum. "Give me forty-five
more seconds." The words were barely out of the waist gunner's mouth
when Jay spotted the first wave of bogeys climbing straight at them on
a 45-degree angle—four Zekes and a twin-engine fighter he took to be a
"Dinah," which the Japanese employed predominantly as a long-range
reconnaissance plane. Some, however, had been modified with cannons.
Each was painted in a dark green or brown camouflage pattern.

Forrest Dillman in the belly ball and Pudge Pugh in the tail turret unleashed a stream of .50-cal rounds from their four guns. The screening fire forced the enemy aircraft to swerve out of the tracers' paths. Then they regrouped and resumed their climb.

Jay could sense they were maneuvering for a frontal attack. It was what any experienced fighter pilot would do: go for the Fortress at what was considered its weakest point. When the Zeros passed Old 666 on either side, near enough for Jay to get a good look, he was taken aback. The planes had stubbier wings and larger engines than he had ever seen on enemy fighters. No wonder they had caught him so fast. He had no idea that the Japanese had moved groups of the newer A6M3 fighter plane into the area.

Within seconds five of the aircraft covered his Fortress like a shroud, at twelve o'clock, two o'clock, four o'clock, eight o'clock, and ten o'clock. They were indeed looping around for a coordinated run. Again Jay was astonished. By now he, like most B-17 pilots, was of course used to enemy fliers coordinating their snap-roll attacks. But he had never seen the Japanese stage such a deft assault with more than two or three aircraft.

YOSHIO OOKI AND HIS TEAM HAD CAUGHT THE BOEING. THE TRACERS from its stinging tail had swept over his canopy as he maneuvered his Zero wide of the American bomber. His men had followed his lead, their timing and precision impeccable. Now they had it surrounded in a nearly closed circle, staying clear only of the aircraft's lethal tail guns.

The Americans must still be shooting their photographs. The pilot did not deviate from his airspeed. He took no evasive action. They would attack him head-on and annihilate him.

THE ZERO AT TEN O'CLOCK MADE HIS RUN AT PRECISELY THE MOMENT George Kendrick asked for another 15 seconds. Through his port window Jay watched the Zeke go into a shallow skid turn and flip onto its back. He caught the bright yellow strobes from the twin 7.7-millimeter machine guns in the plane's nose, and then saw the larger red flare from one of the two 20-millimeter cannons fitted to its wings. Jay held his course steady as Joe Sarnoski hollered "Give 'em hell!" over the interphone and the bombardier, navigator, and top turret gunner responded with a barrage of machine-gun fire. Acrid black smoke filled Old 666 as it vibrated from the violent recoil.

From the flight deck Jay followed the red tracers from Joe's nose gun as they cut bright curving paths before ripping into the first bogey. This Zero had a series of vertical red stripes slanting across its fuselage. Jay marked it as the squadron commander's. The bullets appeared to pass straight through the enemy aircraft.

Then Joe's firing ceased as a three-inch cannon shell crashed through the Greenhouse's thin Plexiglas and exploded in the bombardier's compartment. Joe was catapulted 15 feet backward. He landed facedown with a bone-jarring thud on the aluminum deck almost directly beneath the flight deck.

The concussion from the blast also knocked Ruby Johnston off his feet, but he was able to recover and crawl on all fours toward Joe. He rolled him over and flinched. The shell had lacerated Joe's neck and ripped a hole in his side the size of a bowling ball. He was nearly cut in half but, incredibly, he was still breathing. Johnston ripped open a packet of sulfa powder and doused Joe's wound. Joe's eyelids fluttered, then flipped open. His eyes were red and beginning to swell from the Plexiglas dust they'd absorbed when the Greenhouse shattered. He gurgled, "I'm all right. Don't worry about me." Gouts of blood mixed with the words.

Johnston poured more sulfa. It was now freezing in the open nose cone, the cold air rushing in through the gash left by the cannon shell, and the blood on Joe's face and torso was coagulating into a slushy sheen.

In the cockpit above Joe and Johnston, Jay watched the enemy squadron leader whom Joe had raked spin out toward the sea.

• • •

CHIEF WARRANT OFFICER YOSHIO OOKI WAS FIGHTING FOR HIS AIR-
craft's life. The bullets from the bombardier's nose gun had holed his
fuel tank, and fire shot from his exhaust stacks, a sure sign that he was
leaking aviation fuel. It was only good fortune that somehow prevented
the vaporized propellant drizzling from his wings from igniting and detonating his plane. He was still 80 miles from Buka, and as he raced for
home one of his wingmen fell in beside him as if by sheer force of will
his escort could coax his limping plane back to its base. Perhaps it was
working. As the Buka coastline grew larger, Ooki knew he would make
it. His Zero would never fly again. But he would.[*]

RUBY JOHNSTON HELPED JOE TO HIS KNEES, AND THE BOMBARDIER
crawled along the catwalk back toward his shattered station, like a snail
leaving a trail of gore. Joe gripped the stock of one machine gun with both
hands, pulled himself into a crouch, and resumed firing just as the twin-
engine Dinah banked into a head-on run. The gale-force winds rushing
through the broken Greenhouse slammed the empty shell casings from
the heavy gun back into Joe's face. Yet he continued to switch off from
one .50-cal to another, firing as continuously as he could without burning
out their barrels.

From above Jay again watched the tracers from Joe's nose gun, this
time as they ripped into the second fighter plane. Small sparks erupted
on the enemy's wing roots. The pilot lost control, and Jay was worried
that the wounded aircraft would crash through his windshield. Then, at
the last possible moment, the Dinah's fuel tank exploded in a halo of fire
and it disappeared somewhere beneath the Fortress.

---

[*] That same afternoon, June 16, 1943, Yoshio Ooki took part in the air armada that
attacked Adm. Halsey's convoy assembling at Lunga Point off Guadalcanal in preparation for the invasion of New Georgia. The Japanese lost 28 aircraft during the assault. Ooki and his fighter plane never returned from the action.

Now Jay found himself staring into the coal-black eyes of a third Japanese pilot. He had seen a few Japanese soldiers up close, prisoners of war passing through Port Moresby. Despite their defiant strutting, they were damaged human beings, shamed to have broken their vow to die for the emperor's cause. This was the first time Jay had ever looked into the eyes of a man who not only intended to kill him, but had the means to do so.

He booted his rudder, pinned the Zero on his vertical crosshair, and pressed his thumb hard onto the button on his wheel. The burst from the bore-sighted .50-cal streamed across the sky at the same moment the Japanese pilot sprayed Old 666 with his own machine-gun fire. Jay fired again. Another hit. The Zeke was crippled, fuel streaming from its tanks, about to fall into a death spiral. Just before it did Jay saw a small puff of white smoke emanate from its wing. Cannon blast.

29

THE DESPERATE DIVE

JAY'S EYES WERE STILL FOLLOWING THE ZEKE HE'D BLASTED AS IT twirled toward the water when his cockpit erupted into an effulgence of colors—white, magenta, tangerine, a rainbow of acute pain, followed by an acrid smell thick enough to slice. Suddenly filling his mind was an image of his mother, Marjorie. He saw her face as clearly as if she were sitting there beside him in the copilot's seat. Staring into her eyes, Jay wondered, "Is this it?"

Machine-gun fire from somewhere above him snapped his reverie. Johnnie Able in the top turret. Jay stiffened, and forced his brain to assess the damage to the flight deck. J. T. Britton was slumped forward in the right-hand seat, his body straining against his seat belt. His eyes were closed and his chin rested on his chest. Jay saw no blood.

The cannon shell that had pierced the cockpit had blown away Old

666's instrument panel and severed the control cables connecting the rudders and horizontal stabilizers. The force of the explosion had also torn away the left window and peeled back the plane's aluminum skin beside him. His bucket seat was open to sky above and sea below; it was like riding a motorcycle, "sitting out in the breeze."

For a brief instant Jay thought his eardrums would burst. The roar of the Wright Cyclone engines, the machine-gun reports, the clatter of hot brass shell casings bouncing off metal floors, the wild rush of the 200-miles-per-hour slipstream through the torn-away skin beside him, the crash of enemy cannons—all formed a deafening cacophony that seemed to squeeze his brain down to the size of a fist. He glanced up and was shocked to see the windshield still intact. But the shell had opened a gaping hole in the bulkhead between the cockpit and the navigator's compartment below. He could see Ruby Johnston firing short, frantic bursts through his open window and, beyond, Joe slumped over his machine gun. He wondered if Joe was in much pain. Then the initial shock wore off, and Jay felt as if the bottom half of his body was on fire.

He lowered his gaze. His boilersuit was shredded and his left leg was sliced from the calf to the thigh. It was a carnivore's delight—thick ugly slabs of blackened flesh, like rashers of seared Canadian bacon, dangled from his exposed shinbone and his left knee resembled a mound of raw hamburger meat. It took him a moment to realize that the machine-gun rounds had also torn through his right leg and both of his arms. Each time his heart pumped, a thin stream of pinkish liquid from a nicked artery spurted from his ruptured left wrist and began to pool in his lap. Though Jay did not know it, the exploding cannon shell had propelled nearly 150 pieces of shrapnel—including chunks of the plane's rudder pedals and its control cable—into his body. It occurred to him that had he not pulled his flight boots back from the pedals at the beginning of the mapping run in order to keep the bomber at a perfectly level altitude, he might have lost both feet.

He lifted the interphone mouthpiece with his bleeding right hand to ask for a damage report. Nothing. The shell had also destroyed the bomber's communications system. He cursed under his breath as Ruby Johnston's head and shoulders popped up through the hole in the bulk-head left by the explosion. Johnston was covered by purplish ooze—Jay recognized it immediately as the plane's hydraulic fluid. The navigator re-ported that the hydraulic reservoir was completely destroyed. They could still lower the landing gear with manual hand pumps, but there was no manual alternative to the hydraulic brake system. They'd need an awfully long runway to put down on. If they even made it that far.

As Johnston spoke, J. T. Britton groaned and lifted his head. His face was as pinched as a hatchet blade and he opened his eyes in stages, like a boxer coming to after the count. Britton gathered his wits and patted him-self down. There were no wounds other than the large egg on the back of his head. He took in the damage to the instrument panel. It took him a moment to comprehend that the plane's control cables were smashed and its rudder pedals obliterated. The only instruments still working were the manifold pressure gauge and the magnetic compass in the center of the charred dashboard.

With no tail rudder, Jay's control of the pitch and roll of the aircraft had virtually vanished. He could still try to steer the Fortress by slow-ing the engines on one wing to make the plane turn. If he stayed con-scious. He had never felt such pain in his life; he wanted to scream. But he wouldn't. He needed to keep his head. He was the only one who could fly them out of this mess.

Britton unclasped his safety belt and ducked back onto the catwalk. He returned within minutes and informed Jay that George Kendrick had stowed the camera film and was manning the waist guns against a series of furious attacks. He also said that a shell had destroyed the yellow, keg-like oxygen tanks behind the cockpit. They had only seconds before the little air left in the personal bottles supplying their masks ran out. Unless they got below 10,000 feet they would all pass out and die, either from hypoxia or in the subsequent crash.

At this Jay rolled the bomber hard right and used his ailerons and elevators, miraculously still functioning, to push the nose straight down. The plane dived at 275 miles per hour. The engines screamed and the fuselage groaned. Johnnie Able, thinking the bomber was out of control, jumped down from his top turret to see if the pilots were wounded or dead. The rest of the crew maintained their positions. None of them donned parachutes.

The altimeter on the instrument panel was hanging limp by its wires, but Jay knew he could estimate his altitude by the increases in the engine's manifold pressure. Old 666's rivets were rattling when it reached what he guessed was close to 6,000 feet. Jay leveled off, removed his mask, and took a deep breath. His body contorted with pain at the mere act of forcing oxygen into his lungs, but at least now the crew would be able to breathe.

Johnnie Able, who had hoisted himself back into the top turret, yelled that more enemy fighters were screaming down after them.

Jay banked left, and George Kendrick counted 17 Zekes on either side of the Fortress, flying three and four abreast. Jay saw them a moment later as they raced out in front of him in columns of two. They were setting up another frontal assault. One more big hit, he knew, and Old 666 was done for.

Up in the turret, Johnnie Able cleared a jam from his ammunition belt and lined up a bogey with his twin .50s. He let loose a burst. Jay peered up through the glass ceiling hatch and saw the Zero's engine erupt into orange flames that winked along its fuselage and spread to its fuel tanks. When the fighter spun toward the sea, a funeral pyre of jagged flame leaving a contrail of greasy black smoke, it barely missed clipping Old 666's right wingtip.

Jay wanted to shout to the young flight engineer. But he didn't have the strength. He tried lifting a thumbs-up, but Able had already dropped out of his swing-seat harness and crumpled to the ground behind him. He had been hit in both legs by machine-gun fire. When he landed on the catwalk Able saw that the damaged hydraulic tubes and the oxygen bottles behind the pilot's seat were on fire. He crawled toward the flames, tore the bottles from their stabilizing hinges, and began beating out the blaze with his bare hands. He was joined a moment later by Ruby Johnston, who had scrambled up from the navigator's compartment in search of bandages to stem the bleeding after shrapnel from an exploding shell had punctured his left forearm and creased his skull.

Jay used the morning sun over his left shoulder to set a southwest course. Over the next 30 minutes he lost count of how many head-on runs, one after another, the Zekes made on his bomber. Six? Eight? A dozen? The enemy pilots formed a rotating circle around Old 666's nose and attacked from 11 o'clock to 1 o'clock. When one dropped out, another took his place. Jay felt as if he were flying through a vortex of iron rain—at first a light patter, then a heavy downpour.

30

GET IT HOME

IF JAY KNEW IT, THE JAPANESE KNEW IT. WITH THE NOSE OF HIS FLYING Fortress shot to hell, the bomber was in effect defenseless against frontal attacks. Joe was either dead or dying next to his gun. Johnnie Able was back on the catwalk tending to his leg wounds and burned hands, leaving the top turret empty. And the wire that connected Jay's .50-cal "snozzola gun" to its solenoid had been snapped by the cannon shell.

Though Ruby Johnston had returned to his .50s in the navigator's compartment, he was basically firing blind. The blood from his head wound had clotted over his eyes—his face reminded Jay of a "red beet"—and Johnston's only recourse was to wheel his gun barrels in the general direction of the distinctive whine of a Zero's radial engine and clutch the triggers in fits of firing.

Behind Jay, Willy Vaughan's twin .50-cals had gone silent after a shell fragment sliced open his neck not far from his bayonet scar, but at least Pudge Pugh's tail guns continued to repel attacks from the rear. The enemy pilots had also learned to give Old 666 a wide berth when circling for frontal assaults after George Kendrick flamed one Zeke at four o'clock with his starboard .50-cal, spun, took up his port gun, and shot up another at eight o'clock. He watched it roll on its back and "fall like a leaf," trailing a ball of flame.

The Japanese onslaughts, however, were coming too fast and furious for Kendrick to operate the extra machine gun mounted in the floor behind the wheels, a situation that was exacerbated when a bullet sliced the power line to Forrest Dillman's high-speed rotator, leaving his belly turret stuck facing aft. There was a hand crank to turn the turret on the catwalk behind the bomb bay, but with J. T Britton still woozy—and needed in the cockpit in case Jay passed out—there was no one to operate it.

At least Kendrick's deadly accuracy was buying them some time. The Zeros were capable of closing speeds of nearly 500 miles per hour, but because of Kendrick's waist guns the enemy pilots were being forced to take almost ten minutes to circle out before turning for their strafing runs on Old 666's nose. During these slack periods Jay used his magnetic compass and the position of the sun to make sure he remained on a southwesterly course, the throttles opened to the firewall. Just before he'd lost his sight, Ruby Johnston had checked the rpm of each engine on the tachometer. None, he'd reported, looked to be failing. So with all four engines running on full power Jay felt confident enough to wait until he saw an enemy fighter bank into his turn in front of him before cutting back his throttles and rolling hard either right or left.

This was where all his bull sessions about teamwork would need to pay off. He had convinced his crew that as long as he remained in the pilot's seat nothing could happen to the ship. But with the interphone gone, Jay had no way of signaling the aft gunners which evasive maneuvers he planned to take. They would have to intuitively recognize the zigzagging

aiming runs he was attempting in order to give them the maximum opportunity for a shot. And it was working. As Zeke after Zeke swept past, either
Kendrick's waist guns or Pudge Pugh in the tail would rake the bogey. Yet
still they came, flying into and through the curtain of fire his gunners were
throwing up. In a way, Jay could not help admiring their sense of duty.

Yet without their squadron leader the attacks were uneven. No longer were they coming at Old 666 with the coordinated strikes that had
caused so much early damage. Now they flew almost in single file, swooping dead-on at him one at a time, splashing their ammo all over the sky. It
was their biggest mistake, allowing time for Jay's maneuvering to set them
up for his waist gunner and tail gunner. When they raced out in front and
turned toward him, the leading edge of their wings suddenly blazing with
fire and spitting black smoke, Jay would wait, gritting his teeth, waiting,
waiting, until the enemy pilot committed himself totally. Only then would
he yank hard on the yoke and skid out to either side.

But Jay was bleeding out at an alarming rate. His legs were useless,
and both of his boots had filled with blood. The wheel was also slippery
with blood from the bullet holes in his wrists, and he could grip it only
with his fingertips. During one lull in the attacks he pulled off his belt and
tried to tie a tourniquet around his left thigh. The effort proved too painful and time consuming; the Japanese would not give him enough breathing room to concentrate. Then he became aware of a stroke of luck—the
icy wind whistling past his legs through the plane's open skin was fast
coagulating his wounds.

Jay had ordered J. T. Britton back to the catwalk to see to the wounded,
yet several times Britton stuck his head back into the cockpit and pleaded
to take over the controls so Jay himself might be patched up. Each time
Jay refused. He felt that only he, with his months of experience flying the
Fortress like an agile fighter plane, could keep Old 666 in the air. At least
the pain was keeping him awake.

After 40 minutes and 100 miles or so the enemy fighters, low on fuel
and ammunition, began to peel away. Finally the last of them made one

more ineffectual run before it, too, turned back for its base. There was no way the Japanese pilots could have known that the American "Boeing" was down to its final few bullets.

FLIGHT PETTY OFFICER SECOND CLASS SUEHIRO YAMAMOTO, YOSHIO Ooki's subordinate, was the last flier to break off from the dogfight. That made it his job to file the After-Action report to his squadron commander. Yamamoto reported that the squad had unleashed over 500 20-millimeter cannon rounds and more than 700 machine-gun bullets at the American bomber. The Japanese fighters out of Bougainville flying under Lt. Cmdr. Naboro Hayashi had expended another 35 cannon shells and 1,400 machine-gun rounds.

"Enemy aircraft generates smoke and disappeared in the cloud," Yamamoto wrote. "Later, it was found having crashed in the mountains of Bougainville."

Before filing Yamamoto's report to his own superior, Ooki amended the last sentence. The American bomber, he wrote, was last seen struggling not to crash into the ocean.

THE JAPANESE AFTER-ACTION REPORT WAS NEARLY CORRECT. WITH close to 500 miles of shark-infested waters still to cross before they reached New Guinea's north coast, Jay knew that their ordeal was far from over. He was sitting on his parachute, and he eyed the open sky to his left. Under normal circumstances, a pilot and copilot deciding to "hit the silk" would make the three-foot drop behind their seats, crawl through the tunnel leading past the navigator's table to the nose, pop off the front hatch of the chin turret, and leap. It struck Jay that in this situation none of that would be necessary—he would merely have to lunge sideways. But he never gave serious thought to activating the bail-out alarm, if it still worked. Under the circumstances, he thought, he probably could not have survived a jump even if he tried, and he was not yet ready to allow his crew to jump into the sea without their captain. Still, given Old 666's shot-up condition, he calculated that there was a better than even chance they would have to ditch. He also estimated their chance of surviving an ocean crash landing at about 50 percent.

Unlike the B-26s with their elevated wings that he'd flown with the 22nd Bomb Group, a B-17 had wings that extended evenly from its fuselage, theoretically making it able to "surf" onto the water while ditching. And as its bomb bay doors were built flush to the fuselage's belly, it tended to stay afloat longer than even the newer B-24 Liberators with their protruding bomb bays. This structural modification was credited with keeping three quarters of the B-17s that had glided into the sea from breaking apart—compared with about two thirds of most other American bombers. Jay felt a deep personal responsibility for each of the men who flew with him, and he simply wanted them to have the best chance possible to return alive from this mission. He knew that he had trained the crew well, and if it came to an ocean ditch, he could count on them to brace themselves correctly and to remember their postcrash duties precisely at the instant the plane stopped in the water. If they did that, they would all be likely to live through any ditch. That was the good news.

The bad news was that Pacific Ocean currents could carry a life raft dozens of miles a day in so many directions, depending on wind and tide, that grid searches by rescue aircraft could expand to cover thousands of miles. All Allied aircrews recognized that the larger the search grid, the less chance of spotting downed Airmen. Rescue teams might pull out every stop for a missing general like Ken Walker or a famous touring celebrity or politician. But for ordinary Airmen who ditched into the sea, the rule of thumb was that if no survivors were found within 24 hours, chances are none would ever be.

But all of Jay's hypothetical calculations were pushed aside by one paramount thought: they had completed only half the mission. If they did not return with the photographs, the entire exercise, the blood expended, would have been for naught. Jay had heard stories of Airmen who'd been forced to ditch their damaged aircraft after successful bombing runs.

Some who'd survived told tales of at least having had the satisfaction of watching their ordnance take out an enemy installation or ship before losing their plane. There would be no such solace for Jay or his crew if they went down now. Not with that vital film resting at the bottom of the sea.

Once more Jay envisioned the Marines and soldiers being torn apart before they even reached the Bougainville beaches. Or, at the very least, another American recon bomber crew being sent back up over the island to fly through the same hell that he had just survived. He looked down at Joe, lying still in the nose. He thought of the blinded Ruby Johnston, and Johnnie Able's shot-up legs.

No, he would get this plane home. Only one question remained. How?

31

"HE'S ALL RIGHT"

EVEN WITHOUT HIS ALTIMETER JAY COULD SENSE THAT OLD 666 WAS steadily losing altitude. It was "mushing"—the tail dragging below the nose—and the lower it descended, the more fuel it would eat up plowing through the thicker atmosphere. He could jockey the prop pitch and "lean" the air-to-fuel ratio only so much for fear of the engines either starving or running too hot. And even if the aircraft somehow managed to remain aloft for the next few hours, it would never be able to clear the Owen Stanleys and make Port Moresby. Given the amount of blood Jay was losing, he doubted he would live that long anyway.

Their only hope, he knew, was to try to reach the Allied airfield complex hacked out of the jungle at Dobodura, some 100 miles closer than Port Moresby on the north side of the mountain range. The main grass strip at Dobodura was just under 7,000 feet long. They would need every foot of it. Even at that, with no brakes or flaps Jay would have to ground-loop the landing on the slick surface and maybe even open the bomb bay doors in order to let the plane suck in air to slow down. It would be dicey, but it was their best chance of survival. Yet where the hell were they in relation to Dobodura?

Jay was contemplating this question when Willy Vaughan, his bleed-ing neck bandaged with a rag, lurched into the cockpit. Jay didn't know that Vaughan had even been hit, but the radioman waved off the wound. He looked more surprised than hurt, and said that the rest in the back were fine, although machine-gun fire had holed the fin badly and For-rest Dillman's turret remained stuck. Jay asked for a morphine syrette. Vaughan shook his head. They were all gone. Then he reported that the plane's command radio and radio compass were shattered, knocked out by a cannon shell. The only set still working was an experimental Navy-issue liaison he'd picked up in Port Moresby and had been tinkering with ever since. Its voice mode was inoperative, but he could try to send Morse Code signals.

Jay nodded and told Vaughan of his plan to make for Dobodura. The radio operator hobbled back to his wrecked compartment. A mo-ment later Dillman emerged from the belly bubble to the sight of Vaughan "working the key and dials with his left hand while holding a bloody patch on his neck with his right hand."

Jay was still pointing Old 666 southwest when Vaughan reappeared in the cockpit 30 minutes later. He handed Jay a scrap of paper. On it was written the heading "222 degrees M." Two hundred twenty-two de-grees magnetic north, as opposed to true north. (True north and magnetic north vary over time.) Vaughan's Morse Code messages had been picked up by an American patrol vessel and Australian coastwatchers, who had shot azimuths to triangulate the transmissions in order to get a fix on the bomber's position. This allowed Vaughan to plot a course to Dobodura. Jay swung the nose to 222 degrees magnetic north and stayed on it.

A moment later Johnnie Able limped into the cockpit and slid into the copilot's seat. Jay managed a grunt and said, "Pretty tough time." Able informed Jay that J. T. Britton and George Kendrick had broken out clean bandages to patch up Vaughan and Ruby Johnston, and asked how he could help. Most American Airmen arriving in-theater learned quickly that navigation by radio was of little use to pilots over the trackless Pacific, and dead reckoning was the most useful skill a pilot could rely on to bring his aircraft and crew home alive. Jay, his pain spiking, handed over his compass to the teenage flight engineer and showed him how to cut back the throttles to conserve gas. Then he gave him control of the aircraft.

Britton and Kendrick now squeezed into the flight deck and turned their medical attention to Jay. They cut away his pants legs and the sleeves of his boilersuit and applied tourniquets to his limbs. Jay never completely lost consciousness, but his vision was strained as he squinted in search of any sign of shoreline on the western horizon. He was falling deeper into that liminal state between wake and sleep, but he fought with all his willpower the desire to allow his eyes to remain closed.

He determined that one way to keep his mind working was to total up the crew's kills. He counted five enemy fighters definitely destroyed—Joe's two, two more by George Kendrick, and Johnnie Able's one. There were at least two more probables, including the Zero he'd blasted, and perhaps another half dozen severely damaged. Later, he'd have to speak to Pugh and Dillman to see how they fared.*

* Contrary to official U.S. Army Air Force records, postwar documents recovered from the Japanese indicated that no fighters sent up from Buka to intercept Old 666 were shot down. Piecemeal reports of planes sent up from Bougainville are incomplete. The differences between the American and Japanese versions are undoubtedly the result of a number of factors, not least the fog of war. Moreover, attacking aircrews on both sides were known to inflate the damage they inflicted, just as commanders on the ground were given to minimizing negative results. In any event, for our purposes we found it more prudent to rely on official American records, including Jay Zeamer's Medal of Honor citation, and the papers of eyewitnesses, most notably

J. T. Britton implored Jay to move back to the catwalk, where he and George Kendrick could lie him down to better treat his multiple wounds. Jay shook his head.

"I don't move," he said, "until the mission is ended."

PUDGE PUGH INCHED FORWARD THROUGH THE TAIL SECTION AND INTO Willy Vaughan's radio compartment. It was so much warmer in the center of the fuselage, and Pugh lingered to watch George Kendrick and Forrest Dillman re-bandage Vaughan's neck. When Pugh judged that they had the task under control he continued forward, gripping the thick, waist-high ropes on either side of the slim catwalk that spanned the bomb bay. He squeezed past the landing gear and ducked into the crawl space that led to the nose.

There was blood everywhere. He saw J. T. Britton tending to Ruby Johnston's head, and farther up he spotted Joe. The bombardier was still slumped over one of his guns, his finger still curled around the trigger. Pugh scampered forward. Joe's ammunition belts were empty, and one of the .50-cal barrels was burned out. It was colder in the Greenhouse than it had been in the tail, and small rivulets of frozen blood formed spidery lines flowing from Joe's body.

Pugh lifted the bombardier away from the jagged edges of the shattered glass and rolled him faceup into his lap. He removed the ever-present rosary from the pocket of Joe's boilersuit and pressed it into his friend's bloody hand. Pudge Pugh cradled Joe Sarnoski in that position for ten minutes, until his own body heat began to melt the frozen blood streaking Joe's boilersuit. He saw Joe open his eyes once, lift the rosary to his lips, and kiss it. Then Joe closed his eyes for good—"wounded to the death," as *The New York Times* phrased it—and breathed his last.

Pudge Pugh was still cradling the corpse when Ruby Johnston

Zeamer himself and the statements from his crew, than the documents of a defeated enemy proved time and again to have lied about its military losses.

crawled forward as far as his pockmarked navigator's table to ask how Joe was.

"He's all right," Pugh uttered in a barely audible voice. "He's all right."

He didn't know what else to say.

32

DOBODURA

THE SUN WAS ALMOST DIRECTLY OVERHEAD WHEN JAY SPOTTED THE lush coastline. The green jungle canopy beyond the beach looked so far away that it seemed to be sprouting from below the earth's curvature. Johnnie Able let out a soft, coughing whoop as J. T. Britton reentered the flight deck to take his place in the copilot's seat. Despite his impaired vision, Jay recognized the familiar outline of the American PT Boat base at Oro Bay, and a few moments later the contours of Cape Endiaidere. Twenty-five miles beyond it lay the Dobodura strip.

Jay remained semiconscious, as if discerning only shadows in fog, as Britton swung Old 666 wide over the water, banked, and pointed the plane's nose inland. The copilot yanked back the throttles until the yoke was pressed into his gut, and approached the ground low and hot. There was no time to fly a field pattern, and Britton could only guess at the wind direction. Johnnie Able was kneeling between the two pilots, one hand on Britton's shoulder and the other bracing Jay to keep him from tumbling out of his seat. Everyone else assumed ditch positions in the rear of the craft.

Someone had opened the bomb bay door in an attempt to catch some air to slow the aircraft down. It didn't seem to work, and Britton swung the bomber over the strip so fast that it looked as if the tops of the palm trees were shooting up at them. Despite his pain Jay instinctively lifted his feet from the deck so they would not be clipped by the treetops. He saw the airfield's rickety control tower flash by on his right and then they hit the dirt hard and bounced once, twice, three times. The old B-17 stuttered and croaked as if the rivets would pop.

With no brakes they were approaching the end of the runway much too fast, and Britton spun the steering wheel with all his strength until the Fortress's left wing dug into the dirt and its right wing caught air—what pilots called pulling a "Lufbery," after Eddie Rickenbacker's old World War I commander. Rocks and chunks of turf flew like sparks from a grindstone as the skidding, circular movement gradually tightened. Finally the bomber rolled to a stop in a cloud of dust, a yard from the end of the strip. Britton would later explain, "I just greased it in."

Someone noted that it was 12:15, more than eight hours since they'd lifted off from Port Moresby. When Britton cut the engines, Jay took a deep breath. Then his world turned to rust, sick and livid.

JAY WAS NOT SURE WHERE HE WAS, BUT HE WAS IN NO PAIN. IT WAS AS IF his body was numb from head to toe. He could smell the sizzling oil and fuel weeping from Old 666 onto the dusty airstrip, and he thought he heard men talking, shouting, though it sounded as if their voices were coming from underwater.

Then, more clearly, a husky whisper, close, near his ear, beside his missing cockpit window: "Get the pilot last. He's dead."

Jay wanted to shout, "The hell he is, you SOB!" But his world was dimming and he could not find the strength to move his mouth. He lay motionless as the hatch above him cracked open and two strong hands unbuckled his safety belt. He felt himself being lifted by his shoulders. The pain returned, unbearable. He passed out again.

A fire brigade hosed down the engine, and the medics from the meat wagon that rushed out to evacuate Old 666 triaged and treated Ruby Johnston, Willy Vaughan, and Johnnie Able on the ground beside the wrecked aircraft. The remainder of the bomber crew walked the aircraft's perimeter, astounded at the damage it had sustained. They counted upwards of 180 bullet holes and what looked to be at least five cannon blasts.

Finally, two medics gingerly lifted Joe Sarnoski's body from the blasted nose. His sister Matilda would graduate from high school the next day as class valedictorian. She would never receive her wristwatch.

THE FINAL FLIGHT OF OLD 666 WITH CAPT. JAY ZEAMER AT THE HELM COMmanding his crew of Eager Beavers was—and remains—the longest continuous dogfight in the annals of the United States Air Force.

For the comrades in arms aboard the Flying Fortress on that day, the mission over Buka and Bougainville forged a brotherhood for whom distance and time meant nothing, compared with the love and friendship that continued to connect them by what Lincoln called the mystic chords of memory.

For Jay, the born renegade, it was the culmination of a series of events that, in retrospect, appears almost preordained. But as any soldier who has ever faced an enemy knows, combat is never predetermined. It takes fortitude, training, insight, and luck to affect the outcome of an armed engagement. What Jay and Joe and the Eager Beavers accomplished that day was more than a contribution to America's war effort. It was a feat above and beyond the call of duty.

In their simple elegance, the words of Gen. George Churchill Kenney, written with the benefit of looking back on the horrors of a world war, perhaps say it best.

"Jay Zeamer and his crew performed a mission that still stands out in my mind as an epic of courage unequaled in the annals of air warfare."

Not bad for a bunch of screwups and misfits.

EPILOGUE

WHEN JAY WAS PULLED FROM OLD 666, THE MEDICAL STAFF AT DOBO-dura's small field hospital determined that he had lost nearly half the blood in his body. An all-points call was put out seeking Type O volunteers, and scores of Airmen formed a line that stretched outside the door of the little building. Jay received constant transfusions over the next 72 hours, while doctors removed more than 120 ragged pieces of steel and rubber from his legs, arms, and torso.

Twenty-four hours later he, Johnnie Able, Willy Vaughan, and Ruby Johnston were airlifted across the Owen Stanley Range and back to the larger base hospital near Jackson Field. There the medical staff prepared to amputate Jay's left leg until it was decided that he had lost too much blood and would never survive the procedure. Jay was conscious for none of this. He did have a hazy memory of being lifted onto a stretcher and carried into the belly of a cargo plane. But he had no recollection of George Kendrick, J. T. Britton, Pudge Pugh, and Forrest Dillman accompanying him and the others to Port Moresby.

When he awoke in the base hospital the first thing he said was, "Where is Joe?"

Kendrick, Britton, Pugh, and Dillman, standing vigil at his bedside, exchanged glances. They knew that Joe's body had also been brought back to Port Moresby on a separate flight. "In another ward," one of them said. Then Jay asked after the wounded members of his crew. He received the same reply.

Two weeks later, when his crew thought he was strong enough to bear the news, he was finally told that Joe had been killed on the mission.

On June 18, 1943, two days after Old 666's solitary flight over Bougainville Island, a Western Union telegram arrived at the Zeamer residence on Ridge Street in Orange, New Jersey. Jay's mother, Marjorie, was home alone when she opened it. It stated that the War Department regretted to inform her and her husband that their oldest son, U.S. Army Air Force Capt. Jay Zeamer Jr., had been killed in action in the Southwest Pacific.

Marjorie's first instinct was to hide the bad news from the rest of the family. But she couldn't. Jay's brother Jere, who had recently joined the Army as a second lieutenant upon his graduation from M.I.T., was granted bereavement leave and rushed home from his posting at the General Motors Tank Proving Grounds in Michigan. Meanwhile Jay's sisters Isabel and Anne, matriculating at Wellesley and Bryn Mawr respectively, also dropped everything and joined their parents in Orange.

Three days later, as the mourning family made arrangements for a memorial service for Jay, another telegram arrived at the Zeamer home. It was from the Army's Adjutant General's office. It read:

PLEASE DISREGARD TELEGRAM INFORMING YOU THAT YOUR
SON CAPTAIN JAY ZEAMER WAS KILLED IN ACTION ON SIXTEEN
JUNE IN SOUTHWEST PACIFIC AREA I AM HAPPY TO ADVISE THAT

INFORMATION HAS JUST BEEN RECEIVED REPORTING HIM WOUNDED
IN ACTION ON SIXTEEN JUNE WITH STATEMENT THAT FURTHER
INFORMATION WILL BE FURNISHED WITHIN TEN DAYS THIS REPORT
FURTHER STATES HE RECEIVED SHRAPNEL WOUNDS LEFT LEG YOU
WILL BE PROMPTLY ADVISED AS REPORTS ARE RECEIVED

Jay spent the next 15 months in a succession of hospitals recovering
from his wounds.

THOUGH JAY AND THE NAVIGATOR RUBY JOHNSTON WERE NOT STRONG
enough to be present, the rest of the Eager Beavers—including Johnnie Able and Willy Vaughan, who had begged permission to leave their
hospital beds—stood at attention as a makeshift honor guard in front of
fifty Airmen at the burial of Second Lt. Joseph Raymond Sarnoski beside
a small, sun-kissed knoll in Port Moresby. Joe was one of over 40,000
United States Airmen killed in combat during World War II.

A few weeks later, Pudge Pugh wrote to John and Josephine Sarnoski.
"Even though you are both terribly upset," he told Joe's parents, "it might
comfort you to know that your son was one of the finest, cleanest and
bravest boys I have ever known or chummed with.

"In trying to tell you how much he meant to me as a real buddy,"
Pudge continued, "words are just too inadequate to describe. His character was the highest and finest of any young man I have ever known. If
these few words ease the pain you feel, if only for a second, I will feel a
little better also."

THE GROUND CREW THAT HAULED OLD 666 OFF THE DOBODURA AIRSTRIP
confirmed what the dazed aircrew had seen, counting 187 bullet holes
and five gaping cannon holes in the shredded skin. But the K-17 trimetrogon cameras were undamaged. The film from them was flown to Port
Moresby the day Old 666 landed. Once developed, the photos proved to
be invaluable to Adm. Halsey and his invasion planners. Because of those

images, Empress Augusta Bay's perilous coral reefs were located, delineated, and charted, and the topography of Bougainville's beachheads was
revised for the LST craft that would carry the American landing force.

On the last day of June 1943, fourteen days after Old 666's photo-
mapping mission of Buka and Bougainville, Gen. MacArthur and Adm.
Halsey launched Operation Cartwheel, their grand Pacific strategy. Mac-
Arthur's infantry landed at Nassau Bay on the north coast of New Guinea,
and by September Lae was in Allied hands. Simultaneously, Halsey directed the 4th Marine Raider Battalion's successful invasion and capture
of New Georgia in the central Solomons.

The climactic event in Operation Cartwheel took place on November 1, when the 3rd Marine Division and the Army's 2nd Raider Regi-
ment stormed ashore at Torokina Point on the west coast of Bougainville
Island. Much of the credit for the successful landings was given to the
drivers of the Marine landing craft who, using maps and charts developed
by the Army Corps of Engineers from the photographs taken by the crew
of Old 666, successfully avoided the deadly reefs lacing Empress Augusta
Bay.* Those maps and charts were credited with saving countless American lives.

Perhaps more important, persuasive revisionist historians such as
John Prados at the University of Tennessee have recently begun to credit
the Solomon Islands campaign, which culminated with the landings on
Bougainville and the neutralization of Rabaul, as the true turning point

---

* It was during the Bougainville invasion that a case of mistaken identity on a starless
night provided one of the classic ripostes of the war. The destroyer USS *Spence* was
mistakenly sideswiped by a sister destroyer, USS *Thatcher*, and was limping home
under blackout conditions when the crew was rattled by a shower of shells that had
been fired from the direction of the *Spence*'s own picket lines. Commander Bernard
Austin, the skipper, raced for his TBS phone and shouted frantically to the commander of the picket line, Capt. Arleigh "31-Knot" Burke, "We've just had a close
call. Hope you are not shooting at us." To which Burke replied, "Sorry. But you'll
have to excuse the next four salvos already on their way." Burke's second bombardment narrowly missed the *Spence*.

of the Pacific war. "It seemed almost an entrenched interpretation among participants and historians that the Battle of Midway in June 1942 represented that decisive event," Dr. Prados writes in *Islands of Destiny*. He argues, however, "My reading and research eventually supplied convincing evidence that the moment of decision occurred during the campaign for the Solomon Islands."

The eminent naval historian Bruce Gamble is even more specific regarding the importance of the capture of Bougainville, calling the primitive runway that American Seabees blasted and bulldozed out of the island's swampland "the most important Allied airstrip of the South Pacific war."

Indeed, though the fighting on Bougainville would continue for over a year, the American landings on the island's west coast for the first time truly put the Japanese on the defensive not just in the Southwest Pacific but across the entire Asian rim. Moreover, Halsey's control of Bougainville combined with Nimitz's advances in the Central Pacific served to make MacArthur's long-desired invasion of Rabaul unnecessary. Instead, with Rabaul isolated and its lines of resupply ultimately severed, the Supreme Commander was free to concentrate on the successful American and Australian counteroffensive in western New Guinea. The capture of Bougainville led directly to MacArthur's return to the Philippines, and Nimitz's island-hopping campaigns weakened the Japanese military to the point where it no longer presented a viable fighting force.

This is not to say that the capture of Bougainville completely eliminated Rabaul from the war's calculations. The Japanese hung on in the town and, shortly after Halsey's troops landed on Bougainville, even managed one major reinforcement consisting of hundreds of aircraft. But as the Allies had foreseen, with American single-engine fighters now based on Bougainville and available as screening escorts, U.S. bomber formations turned the skies over Rabaul black with near-daily air flotillas. In addition, with Bougainville in hand, Halsey was confident enough to conduct two carrier strikes against Rabaul. Within four months the once-vaunted enemy citadel that had sprung up around Simpson Harbour had

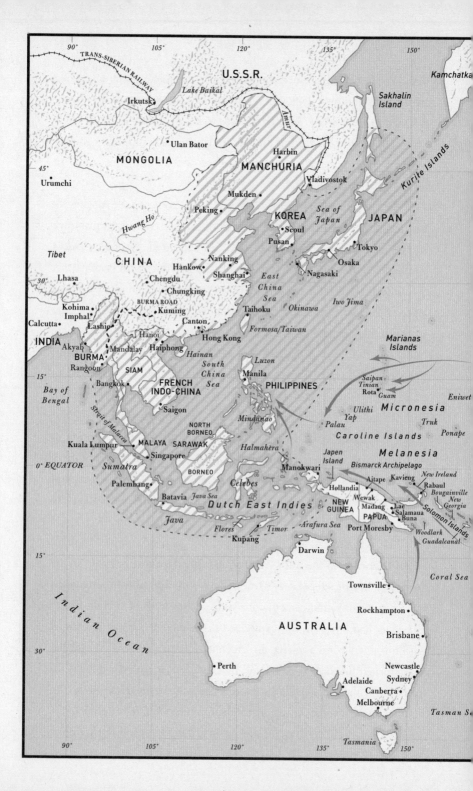

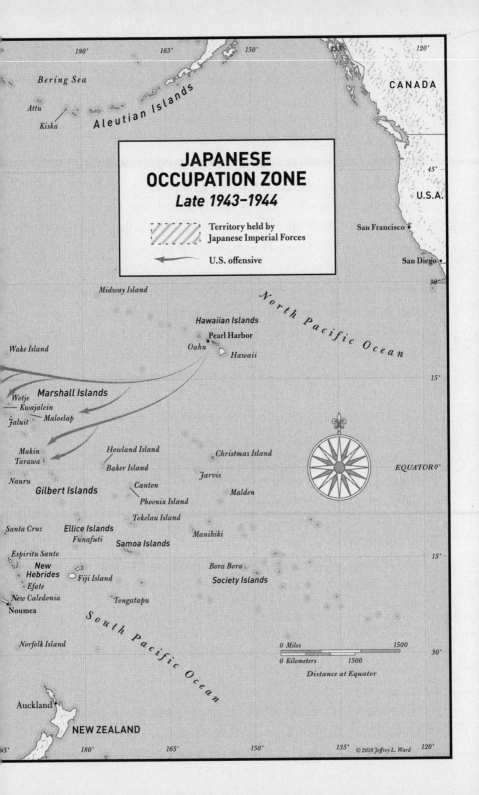

180° 165° 150° 135° 120°

Bering Sea

CANADA

Attu

Kiska

Aleutian Islands

45°

U.S.A.

JAPANESE OCCUPATION ZONE
Late 1943–1944

San Francisco

Territory held by
Japanese Imperial Forces

U.S. offensive

San Diego

30°

Midway Island

North Pacific Ocean

Hawaiian Islands

Pearl Harbor

Wake Island

Oahu   Hawaii

15°

Wotje   **Marshall Islands**

Kwajalein

Jaluit   Maloelap

Makin   Howland Island   Christmas Island

Tarawa

Baker Island

Jarvis

Nauru

Gilbert Islands   Canton   Malden

Phoenix Island

EQUATOR 0°

Tokelau Island

Santa Cruz   **Ellice Islands**   Manihiki

Funafuti

Samoa Islands

Espiritu Santo

15°

**New
Hebrides**   Fiji Island   Bora Bora

Efate   **Society Islands**

New Caledonia

Noumea   Tongatapu

South Pacific Ocean

Norfolk Island

0 Miles   1500

0 Kilometers   1500

30°

Distance at Equator

Auckland

NEW ZEALAND

180°   165°   150°   135°   120°

© 2016 Jeffrey L. Ward

been almost completely razed. As the historian Gamble further notes, the Allied air attacks on Rabaul—which began in January 1942 and continued through the end of the war in August 1945—constituted the longest battle of World War II.

While it continued to be overshadowed by the European-based 8th Air Force, Gen. Kenney's 5th Air Force grew stronger as Allied forces crept inexorably closer to the Japanese homeland. The 5th was spearheaded by the 43rd Bomb Group—the "First Team," as they came to call themselves—and the Group's Airmen were able to cite a series of "firsts" to back up their claim. They were the first to make practical use of skip bombs, the first to operate out of New Guinea, the first to attack the seemingly impregnable "Fortress Rabaul," the first to sight and smash the Japanese during the decisive Battle of the Bismarck Sea, and the first outfit in the Southwest Pacific Theater to lay mines from the air (dropping 18 from an altitude of 300 feet into the mouth of northeast New Guinea's Sepik River in May 1943). Perhaps above all, the pilots of the 43rd Bomb Group were also the first to prove the deadly fighting qualities of the Flying Fortress against the Zero.

As for Old 666, despite the beating it took over Bougainville, it was somehow patched up, made ready to fly again, and assigned to the 8th Photo Reconnaissance Squadron of the 6th Photographic Reconnaissance Group. Finally, in February 1944, with the E series of B-17s having been gradually rotated out of combat and replaced by the newer F and G Flying Fortress models, Old 666 was flown to Albuquerque, New Mexico, and, as the Bomb Group's Official History sardonically notes, "farmed out to pasture like a good old fire horse."

Though it technically remained in reserve service until the end of the war, 18 months later, not long after V-J Day in August 1945, Old 666 was chopped up and melted for scrap.

THREE AND A HALF WEEKS AFTER HIS FINAL FLIGHT, WHILE STILL BED-
ridden in Australia, Jay was given a field promotion to major. Ten months

later he was promoted again, to lieutenant colonel, while convalescing at the Walter Reed Medical Center in Washington, D.C. There he shared a hospital room with Capt. Ted Lawson, whose first-person account of Jimmy Doolittle's dramatic raid, *Thirty Seconds Over Tokyo*, was an instant bestseller and was soon adapted into a movie starring Spencer Tracy as Doolittle and Van Johnson as Lawson.

It was the adventuresome Col. Merian C. Cooper—the cocreator of *King Kong*, who after the war went on to collaborate with John Ford on such classic films as *The Quiet Man*—who recommended that Jay Zeamer and Joe Sarnoski be nominated to receive the Medal of Honor. Cooper knew heroism. Following the armistice that ended World War I and before volunteering for Kosciuszko's Squadron, Cooper had scoured the French countryside and finally located the grave of Lt. Frank Luke, America's second-highest-scoring ace in the Great War. Luke was posthumously awarded the Medal of Honor.

Now, Cooper wrote of the final flight of Old 666, "I consider Captain Zeamer's feat above and beyond the call of duty, comparable to that of Lieutenant Luke, who stands with Captain [Eddie] Rickenbacker as one of the leading flying officers of exceptional courage and daring."

When Cooper's narrative made its way up the chain of command, Gen. Kenney concurred, and personally wrote Jay's citation. Jay was still recovering at Walter Reed when he received the telephone call informing him he had been awarded the Medal of Honor.

"At that point," he later recalled, "I dropped the phone."

Our nation's highest military award was presented to Jay by Gen. Henry "Hap" Arnold, commander of the Army Air Forces, on January 6, 1944, at a ceremony at the Pentagon. The citation reads in full:

On 16 June 1943, Maj. Zeamer (then Capt.) volunteered as pilot of a bomber on an important photographic mapping mission covering the formidably defended area in the vicinity of Buka, Solomon Islands. While photographing the Buka airdrome, his crew observed about

20 enemy fighters on the field, many of them taking off. Despite the certainty of a dangerous attack by this strong force, Maj. Zeamer proceeded with his mapping run, even after enemy attacks began. In the ensuing engagement, Maj. Zeamer sustained gunshot wounds in both arms and legs, 1 leg being broken. Despite his injuries, he maneuvered the damaged plane so skillfully that his gunners were able to fight off the enemy during a running fight which lasted 40 minutes. The crew destroyed at least five hostile planes, of which Maj. Zeamer himself shot down 1. Although weak from loss of blood, he refused medical aid until the enemy had broken combat. He then turned over the controls, but continued to exercise command despite lapses into unconsciousness, and directed the flight to a base 580 miles away. In this voluntary action, Maj. Zeamer, with superb skill, resolution, and courage, accomplished a mission of great value.

Seated in the front row for the awards ceremony were Jay Sr. and Marjorie Zeamer, who beamed when Gen. Arnold placed the medal around their son's collar to complement his two Silver Stars, his Distinguished Flying Cross, his Air Medal with Oak Leaf Cluster, and his Purple Heart.

"This reminded me more and more that I represent *many* people," Jay would say later about the awards ceremony. "My comrades who did something special but ended up dead and nobody noticed. In many cases there was no recognition at all. I received the award for all those who died, especially my own bombardier, Joe Sarnoski."

Jay's physicians had told him he would never walk again. Ever the renegade, he proved them wrong. Later that year he was released from Walter Reed and, though still in pain, returned to active duty as a field air officer in charge of inspecting training bases to ensure that Airmen heading into overseas combat were receiving the proper indoctrination and equipment.

• • •

JAY ZEAMER JR. WAS ONE OF ONLY NINE EAGLE SCOUTS TO BE AWARDED
the Medal of Honor. When he finally made it home to Orange, New Jersey, he was naturally feted as a returning hero and awarded a gold medal from the Merchants Association of Orange. A year later he was named the town's Outstanding Citizen for 1945. Jay, whose hair had turned prematurely gray, accepted both awards with his usual humility, telling the men and women who had gathered in his honor that any awards presented to him were emblematic of his community's appreciation for the hard work of all men and women serving in the armed forces.

A local reporter who interviewed the 27-year-old Jay at the ceremony noted that his eyes bore "a seriousness generally not expected in men of his years." It was also reported that though he walked with a noticeable limp, he moved through the adoring crowds briskly.

During his remarks at the many stateside dinners and receptions held in his honor upon his return, Jay consistently returned to his humble roots. That attitude had been encapsulated when, six months after his Medal of Honor flight, Jay sat for an interview with his hometown *Newark News*. "Do me a favor when you write this story," he had implored the reporter. "Leave out the melodrama."

In keeping with his aversion to melodrama, Jay rarely mentioned the painful trip he had undertaken to visit the Sarnoski homestead in Carbondale, Pennsylvania, shortly after his release from Walter Reed. It was late 1944, and after being dropped off at the closest paved road to the Sarnoski farm, with the help of a cane Jay trudged over a mile uphill to the family's front yard, every step more agonizing than the previous one. When he reached the property one of the first things he noticed was the rows of carrots, tomatoes, beets, and peas in the beautifully tended victory garden the family had planted in Joe's honor.

Joe's father, John, was not home that day, but Josephine invited Jay into her parlor, poured him a glass of *swojskie wino*, the Polish sweet red wine she always had at the ready for visitors, and listened in silence as he told her the story of her son's heroism in the Southwest Pacific Theater of War. "He was my best friend," Jay told her, "and I'm sorry for your loss."

What he did not tell her was how responsible he felt for her son's death, a burden, however undeserved, he carried with him for the rest of his life.

Jay had brought along a few of Joe belongings to return to John and Josephine, including Joe's bombardier's trooper hat and his flight goggles. When he presented these to Josephine, she finally cried.

It was Cicero who observed that in peace, sons bury fathers; in war, fathers bury sons. So do mothers.

AT THE WAR'S END IN 1945, JAY WAS MEDICALLY DISCHARGED FROM THE United States Army Air Force. He returned to M.I.T. and, a year later, earned a master's degree in aeronautical engineering. He proceeded to work for a string of aerospace companies—Pratt & Whitney, Hughes Aircraft, and Raytheon—designing test installations for new aircraft engines as well as new cockpit configurations.

In 1949, Jay married Barbara Ferner, whom he had met on a snowbound train to the Pacific Northwest. Together the couple raised five daughters—Marcia, Jacquie, Jayne, Susan, and Sandra. Nineteen years later, having lived for periods on both coasts, the Zeamers moved permanently to Boothbay Harbor, Maine, his family's old summer vacation spot. There, as Jay put it, he "just lived the local life" until his retirement in 1975.

Although he enjoyed golf, tennis, and even skiing, Jay admitted that his injured left leg, pocked with holes "big enough to put your fist in" and hampered by only a 60-degree arc of flexibility, prevented him from chasing tennis balls very far and even from walking downstairs. "I have to skip, and people are always asking me what's my hurry," he told a reporter. Late in life Jay also lost the tops of both ears to skin cancer, which he attributed to the "wicked sunburns" he suffered in the Southwest Pacific.

• • •

EXACTLY ONE MONTH BEFORE GEN. ARNOLD PLACED THE MEDAL OF
Honor around Jay's neck at the Washington, D.C., ceremony, Second
Lt. Joseph Raymond Sarnoski's Medal of Honor nomination was also
approved. His posthumous award was presented to his wife, Marie, at
Virginia's Richmond Army Air Force base on June 7, 1944, a year nearly
to the day after his heroic flight. Joe's father was too ill to attend the ceremony, but Marie gave the medal to Joe's mother, Josephine, who in turn
bequeathed it to the Congressional Medal of Honor Society.

For their valor on that June 1943 flight over Buka and Bougainville,
J. T. Britton, William Vaughan, Herbert "Pudge" Pugh, Forrest Dillman,
Johnnie Able, Ruby Johnston, and George Kendrick were each awarded
the Distinguished Service Cross, the nation's second-highest military
commendation for heroism in armed conflict. This gave Old 666's crew
the distinction of becoming, as it still remains, the most highly decorated
combat aircrew in the history of American military service.

Following their final flight in Old 666 the Eager Beavers scattered
across the globe, some still flying missions.

The radioman Willy Vaughan spent two months recuperating from
his wounds before being assigned to a new Flying Fortress. In October
1943, he took part in the Battle of Finschhafen, near Lae, as part of the
ongoing Operation Cartwheel. When Vaughan's bomber was caught in
a hailstorm of anti-aircraft fire, the crew was forced to bail out over the
Bismarck Sea. Vaughan and several crewmates washed up on the shores
of Manus Island, the largest in the Admiralty chain, where they were res-
cued by sympathetic tribesmen. It took them two weeks to surreptitiously
make their way from Manus to the Allied base at Buna, from which they
were flown back to Port Moresby.

Soon thereafter Vaughan returned to the United States, having flown
73 missions over 22 months of service in the Pacific Theater. He was officially credited with shooting down nine Japanese fighter planes, with four
more "probables." Despite his harrowing war experiences he never shed

his reticence and only reluctantly spoke to newspapermen clamoring to hear his story of the dogfight over Bougainville. Typical of Vaughan's droll responses was his answer to a reporter who inquired about his Purple Heart with two clusters indicating not only the shrapnel wound he had received that day, but also the bayonet wound incurred during the hand-to-hand combat at Milne Bay: "I was always getting it in the neck," he said.

Back in the States, Vaughan applied to and was accepted by the Army Air Corps' bomber pilot flight school, and after the war he served in the Air Force Reserves, attaining the rank of lieutenant colonel. By then he had returned to his hometown, Youngstown, and there he remained for the rest of his life. William Vaughan died in 1999 at the age of 79.

Following World War II, Old 666's navigator Lt. Ruby Johnston also remained in the Army Air Corps and, later, the U.S. Air Force. He finished college and served during both the Korean and the Vietnam wars before leaving the service with the rank of colonel to become a high school guidance counselor and special education teacher in his home state, Florida. Along the way he married and had five children before retiring from his career in education in 1984. He died 11 years later at the age of 77.

Sergeant Johnnie Able was honorably discharged from the service after he recovered from the wounds he received over Bougainville. He returned to his hometown, Myrtle Beach, South Carolina; attended college and law school on the GI Bill; and married his high school sweetheart, with whom he had two daughters. Able became one of the most beloved attorneys in town, and he was known for offering his services pro bono to those in need of legal advice. He died when he was only in his late forties, and was deeply mourned by the community.

The waist gunner and the crew's "Photo Joe," Tech. Sgt. George Kendrick, seemed to fall off the map after the war. It is known that he returned to his Northern California home after his honorable discharge, but there Kendrick disappeared from any records despite efforts, including several by Jay Zeamer, to locate him. It is believed that Kendrick died in his fifties somewhere in the Berkeley area.

After his combat service the belly gunner Forrest Dillman returned to Nebraska and completed his college education. He remained in the Army Reserves and was recalled to active duty at the outbreak of the Korean conflict in 1950. He was honorably discharged three years later. Dillman worked as an insurance salesman and real estate broker, first in Nebraska and then, after moving west in 1959, in California. He died in 1975 at the age of 54, and is buried in the National Cemetery in Visalia, California.

A funny thing happened to Herbert "Pudge" Pugh one summer afternoon in 1973. It was hot that day, and after clocking out of his job at the Navy shipyard in Mechanicsburg, Pennsylvania, he dropped by a corner bar in the nearby town of New Cumberland for a cold beer. The female bartender who served him looked awfully familiar, and Pudge told her so. Assuming this was one of the thousands of pickup lines she had heard too many times, the bartender nonetheless played along and introduced herself as Agnes Sarnoski Rembisz, from Carbondale. Pugh nearly fell off his bar stool.

Thirty years earlier, weeks after Pudge had sent his letter of condolence to John and Josephine Sarnoski, he received a letter back from Joe's younger sister Agnes—the same Agnes to whom Joe had sent the poem "We Swoop at Dawn." In her missive, Agnes had asked Pudge to tell her "all about my brother Joe."

Pudge had written back to Agnes about how close he was with the bombardier, describing Joe's heroic death over Bougainville in terms he felt would not overly upset a 25-year-old girl. "Agnes, I want you to know," he'd written, "that even though Joe was seriously hit once and knocked away from his guns, he struggled back to his position and definitely disintegrated two Jap fighters." In the same letter Pudge also promised Agnes that her big brother's death would be "avenged many many times before this war is over."

Now, three decades later, here he was face-to-face with his former correspondent. "We got misty-eyed, we choked up," Pugh recalled to a newspaper reporter. "We could never stop talking about Joe."

Joe Sarnoski's younger sister invited Pugh back to her home, where over "great laughter and oven fresh cookies" the two reminisced about that June day in 1943. Pudge and Agnes remained in touch until Pugh's death in 1997 at the age of 77. Herbert Pugh was survived by his wife, four daughters, and ten grandchildren.

Not long after his final flight in Old 666 as copilot, John "J. T." Britton was transferred from the Southwest Pacific to the China-Burma-India Theater. There he served out the remainder of the war as, first, an Operations Officer and, later, the commander of a forward airbase in Burma overseeing transport planes ferrying troops and matériel into China.

Like Vaughan and Johnston, Britton made a career in the service, retiring from the U.S. Air Force in 1961 with the rank of colonel. After he and his first wife divorced, he returned to college at the age of 41; received degrees in forestry and veterinary studies from the University of Texas at El Paso; and purchased a farm in Midland, Texas, where he met and married his second wife, Josephine. Ever the gaming shark, when not farming and raising livestock, Britton crisscrossed the country playing in bridge tournaments and accruing master points.

In 1993, half a century after the Bougainville mission, Britton surprised Jay by arriving in Boothbay Harbor to take part in the festivities surrounding "Jay Zeamer Day." Britton was the last of Old 666's crew members to die, in 2011 at the age of 91.

AFTERWORD

IN SEPTEMBER 1995, WHEN JAY ZEAMER WAS 77, HE WAS AMONG THE
hundreds of World War II veterans invited to Pearl Harbor to commemo-
rate the fiftieth anniversary of V-J Day. While there he visited the National
Memorial Cemetery of the Pacific, known as the Punchbowl, on the outskirts of Honolulu. In the Punchbowl can be found, nestled in the crater
of an ancient volcano, the 33,143 graves and commemorations of American soldiers, sailors, Marines, and Airmen who gave their last full measure
of devotion in the war against Japan.

By this time Jay was using a crutch, and the ceremonies at Pearl involved much standing for an elderly man with a frail leg. Still, during a
break from the official events, Jay opted to forgo a rest back in his hotel
room and instead walked among the cemetery's headstones. Of the tens
of thousands of men buried in the Punchbowl, he had known more than

a few, and had flown with some of them. But it was the memory of Joe Sarnoski, left behind in a hastily dug grave in New Guinea, that so often occupied his mind, never more so than on this anniversary.

Family and friends had often admonished Jay for being too hard on himself, for thinking that he had been responsible for his best friend's death. Yet even the passage of more than half a century had not changed his belief. As he once told his wife, "I got him promoted and I got him killed."

That afternoon in Honolulu, Jay was accompanied on his slow walk through the graveyard by a small coterie of family and friends, as well as a reporter for the *Air Force News*. It was the reporter who led the limping Jay to Section A of the Punchbowl. There, in grave 582, was the final resting place of Second Lt. Joe Sarnoski.

Unbeknownst to Jay, Joe's body had been disinterred from the makeshift grave in Port Moresby in 1945; briefly reburied in Ipswich, Australia; and in early 1949 flown to Hawaii, to be interred in American soil. Jay was stunned. "I didn't know he was here," Jay said, and he began to cry.

Leaning heavily on his crutch, Jay bent painfully over the headstone marking Joe's grave and placed a lei of flowers on the plaque commemorating his bombardier. The plaque was decorated with a blue flag bearing the likeness of the Medal of Honor. Tears continued to streak his cheeks as he straightened, came to attention, and saluted his old comrade.

Then, his voice cracking with emotion, he turned toward the small group surrounding him and said, "It's very important for me to place this wreath here. Because without him, I wouldn't be here today."

And with that he palmed away another tear and bowed his head in silent prayer.

JAY'S LAST YEARS WERE PEACEFUL ONES. HE DIED AT AGE 88 ON MARCH 22, 2007, in his beloved Boothbay Harbor. He is buried in Arlington National Cemetery. His family members recall that not long before his death he shared his guiding philosophy with them.

"You can always find a way to do anything you want if you are dead set on doing it, come hell or high ack-ack," he said. "I think that is the most valuable thing anyone can learn from life."

At Jay's memorial service, hundreds of people, including the governor of Maine, attended what was in essence a celebration of the life of a man his wife, Barbara, called "a true maverick."

As Barbara, her five daughters, and the Zeamer grandchildren filled the front row of seats at the service, one of Jay's favorite quotations, from Theodore Roosevelt, was read:

> It is not the critic who counts; not the man who points out how the strong man stumbles or where the doer of deeds could have done them better. The credit belongs to the man who is actually in the arena, whose face is marred by dust and sweat and blood, who errs and comes up short again and again, but who spends himself in a worthy cause; who, at the best, knows, in the end, the triumph of high achievement, and who at the worst, if he fails, at least he fails while daring greatly.

Jay Zeamer and Joe Sarnoski and the Eager Beavers had dared greatly. They had not failed.

ACKNOWLEDGMENTS

THIS BOOK WOULD NOT HAVE BEEN POSSIBLE WITHOUT THE MANY PEO-ple, organizations, and institutions that provided us with a wealth of personal and professional material. We must begin by thanking the extended family of Jay Zeamer, particularly his wife, Barbara; his daughter Sandra; and his nephews Warwick and Geoffrey Zeamer. An equal amount of gratitude must be sent to members of Joe Sarnoski's family, most especially his nephew Jim Rembisz, who provided us with invaluable documentation; and Joe's sister Matilda Spodnewski and his nieces Judith Thompson and Kathy Stees. We are also indebted to Boyd Britton and Richard Vaughan for recollections about their fathers, brave crewmates of Capt. Jay Zeamer Jr. and Lt. Joe Sarnoski.

We are also grateful to the men and women who were generous enough to take the time to share their intimate memories and special knowledge of the 5th Air Force during World War II. These include George Anderson, Linda Burton, James Cherkauer, James Diefenderfer, Barbi Greene Evans, Bruce Gamble, Edward Gammill, Kensmen.com and its resources, Michelle Krell Malone, Jack and Alan Matisoff, John McDowell, Melissa Parker, Louise Terrell, and Susan Lanson and all the members of the 43rd Bomb Group Association. More specifically, we are deeply grateful to Daniel Knickrehm, formerly the 43rd Bomb Group historian, who not only assisted us during the early stages of our research but was there toward the end too, by giving the manuscript a thorough read and helping us correct factual errors.

There were many individuals and institutions that were indispensable to us in our research, and we are thankful for their efforts, especially in those instances when they responded to repeated requests for material; they include Mike Leister of the Air Mobility Command Museum at Dover Air Force Base; James Amemasor and the New Jersey Historical Society; Randy Andrews; Autumn Arnett and *Air Force Magazine*; Richard Baker; Rich Bowra; Kevin Burnham and the *Boothbay Register*; the Carbondale Historical Society; the Carlisle Public Library; Keegan Chetwynd and the Air Force Heritage Museum; Bill Cronauer and the Scranton Public Library; Bruce Crosby and the *McCook Gazette*; Cara Curtis and the Cumberland County Historical Society; the Dauphin County Library System; Archangelo DiFante; Cindy Drake and the Nebraska State Historical Society; Dennis Fabiszak and the East Hampton Free Library; Double Delta Photo Research; Brian George; Lesta Sue Hardy and the Chapin Library; the Harrisburg Public Library; Clint Hayes; the John Jermain Memorial Library, especially Cathy Creedon and Sue Mullin; the Joseph Clark Collection; the Leesville Public Library; Sharon Leon and the Pacific War Archives at George Mason University; and Richette Wilson Lobban.

In addition, our research would not have been complete without the assistance of the McCook Public Library; Tim McFadden and the Boothbay Harbor Memorial Library; Darla Moore and the Winter Park Public Library; Newark Public Library; New Jersey Historical Society; Lydia Olszak; Ryan O'Malley; Janice Olson; the Orange, New Jersey, Public Library; Melissa Parker; Pensacola Public Library; Jessica Pratt and the Carbondale Library; Holly Reed at the National Archives and Records Administration; the Richmond Public Library, especially Linda Holmes, David Kilmon, and Karen Roy; Barbara Rumsey and the Boothbay Harbor Historical Society; Denise Shellehamer; Robert Sligh; the Steelton Public Library; Sara Swan and the National Museum of the U.S. Air Force; Justin Taylan and Pacificwrecks.org; U.S. Army Heritage and Education Center; Peggy Vignolo; Alisa Whitley and the Library of the Marine Corps; and the Youngstown Public Library.

Words cannot convey the appreciation we feel for the expertise and enthusiasm of our editor, Jofie Ferrari-Adler, and the other members of the Simon

& Schuster team, particularly Jonathan Karp, Richard Rhorer, Leah Johanson, Stephen Bedford, Susan Gamer, Marie Florio, and Julianna Haubner. Moreover, with us at every step of the way during the reporting and writing of this book walked our literary agent, Nat Sobel, and his invaluable instincts, as well as Adia Wright and the helpful elves of Sobel-Weber Associates. Further support was provided by Michael Prevett at the Rain Management Group.

Fortune plays a role in all facets of a book project, and we were fortunate enough to be able to fall back on the crack if unofficial editorial committee of Marty Beiser, Bob Kelly, and David Hughes.

Finally, we have been blessed with family support systems that not only endure through thick and thin, but also inspire. For that we owe a huge debt of gratitude to Denise McDonald, Liam-Antoine DeBusschere-Drury, Leslie Reingold, Kathryn Clavin, and Brendan Clavin.

NOTES ON SOURCES

AS WITH OUR PREVIOUS BOOKS, THE GENEROSITY OF STAFFERS AT LIbraries, museums, and other institutions has been our salvation. In wars since time immemorial it has been said that history is fable agreed upon, but contrary to that perceived wisdom it was indeed fortunate for us that World War II has been so well chronicled by historians and others in Japan, Germany, and other countries as well as in the United States. However, learning what the most authoritative sources of information are, and gaining access to them, is another matter. From major government institutions to military facilities to community libraries and historical societies, we were blessed by the competence, curiosity, and even enthusiasm of the caretakers of those sources of information.

Sadly, it is increasingly difficult to gain firsthand accounts of World War II events because of the aging of that generation. Even the youngest participants in the Pacific war of 1942 and 1943 are in their nineties. We were fortunate to find sons, daughters, grandchildren, and other family members who were willing to share the memories and documents passed down to them. Letters, recollections, and other papers provided to us by members of the Zeamer, Sarnoski, Vaughan, Britton, and other families offered invaluable and irreplaceable information. The 43rd Bomb Group Association was especially helpful, particularly its surviving members who were stationed in the Southwest Pacific as well as the descendants of those who fought there but are now no longer with us. For more information about the men and exploits of the 43rd that we could not include in our narrative, please visit the website kensmen.com.

Also of enormous help to us were the hundreds of pages of declassified documents, After-Action reports, and official records and histories of units deployed to Australia and New Guinea during the first two years of the war. A particular wellspring of research was the official history of the 43rd Bomb Group. This history's clarity, attention to day-to-day detail, and even humor under such trying circumstances are a credit to its compilers, who were no doubt motivated by a combination of pride and desire for thoroughness. Its inclusion of contemporary newspaper accounts, maps, magazine articles, and photographs lent our research into the era a true sense of "You are there."

Our goal in researching and reporting *Lucky 666* was, as always, to tell as fully and accurately as possible a story about ordinary men rising to extraordinary circumstances. As we sifted through the stacks of collected documents, letters, diaries, and transcripts, we had to acknowledge that inevitably there were contradictions. To the best of our ability, we resolved them with even further reporting. Nonetheless, the responsibility for any inaccuracies herein is ours and ours alone.

NOTES

CHAPTER 1: WANDERLUST

10 *"The job involved bookkeeping . . .":* Jay Zeamer Jr. papers.

10 *Sensing that revolution was imminent:* Ibid.

11 *These rural areas virtually called:* Marjorie Zeamer biography.

11 *Foremost in the Zeamer family's memory:* Jere Zeamer remembrance.

13 *Jay's little rowboat:* Marjorie Zeamer biography.

15 *Within a year he had risen:* Jay Zeamer Jr. papers.

15 *After several warnings:* Ibid.

CHAPTER 2: THE WILD BLUE YONDER

17 *Culver's mission statement:* https://en.wikipedia.org/wiki/Culver_Academies.

19 *Jay graduated from Culver:* Jay Zeamer Jr. papers.

21 *The two boys refused:* Geoffrey Zeamer interview.

21 *"by the bushel":* Ibid.

21 *When Jay Sr. was a newborn:* Sketch of Jay Zeamer, Sr., p. 1.

21 *He had also been the victim*: Ibid.

21 *As Jay Sr. noted*: Ibid.

23 *The slow train that transported Jay*: Geoffrey Zeamer interview.

CHAPTER 3: JAY & JOE

27 *But like Jay*: http://en.wikipedia.org/wiki/Eddie_Rickenbacker.

28 *This did not mean Jay*: Rembisz, "Wings of Valor," p. 6.

28 *Though he never did find his man*: Zeamer letter to Victoria, December 21, 1995.

29 *As he would one day*: Ibid.

30 *For reasons that baffled*: Judith Thompson memo 2.

31 *Most of the money*: Matilda Sarnoski interview, June 22, 2015.

31 *"When he tried to teach us"*: Ibid.

31 *"He wanted us to grow up"*: Ibid.

32 *Through all his travels*: Ibid.

33 *More urgently, by the summer of 1941*: Rembisz, "Wings of Valor," p. 6.

CHAPTER 4: "THE SACRED DUTY OF THE LEADING RACE"

36 *Like most seasoned military men*: Hennessy, *USAF Historical Studies No. 98*.

37 *Yet the plane's colorful nickname*: Dewan, *Red Raider Diary*, p. 13.

38 *Referring to the aircraft's developer*: Ibid.,

38 *But it was landings*: Gamble, *Fortress Rabaul*, p. 135.

38 *Or he would come in*: Jay Zeamer Jr. papers.

38 *"For some reason Jay"*: Walt Krell remembrance.

39 *"Nothing ever seemed to bother him"*: Caidin, *Flying Forts*, p. 22.

39 *But once in the air*: Walt Krell remembrance.

39 *The fact that Jay was not alone*: Caidin and Hymoff, *The Mission*, p. 47.

39 *Despite these setbacks*: Jay Zeamer Jr. papers.

41 *Unlike Western white supremacists*: Dower, *War Without Mercy*, p. 203.

41 *In 1940 the influential Japanese politician*: Ibid.

41 *Headquarters had other plans*: Goldstein and Dillon, *The Pacific War Papers*, p. 4.

42 *Finally, with Australia overrun:* Dower, *War Without Mercy,* p. 258.

42 *One American Army general said that:* George C. Kenney Papers, Center for Air Force History.

43 *From early childhood Japanese boys:* Keneally, *Shame and the Captives.*

43 *This attitude was summed up:* Dower, *War Without Mercy,* p. 260.

CHAPTER 5: THE FORTRESS

44 *They planned to call it:* Salecker, *Fortress Against the Sun,* p. 46.

46 *When Hitler's forces invaded Poland:* Mason, *The United States Air Force,* p. 119.

46 *As a pilot of a B-17:* Caidin, *Flying Forts,* p. 3.

47 *As it happened, once aircraft:* http://en.wikipedia.org/wiki/Circular_error _probable).

49 *If he had been familiar with:* Costello, *The Pacific War,* p. 4.

49 *Only a few months earlier:* Davenport, "Impregnable Pearl Harbor."

50 *Toward the end of his dispatch:* Ibid.

50 *Within hours the simultaneous attacks:* James, *A Time for Giants,* pp. 196–97.

CHAPTER 6: THE WINDS OF WAR

53 *He feared that this could be:* Jay Zeamer Jr. papers.

53 *Worse, to Jay's everlasting disgust:* Ibid.

59 *Eleven days before the assault:* Edmonds, *They Fought with What They Had,* p. 56.

59 *This air fleet was:* Costello, *The Pacific War,* p. 105.

59 *The unofficial military grapevine:* Connaughton, *MacArthur and Defeat in the Philippines.*

60 *In his definitive biography:* Manchester, *American Caesar,* p. 230.

60 *And after MacArthur escaped Corregidor:* Connaughton, *MacArthur and Defeat in the Philippines.*

60 *This was too much for Gen. William Brougher:* Ibid.

61 *But as one of Joe's fellow bombardiers noted:* Dunbar letter to Rembisz, December 16, 1985.

62 *The mess room, one Airman wrote*: kensmen.com general history.

63 *The* Argentina *made refueling*: Ibid.

63 *Joe was no stranger*: Ibid.

CHAPTER 7: THE JAPANESE CITADEL

64 *The pilots were also ordered*: Evans and Gaylor, *Revenge of the Red Raiders.*

65 *Indeed, his first commanding officer*: Hillenbrand, *Unbroken*, p. 80.

65 *Despite his famous promise*: Drury and Clavin, *Halsey's Typhoon*, p. 37.

66 *Marshall's proposal was rejected*: Sears, *Pacific Air War*, p. 111.

67 *This "insult" to the supreme commander*: James, *A Time for Giants*, pp. 196–97.

68 *In a bizarre development*: Lardner, *Southwest Passage*, p. 172.

69 *The results were disheartening*: Griffith, *MacArthur's Airman*, p. 56.

70 *Prior to December 7*: Agawa, *The Reluctant Admiral*, p. 293.

70 *Yamamoto had gone so far*: Ibid., p. 292.

73 *They continued, brutally and illegally*: Gamble, *Fortress Rabaul*, p. 64.

74 *This renovation included*: www.ibiblio.org/hyperwar/USMC/USMC-M -NBrit/USMC-M-NBrit-1.html, p.3.

75 *The results of the bombing run*: Gamble, *Fortress Rabaul*, p. 100.

75 *The lead pilot's After-Action report*: Ibid.

CHAPTER 8: INTO THE FIGHT

76 *When in early April*: Dewan, *Red Raider Diary*, p. 10.

77 *These often resulted in clandestine*: Evans and Gaylor, *Revenge of the Red Raiders.*

77 *Though Australia is roughly*: Lardner, *Southwest Passage*, p. 60.

77 *This was particularly true*: Benefield memoir excerpt (chapter 4).

78 *In the winter months*: Lardner, *Southwest Passage*, p. 60.

78 *Those troops, Lardner reported*: Ibid.

78 *What this meant for the*: Ibid., p. 61.

79 *They discovered, for instance*: Griffith, *MacArthur's Airman*, p. 98.

79 *And in a pinch the Australian*: Ibid.

79 *As one of the 22nd*: Dewan, *Red Raider Diary*, p. 25.

85 *Thus, when the three*: Jay Zeamer Jr. papers.

86 *When the war began*: Lardner, *Southwest Passage*, p. 106.

86 *The Japanese took notice*: Gamble, *Fortress Rabaul*, p. 138.

87 *When the lyrical propagandist*: Stahl, "A Monkey Rides My Shoulder," p. 1.

CHAPTER 9: BREAKING THE CODE

92 *This would not only eliminate*: Lardner, *Southwest Passage*, p. 79.

93 *By early May the Americans*: Sears, *Pacific Air War*, p. 110.

93 *This intelligence breach outraged*: Ibid.

95 *luckily, and typically*: Griffith, *MacArthur's Airman*, p. 54.

97 *He was also an ardent*: Drury and Clavin, *Halsey's Typhoon*, p. 23.

99 *Some months earlier*: Sears, *Pacific Air War*, pp. 110–11.

99 *Written by a vice president of research*: Ibid.

100 *Of equal importance, more skilled*: Gamble, *Fortress Rabaul*, p. 190.

100 *As one Army Air Force general*: Letter, Kenney to Arnold, January 1, 1943.

101 *Now, with four airstrips operational*: Costello, *The Pacific War*, p. 375.

102 *And the confrontations*: "World Battlefronts," *Time*, January 18, 1943.

103 *Back in Australia*: Dewan, *Red Raider Diary*, p. 13.

103 *Jay, in turn, marked this shift*: Jay Zeamer Jr. papers.

CHAPTER 10: THE RENEGADE PILOT

104 *The Japanese caricatured*: Dower, *War Without Mercy*, p. 85.

105 *American cartoonists could not resist*: http://ww2cartoons.org/june-1942
     -battle-of-midway-turns-the-tide-in-the-pacific.

105 *General MacArthur also benefited*: http://bfedoriwchapter16.blogspot.com
     /2013/05/politcal-cartoons-and-propaganda.html.

105 *And in London* Punch *published*: http://punch.photoshelter.com/gallery
     -image/Bernard-Partridge-Cartoons/G0000_xSMzDQG4iQ/I00004.3U
     ax6HjeU.

105 *As one family member*: Geoffrey Zeamer interview.

108 *Back on the ground, Seffern wrote*: "Screwball Aces," p. 60.

108 *Jay would later gloss over*: Letter to Bob Butler, 1983.

108 *He was fast running not only*: Hyde, "Medal of Honor Mission," p. 60.

109 *After two of the 22nd's bombers*: Stanaway and Rocker, *Eight Ballers*, p. 42.

110 *The colonel sensed that*: Dewan, *Red Raider Diary*, p. 16.

110 *Another pilot from the 22nd added*: Caidin and Hymoff, *The Mission*, p. 54.

110 *One of the Bomb Group's senior officers*: Dewan, *Red Raider Diary*, pp. 16–17.

111 *Four-engine bombers like*: 43rd Bomb Group Official History, p. 29.

CHAPTER 11: THE BULLDOG

115 *And during his 1940 deployment*: "World Battlefronts," *Time*, January 18, 1943.

115 *Newspapermen and magazine writers*: Boothe, *Europe in the Spring*, p. 171.

116 *When it came Kenney's turn*: Kenney, *General Kenney Reports*, p. 30.

116 *As Kenney recalled in his diary*: Ibid.

116 *Kenney, reacting instinctively*: Gamble, *Fortress Rabaul*, p. 206.

117 *During briefings at the Kila Kila*: Costello, *The Pacific War*, p. 319.

117 *Similarly, he had no answer*: Kenney, *General Kenney Reports*, p. 43.

117 *One mechanic even said*: Benefield memoir excerpt (chapter 6).

119 *Once back in Brisbane he signed*: Manuel, "General Kenney As a Strategic Leader," p. 11.

119 *Kenney explained his thinking*: "World Battlefronts," *Time*, January 18, 1943.

119 *Then he inserted*: Ibid.

119 *Or, as Kenney noted*: Ibid.

120 *It was a move that turned*: Kenney, *General Kenney Reports*, pp. 79–80.

121 *He remedied this by wrangling*: Ibid., p. 52.

121 *"Our only excuse for living"*: Ibid.

121 *He was true to his word*: Ibid., p. 215.

CHAPTER 12: A MICROSCOPIC METROPOLIS

126 *The entire coast, he added*: Murphy, *Skip Bombing*, p.7.

126 *Clouds of mosquitoes competed*: Jimmy Diefendorfer interview.

126 *The base's "Diggers"*: Lardner, *Southwest Passage*, p. 177.

126 *Still, there was no*: Costello, *The Pacific War*, p. 318.

126 *It was not unusual*: 43rd Bomb Group Official History, p. 27.

126 *Disease ran so rampant*: Ibid.

126 *He was also unofficially*: Jay Zeamer Jr. papers.

128 *Incredibly, with Australian cities*: Caidin and Hymoff, *The Mission*, p. 36.

128 *As the U.S. Army Air Force*: AAF Historical Study No. 9.

129 *Even a third parallel*: Jay Zeamer Jr. papers.

129 *During the month of May*: Caidin and Hymoff, *The Mission*, p. 59.

129 *After each attack*: Ibid, p. 60.

129 *One of Jay's fellow pilots*: Ibid.

130 *One of the 43rd's pilots*: Jimmy Diefendorfer interview.

130 *The RAAF officers club*: Lardner, *Southwest Passage*, p. 190.

131 *Many of the Australian fliers*: Jay Zeamer Jr. papers.

131 *A "microscopic metropolis"*: Lardner, *Southwest Passage*, pp. 171–72.

CHAPTER 13: KEN'S MEN

134 *In 1942, and for much*: Rembisz, "Home of Heroes."

134 *Early on, even MacArthur*: Costello, *The Pacific War*, p. 319.

134 *And though to some*: Claringbould, *The Forgotten Fifth*, p. 29.

135 *After apologizing for waking*: Birdsall, *Flying Buccaneers*, p. vi.

135 *"Don't apologize for news"*: Ibid.

136 *An hour later*: Ibid.

136 *MacArthur laughed*: Ibid.

136 *Kenney's presence brought*: Kenney, *General Kenney Reports*, p. 184.

137 *When a seasoned quartermaster*: Ibid., p. 187.

137 *The last thing he needed*: Ibid.

137 *In the middle of his lecture*: Ibid.

138 *Kenney was mightily impressed*: Gunn, *Pappy Gunn*.

138 *After flight tests gauging*: Griffith, *MacArthur's Airman*, p. 104.

139 *The first time Kenney experimented*: "World Battlefronts," *Time*, January 18, 1943.

139 *"You've got to devise stuff like that"*: Ibid.

139 *In private Kenney*: Evans and Gaylor, *Revenge of the Red Raiders*.

139 *Once, after advising MacArthur*: Griffith, *MacArthur's Airman*, p. 99.

139 *For all of the "stuff"*: http://www.quora.com/During-WWII-how-did-the
     -USMC-hold-the-island-of-Guadalcanal-for-such-a-long-time-against
     -such-a-numerous-enemy

142 *But enough of the dropped*: Kenney, *General Kenney Reports*, p. 22.

142 *"The lads in Fiji"*: Ibid.

142 *This freed the major*: Birdsall, *Flying Buccaneers*, p. 25.

143 *Instead his crews*: Ibid., p. 26.

143 *"Just as one would"*: Murphy, *Skip Bombing*, p. 24.

143 *Knowing that the general*: "World Battlefronts," *Time*, January 18, 1943.

CHAPTER 14: A PLACE WHERE TROUBLE STARTED

145 *A sophisticated ladies' man*: Kenney, *General Kenney Reports*, p. 143.

145 *The scion of New Mexican*: Rembisz, "Wings of Valor."

145 *But Kenney liked and admired*: Ibid.

146 *"General Walker stepped"*: pacificwrecks.com.

146 *As one of the 43rd's flight*: Seattle *Daily Times*, September 9, 1942.

146 *Accordingly, he argued*: www.homeofheroes.com/wings/part2/03_walker
     .html.

147 *As Kenney explained*: "World Battlefronts," *Time*, January 18, 1943.

147 *Moreover, as opposed to carpet bombing*: Griffith, *MacArthur's Airman*,
     p. 81.

148 *When word began to spread*: Birdsall, *Flying Buccaneers*, p. 26.

148 *McCullar's combat diaries in particular*: 22nd Bomb Group Official His-
     tory.

150 *With his pilot shielded*: Kenney, *General Kenney Reports*, pp. 169–70.

150 *As Kenney was to put it*: Ibid.

150 *There were no recorded hits*: 22nd Bomb Group Official History.

150 *"Violent explosions and flying debris"*: Ibid.

151 *That final run with McCullar*: Rembisz, "Wings of Valor."

CHAPTER 15: "CLEAR AS A BELL"

152 *Over the previous two months*: Birdsall, *Flying Buccaneers*, p. 29.

154 *None of them was aware*: Jay Zeamer Jr. papers.

154 *Yet a few moments later*: Ibid.

155 *Then the waist gunner's voice*: Zeamer, "There's Always a Way!" p. 102.

156 *After two minutes*: Ibid., p. 104.

157 *The fighter's fuselage spun*: Ibid., p. 103.

158 *Handling his aircraft*: Eaton memo to Jay Zeamer Jr.

158 *As the turret gunner recorded*: Bergerud, *Fire in the Sky*, p. 551.

158 *"That mission," he wrote*: Zeamer, "There's Always a Way!" p. 103.

CHAPTER 16: THE MISSING GENERAL

159 *By any metric, December 1942*: Franklin Roosevelt "Infamy" speech.

160 *Yamamoto in the Imperial Navy*: Goldstein and Dillon, *Pacific War Papers*.

160 *Or, as another aide to Yamamoto*: Ugaki diary, p. 319.

161 *The situation came to a head*: "World Battlefronts," *Time*, January 18, 1943.

161 *"all-out attack"*: Ibid. See also Gamble, *Fortress Rabaul*, p. 278.

163 *The general, who had been*: Boyington, *Baa Baa Black Sheep*, p. 179. https://books.google.com/books?id=GVITAAAAQBAJ&pg=PA179&1pg=PA179&dq=chesty+puller+there+is+only+a+hairline&source=bl&ots=0tF-CgrWBB&sig=IkyG8u9bZWS_5qtnpNuurwpjDBA&hl=en&sa=X&ei=ZmVXVcW9GcyXNpzmgeAP&ved=0CB4Q6AEwAA#v=onepage&q=chesty%20puller%20there%20is%20only%20a%20hairline&f=false.

164 *That night Jay entered*: Jay Zeamer Jr. papers.

CHAPTER 17: PUSHING NORTH

166 *At 60, Adm. Halsey was the self-proclaimed*: Drury and Clavin, *Halsey's Typhoon*, p. 4.

166   *Though he disliked the epithet*: Ibid., p. 12.

166   *When he was presented with his new*: Halsey and Bryan, *Admiral Halsey's Story*, p. 109.

166   *And when word spread*: James, *A Time for Giants*, p. 181.

167   *The raid had been*: Drury and Clavin, *Halsey's Typhoon*, p. 4.

168   *Allied advances half a world*: Costello, *The Pacific War*, p. 374.

168   *King concluded that the path*: Sears, *Pacific Air*, p. 112.

169   *The general vociferously and publicly*: Drury and Clavin, *Halsey's Typhoon*, p. 39.

174   *At the very least*: Jay Zeamer Jr. papers.

174   *By February 1943, Rabaul was*: 43rd Bomb Group Official History.

174   *"[The American] attacks are furious"*: Ibid.

174   *"The position of the command"*: Ibid.

CHAPTER 18: A FINE REUNION

176   *Benn, as Kenney himself noted*: Kenney, *General Kenney Reports*, p. 126.

178   *So they hatched a scheme*: 43rd Bomb Group Official History.

178   *with McCullar's crew*: Cohn, "Z Is for Zeamer," p. 22.

178   *As he told a relative*: Geoffrey Zeamer interview.

179   *"the friction of war"*: "Von Clausewitz on War."

179   *"I caught him by surprise"*: Jay Zeamer Jr. papers.

181   *He described to Jay how*: Dewan, *Red Raider Diary*.

181   *As he'd written to his sister Jennie*: Joe Sarnoski letter to Jennie.

182   *The daily eight-hour classes*: Dale F. Barr letter.

CHAPTER 19: "A MOTLEY COLLECTION OF OUTCASTS"

189   *It was only natural that*: Zeamer, "There's Always a Way!" p. 104.

189   *Jay rarely raised his voice*: Cohn, "Z Is for Zeamer," p. 22.

189   *Quaint as that notion*: Jay Zeamer Jr. papers.

189   *Given his growing combat*: Ibid.

191   *Jay came to think of him*: Ibid.

191   *As a waist gunner George Kendrick*: Ibid.

194 *But it was not often that an Airman*: Hyde, "Medal of Honor Mission," p. 60

194 *"[Zeamer] recruited a crew"*: Cicala, "The Most Honored Photograph."

CHAPTER 20: BLOOD ON THE BISMARCK SEA

197 *One of the American pilots*: Hastings, "No Survivors," p. 18.

197 *He added that the carnage*: Ibid.

197 *As one of the outfit's pilots*: 43rd Bomb Group Official History.

198 *As the Combat Diary continued*: Ibid.

198 *They also gleefully reported*: Stanaway and Rocker, *Eight Ballers*, p. 55.

198 *As another pilot noted*: Hastings, "No Survivors," p. 18.

198 *Clad in full jungle uniforms*: Birdsall, *Flying Buccaneers*, p. 62.

198 *All told, the Americans*: Ibid., p. 63.

198 *Despite reports of Australian*: Johnston, *Whispering Death*, p. 276.

198 *Allied aircraft had dropped*: Prados, *Islands of Destiny*, p. 254.

199 *When Emperor Hirohito learned*: Ibid., p. 255.

199 *He also ordered a shake-up*: Ibid., p. 256.

199 *And as one of Adm. Yamamoto's*: Griffith, *MacArthur's Airman*, pp. 111–12.

199 The New York Times *hailed*: *New York Times*, March 6, 1943.

199 *And MacArthur's description*: Kenney, *General Kenney Reports*, p. 206.

200 *The Battle of the Bismarck Sea*: Cohn, "Z Is for Zeamer," p. 69.

200 *From that moment on the two*: Jay Zeamer Jr. papers.

CHAPTER 21: THE FLIGHT OF THE GEISHAS

202 *Seasoned pilots knew that the first*: 43rd Bomb Group Official History.

202 *But, as Jay noted*: Jay Zeamer Jr. papers.

204 *The flight began as a simple*: Zeamer letter to Victoria.

204 *One day the squadron pooled*: Benefield memoir excerpt (chapter 4).

205 *It was just "bad luck"*: Sarnoski letter to Victoria.

205 *By reporting that the bomber*: Ibid.

207 *"But they gave up on us"*: Ibid.

207 *This, Jay insisted*: Warwick Zeamer interview.

208 *Joe, however, liked to tease*: Cohn, "Z Is for Zeamer," p. 22.

CHAPTER 22: OLD 666

211 *Although it was less than a year old*: "Old 666: Fantastic Voyage of the Cursed Bomber," p. 1.

211 *The aircraft may have resembled*: Jay Zeamer Jr. papers.

211 *Then, just as he had*: Ibid.

211 *"We did what the kids"*: Ibid.

212 *Half of them, he wrote*: Ibid.

216 *Allied war planners took some*: "Expansion to Air Power" documentary.

216 *In a cruel irony*: http://thefedorachronicles.com/worldwar2/menin/menin _metcalf.html.

216 *No other B-17 carried*: Scher, "Death Took a Holiday."

CHAPTER 23: THE OUTLAWS

220 *Jay was hit particularly hard*: Zeamer, "There's Always a Way!" p. 102.

221 *As a fellow bomber pilot*: Rembisz, "Wings of Valor," p. 7.

222 *Jay also recalled how he had personally*: Zeamer, "There's Always a Way!" p. 104.

222 *But Lindsey continued to wrestle*: Ibid.

223 *Yet one visiting reporter*: Cohn, "Z Is for Zeamer," p. 22.

224 *As he later told a friend*: Zeamer, "There's Always a Way!" p. 104.

224 *Despite its added armament*: Jay Zeamer Jr. papers.

224 *To prove this, Jay could not resist*: Ibid.

224 *"The airplane was faster than"*: Ibid.

224 *The next morning the crew*: Ibid.

225 *"You couldn't keep them"*: Rembisz, "Wings of Valor," p. 7.

225 *Most COs on the front lines*: Cicala, "The Most Honored Photograph," p. 2.

226 *It was the United States*: https://www.bc.edu/content/dam/files/schools /law/lawreviews/journals/bciclr/26_1/01_TXT.htm.

226 *John Wilkes Booth notwithstanding*: https://www.bc.edu/content/dam/files /schools/law/lawreviews/journals/bciclr/26_1/01_TXT.htm.

226 *Yet the U.S. Army's World War II*: https://www.bc.edu/content/dam/files /schools/law/lawreviews/journals/bciclr/26_1/01_TXT.htm.

227 *The churchmen gave the attack*: Drury and Clavin, *Halsey's Typhoon*, p. 11.

CHAPTER 24: NO POSITION IS SAFE

229 *It was the lead plane*: Jay Zeamer Jr. papers.

229 *A week later, on a daylight patrol*: Ibid.

230 *That was his cue to throw*: Ibid.

231 *Yet never one to leave*: Ibid.

231 *The raid elicited an unusual congratulatory*: 43rd Bomb Group Official History.

232 *This did not stop the officers of the 90th*: Gamble, *Target: Rabaul*, p. 87.

233 *Emblematic of the outfit's proficiency*: 43rd Bomb Group Official History.

234 *And there was no use waiting*: Costello, *The Pacific War*, p. 375.

234 *As one American Airman noted*: Drea, U.S. Army Center of Military History brochure, 1991.

234 *Cooper was to adventure*: Kenney, *General Kenney Reports*, p. 240.

235 *"Coop," Kenney wrote*: Ibid.

CHAPTER 25: NEW ADDITIONS

239 *American intelligence knew that*: Wukovits, *Admiral "Bull" Halsey*, p. 160.

241 *He stressed that between*: *Newark News*, January 11, 1944.

241 *He guessed that the odds*: Zeamer, "There's Always a Way!" p. 17.

242 *It was about to be tacked*: Zeamer YouTube interview, https://www.youtube.com/watch?v=VGt8gQulPcM.

242 *All he asked was that*: Ibid.

242 *Jay's superiors were not surprised*: Jay Zeamer Jr. papers.

242 *By now his unorthodox*: Ibid.

246 *As his fellow Pennsylvanian*: Pugh letter to Sarnoskis.

247 *They were no longer amiable*: Jay Zeamer Jr. papers.

247 *An insight into Joe's mind-set might*: Sarnoski letter to Agnes.

CHAPTER 26: "HELL, NO!"

249 *What appeared to be the worst damage*: Zeamer, "There's Always a Way!" p. 17.

250 *Within seconds every searchlight*: Ibid., p. 105.

250 *Jay took in the parallel rows*: Ibid.

251 *No one, however, could sleep*: "Richmond Wife of Slain Aviator Receives Award," p. 24.

252 *American bomber pilots knew*: www.lonesentry.com/articles/ttt09/japanese-antiaircraft.html.

252 *Jay lifted the phone back*: Beck, "Jay Zeamer Downplays WWII Heroism,"

252 *"I'm only doing the"*: Zeamer YouTube interview.

253 *Jay was so riled by the request*: Jay Zeamer Jr. papers.

253 *There was little precedent*: Drea, U.S. Army Center of Military History brochure.

253 *As a subsequent report*: Ibid.

253 *Jay had flown more than 45 combat*: King, "Some First Hand Observations on Combat Stress."

253 *Jay knew that once a pilot*: Gamble, *Fortress Rabaul*, p. 294.

253 *So as each of his men*: Jay Zeamer Jr. papers.

CHAPTER 27: BUKA

256 *"unsleeping Eye of the earth"*: Robinson Jeffers, "The Eye."

259 *Jay had time to ponder the wonders*: Jay Zeamer Jr. papers.

260 *As Johnnie Able later explained*: Old 666 crew statement, July 1943.

260 *Or, as Jay heard the collective response*: Jay Zeamer Jr. papers.

260 *From five miles above the rutted*: Ibid.

260 *Below him he counted more*: Cartwright, "Zeamer Maintains He Was Just Doing His Job."

260 *Questions flooded his mind*: Ibid.

261 *Nor did he know that their Japanese*: Gamble, *Target: Rabaul*, p. 77.

261 *For a split second Jay*: Jay Zeamer Jr. papers.

CHAPTER 28: "GIVE 'EM HELL!"

263 *The pilot of a lone Boeing*: Flying Unit Combat Action Report, September 9, 1943.

264 *After ten minutes Kendrick's voice*: Jay Zeamer Jr. papers.

266 *Jay held his course steady*: Old 666 crew statement, July 1943.

266 *He gurgled, "I'm all right"*: Jay Zeamer Jr. papers.

CHAPTER 29: THE DESPERATE DIVE

269 *Suddenly filling his mind*: Jay Zeamer Jr. papers.

269 *Staring into her eyes*: Ibid.

270 *His bucket seat was open to the sky*: Ibid.

270 *For a brief instant Jay thought his eardrums*: Ibid.

271 *He had never felt such pain*: Ibid.

271 *One more big hit, he knew*: Ibid.

CHAPTER 30: GET IT HOME

274 *The blood from his head*: Jay Zeamer Jr. papers.

275 *The enemy pilots had also learned*: Air Information Bulletin, July 14, 1943.

275 *He had convinced his crew*: Jay Zeamer Jr. papers.

275 *They would have to intuitively*: Crosshairs Humphreys, "By Resolute Defense," p. 27.

276 *After 40 minutes and 100 miles*: Old 666 crew statement, July 1943.

277 *Yoshio Ooki's subordinate*: Rembisz, "Wings of Valor."

277 *Under the circumstances*: Zeamer, "There's Always a Way!" p. 106.

277 *Still, given Old 666's shot-up*: Ibid.

278 *This structural modification was credited*: Hillenbrand, *Unbroken*, p. 85.

CHAPTER 31: "HE'S ALL RIGHT"

281 *A moment later Dillman emerged*: Old 666 crew statement, July 1943.

281 *He handed Jay a scrap of paper*: Jay Zeamer Jr. papers.

282 *Jay managed a grunt*: Old 666 crew statement, July 1943.

283 *"I don't move"*: Rembisz, "Wings of Valor."

283 *Then Joe closed his eyes*: *New York Times*, August 10, 1943.

284 *"He's all right"*: Old 666 crew statement, July 1943.

CHAPTER 32: DOBODURA

286 *Britton would later explain*: Britton, Oral History.

286 *Jay was not sure where he was*: Jay Zeamer Jr. papers.

286 *Then, more clearly, a husky whisper*: Ibid.

287 *Jay wanted to shout*: Ibid.

288 *In their simple elegance*: Kenney, *General Kenney Reports*, p. 259.

EPILOGUE

290 *When he awoke in the base hospital*: Zeamer letter to Victoria.

290 *Kendrick, Britton, Pugh, and Dillman*: Ibid.

290 *Three days later, as the mourning family*: Jay Zeamer Jr. papers.

291 *A few weeks later, Pudge Pugh*: Pugh letter to Sarnoskis.

293 *"It seemed almost an entrenched"*: Prados, *Islands of Destiny*, p. xv.

293 *The eminent naval historian Bruce Gamble*: Gamble, *Target: Rabaul*, p. 230.

293 *The Japanese hung on in the town*: Gamble, *Fortress Rabaul*.

296 *Finally, in February 1944*: 43rd Bomb Group Official History.

296 *Though it technically remained*: "Old 666: Fantastic Voyage of the Cursed Bomber."

296 *Old 666 was chopped up*: Ibid. See also Humphreys, "By Resolute Defense," p. 26.

297 *Now, Cooper wrote of the final flight*: *Newark Evening News*, July 22, 1946.

297 *"This reminded me more"*: Beck, "Jay Zeamer Downplays WWII Heroism."

299 *Jay Zeamer Jr. was one of only nine*: Scher, "Death Took a Holiday," p. 34.

299 *A local reporter who interviewed*: Ibid.

299 *That attitude had been encapsulated*: *Newark Evening News*, January 11, 1944.

299 *Joe's father, John, was not home*: Jim Rembisz interview.

300 *There, as Jay put it*: Scher, "Death Took a Holiday," p. 34.

300 *Although he enjoyed golf, tennis*: *Newark Evening News*, July 22, 1946.

300 *"I have to skip"*: Scher, "Death Took a Holiday," p. 34.

300 *Late in life Jay also lost*: Geoffrey Zeamer interview.

301 *He was officially credited with shooting*: *Youngstown Vindicator*, November 1943.

302 *Typical of Vaughan's droll responses*: Ibid.

303 *Thirty years earlier*: Sarnoski letter to Agnes.

303 *"Agnes, I want you to know"*: Ibid.

303 *In the same letter Pudge*: Ibid.

304 *Now, three decades later*: Turner, "Bartender Stirs Memories of WWII Mission."

AFTERWORD

306 *As he once told his wife*: Jay Zeamer Jr. papers.

306 *"I didn't know he was here"*: Rembisz, "Wings of Valor."

306 *Then, his voice cracking with emotion*: Arana-Barradas, "President Honors Pacific War's Fallen Heroes."

307 *"You can always find a way"*: Zeamer, "There's Always a Way!" p. 17.

BIBLIOGRAPHY

BOOKS

Agawa, Hiroyuki. *The Reluctant Admiral*. Tokyo: Kodansha International, 1979.

Anderson, George Olaf. *This Is My History*. Unpublished memoir.

Benefield, James Stough. *Far From the Ballpark*. Unpublished memoir.

Bergerud, Eric. M. *Fire in the Sky: The Air War in the South Pacific*. New York: Basic Books, 2009.

———. *Touched by Fire: The Land War in the South Pacific*. New York: Viking, 1996.

Birdsall, Steve. *Flying Buccaneers: The Illustrated Story of Kenney's Fifth Air Force*. New York: Doubleday, 1977.

Boothe, Clare. *Europe in the Spring*. New York: Knopf, 1941.

Boyington, Gregory. *Baa Baa Black Sheep*. New York: Bantam, 1977.

Caidin, Martin. *Flying Forts*. New York: Meredith Press, 1968.

———, and Edward Hymoff. *The Mission*. New York: Lippincott, 1964.

Camp, Dick. *Leatherneck Legends: Conversations with the Marine Corps' Old Breed*. Minneapolis: Zenith, 2006.

Claringbould, Michael. *The Forgotten Fifth*. Aerothentic Publications, 1997.

Clifford, Harold B. *The Boothbay Harbor Region 1906–1960*. Freeport, ME: Cumberland Press, 1961.

Condreras, Frank J. *The Lady from Hell: Memories of a WWII B-17 Top Turret Gunner*. North Charleston, SC: Booksurge, 2005.

Connaughton, Richard. *MacArthur and Defeat in the Philippines*. New York: Overlook Press, 2011.

Costello, John. *The Pacific War 1941–1945*. New York: Harper Perennial, 2009.

Dewan, Merrill Thomas. *Red Raider Diary*. Pittsburgh, PA: Rose Dog Books, 2009.

Dower, John W. *War Without Mercy: Race and Power in the Pacific War*. New York: Pantheon, 1986.

Drury, Bob, and Tom Clavin. *Halsey's Typhoon: The True Story of a Fighting Admiral, an Epic Storm, and an Untold Rescue*. New York: Atlantic Monthly Press, 2007.

Edmonds, Walter Dumaux. *They Fought with What They Had: The Story of the American Air Forces in the Southwest Pacific, 1941–1942*. New York: Little, Brown, 1951.

Evans, Don, Walt Gaylor, et al., *Revenge of the Red Raiders*. Boulder, CO: 22nd Bomb Group Association, 2014.

Francillon, Rene. *Japanese Aircraft of the Pacific War*. Annapolis, MD: Naval Institute Press, 1987.

Gailey, Harry A. *Bougainville, 1943–1945: The Forgotten Campaign*. Lexington: University of Kentucky Press, 2003.

Gamble, Bruce. *Fortress Rabaul: The Battle for the Southwest Pacific, January 1942–April 1943*. Minneapolis: Zenith Press, 2010.

———. *Target: Rabaul: The Allied Siege of Japan's Most Infamous Stronghold, March 1943–August 1945*. Minneapolis: Zenith Press, 2013.

Goldstein, Donald M., and Katherine V. Dillon. *The Pacific War Papers*. Washington, DC: Potomac Books, 2005.

Griffith, Thomas E., Jr., *MacArthur's Airman: General George C. Kenney and the War in the South Pacific*. Lawrence: University of Kansas Press, 1998.

Guard, Harold, with John Tring. *Pacific War Uncensored*. Philadelphia: Casemate, 2011.

Gunn, Nathaniel. *Pappy Gunn*. Bloomington, IN: AuthorHouse, 2004.

Guy, Sallie. *Flying Without Wings: The Story of Carroll Guy—A World War II Bomber Pilot.* Indianapolis: Dog Ear Publishing, 2008.

Halsey, William, and J. Bryan III. *Admiral Halsey's Story.* New York: McGraw-Hill, 1947.

Hammel, Eric. *Air War Pacific Chronology.* Pacifica, CA: Pacifica Press, 1998.

Hennessey, Juliette. *USAF Historical Studies No. 98.* Montgomery, AL: Air Force Historical Research Agency, 1952.

Hickey, Laurence. *Stories from the Fifth Air Force.* Boulder, CO: International Historical Research Associates, 2015.

Hillenbrand, Laura. *Unbroken: A World War II Story of Survival, Resilience and Redemption.* New York: Random House, 2010.

Holland, James. *Dam Busters: The True Story of the Inventors and Airmen Who Led the Devastating Raid to Smash the German Dams in 1943.* New York: Atlantic Monthly Press, 2012.

James, Clayton D. *A Time for Giants: The Politics of the American High Command in World War II.* New York: Franklin Watts, 1987.

Johnston, Mark. *Whispering Death: Australian Airmen in the Pacific War.* Crow's Nest, New South Wales: Allen & Unwin, 2011.

Keith, Phil. *Stay the Rising Sun: The True Story of the USS Lexington, Her Valiant Crew, and Changing the Course of WWII.* Minneapolis: Zenith Press, 2015.

Keneally, Thomas. *Shame and the Captives.* New York: Atria, 2015.

Kenney, George C. *General Kenney Reports: A Personal History of the Pacific War.* New York: Duell, Sloan and Pearce, 1949.

Lardner, John. *Southwest Passage: The Yanks in the Pacific.* Lincoln: University of Nebraska Press, 2013.

Lindsay, Patrick. *The Coast Watchers: The Men Behind Enemy Lines Who Saved the Pacific.* Sydney: William Heinemann, 2010.

Manchester, William. *American Caesar: Douglas MacArthur, 1880–1964.* Boston: Little, Brown, 1978.

Mason, Herbert. *The United States Air Force: A Turbulent History.* New York: Van Nostrand Reinhold, 1976.

McAulay, Lex. *Into the Dragon's Jaws: The Fifth Air Force over Rabaul.* Mesa, AZ: Champlin Fighter Museum Press, 1987.

McGee, William L. *The Solomon Campaigns 1942–1943: From Guadalcanal to Bougainville*. Santa Barbara, CA: BMC Publications, 2007.

Miller, John, Jr. *Cartwheel: The Reduction of Rabaul*. New York: National Historical Society, 1993.

Murphy, James T., with A. B. Feuer. *Skip Bombing*. Westport, CT: Praeger, 1993.

North, Oliver, with Joe Musser. *War Stories II: Heroism in the Pacific*. Washington, DC: Regnery, 2004.

Perrone, Stephen M. *World War II B-24 "Snoopers."* Somerdale, NJ: NJSG, 2001.

Prados, John. *Islands of Destiny: The Solomon Islands Campaign and the Eclipse of the Rising Sun*. New York: NAL/Penguin, 2012.

Rose, Alexander. *Men of War: The American Soldier in Combat*. New York: Random House, 2015.

Ross, Norman. *Memoirs of a Tail Gunner*. Self-published memoir, 2007.

Salecker, Gene Eric. *Fortress Against the Sun: The B-17 Flying Fortress in the Pacific*. Conshohocken, PA: Combined Publishing, 2001.

Sears, David. *Pacific Air War: How Fearless Flyboys, Peerless Aircraft, and Fast Flattops Conquered the Skies in the War with Japan*. Cambridge, MA: Da Capo Press, 2011.

Smith, Rex Alan, and Gerald A. Meehl. *Pacific War Stories*. New York: Abbeville Press, 2004.

Stanaway, John. *P-38 Lightning Aces 1942–43*. Amazon: Osprey, 2014.

Stanaway, John, and Bob Rocker. *The Eight Ballers: Eyes of the Fifth Air Force*. Atglen, PA: Schiffer Publishers, 1999.

Toll, Ian W. *The Conquering Tide: War in the Pacific Islands, 1942–1944*. New York: Norton, 2015.

Vaz, Mark. *Living Dangerously: The Adventures of Merian C. Cooper, the Creator of King Kong*. New York: Villard, 2005.

Wukovits, John. *Admiral "Bull" Halsey: The Life and Wars of the Navy's Most Controversial Commander*. New York: St. Martin's Press, 2010.

ARTICLES

Arana-Barradas, Master Sgt. Louis A. "President Honors Pacific War's Fallen Heroes," *Air Force News*, September 1995.

Ball, Charles B. "'You Can Always Find a Way to Do Anything,'" *Boston Traveler*, April 3, 1967.

Beck, Robin. "Jay Zeamer Downplays WWII Heroism That Earned Him the Medal of Honor," *Boothbay Register*, June 10, 1993.

Cartwright, Steve. "Zeamer Maintains He Was Just Doing His Job," *Kennebec Journal*, June 16, 1993.

Cohn, Art. "Z Is for Zeamer," *Liberty Magazine*, January 15, 1944.

Cromie, Robert. "Beat Up, Shot Up, but 'Fort' Downs 5 Zeroes," *Chicago Tribune*, June 21, 1943.

——. "M'Arthur Blasts Rabaul," *Chicago Tribune*, October 14, 1943.

Crow, Jonathan. "Dr. Seuss Draws Anti-Japanese Cartoons During WWII," *Open Culture*, August 20, 2014.

Darnton, John. "Swamp Ghosts," *Smithsonian Magazine*, October 2007.

Davenport, Walter. "Impregnable Pearl Harbor," *Collier's*, June 14, 1941.

DeStefano, Dana. "Memorial Honors Medal Winners," *Scranton Times*, July 9, 2006.

Dunn, Richard L. "The Search for General Walker: New Insights," *Air Power History*, Fall 2014.

DuPre, Flint. "USAF and the Medal of Honor," *Air Force Magazine*, March 1967.

Durdin, Tillman. "Skip Bombing Sank Cruiser at Kavieng," *New York Times*, April 1, 1943.

"Dying Flier Downs 2 Japanese Planes," *New York Times*, August 10, 1943.

Flannery, Joseph X. "Irish Heroes Remembered," *Scranton Times*, March 16, 1999.

——. "Rare Honors for Rare People," *Scranton Times*, November 23, 1996.

Futch, Michael. "Members of 5th Army Air Force 43rd Bomb Group Hold Reunion in Fayetteville," *Fayetteville Observer*, September 22, 2013.

Glodek, Sgt. Dan. "Their Last Measure of Devotion," *Lackawanna Historical Society Journal*, Summer 2006.

——. "The Other Medal of Honor Story: Remembering Lt. Joseph R. Sarnoski," *Lackawanna Historical Society Journal*, Winter 2005.

Hanley, Charles J. "An Old Pilot Grieves Bombardier's Death," *Associated Press*, September 4, 1995.

Haskins, Mardell. "Flying B-24s in WWII," *Southwest Aviation Report*, August 2013.

Hastings, H. T. "No Survivors," *Saturday Evening Post*, May 1943.

"Hero Is Now Aviation Engineer," *Newark Evening News*, July 22, 1946.

Humphreys, Ned. "By Resolute Defense—At Price of His Life," *Crosshairs*, June 1990.

Hyde, Ed. "Medal of Honor Mission of Capt. Zeamer's 'Screwball' Aces," *Stag Magazine*, February 1965.

"Jay Zeamer, a Decorated Pilot in World War II, Dies at 88," *Los Angeles Times*, March 26, 2007.

Kashuba, Cheryl A. "Remembering the Valor of Four Area Sons," *Times Tribune* (PA), July 12, 2009.

King, Lydia. "Some First Hand Observations on Combat Stress," *Aging & Mental Health*, March 2007.

Kostka, Del C. "Air Reconnaissance in the Second World War," Military History Online.

"LBJ's Lies About His War Record," History News Network, July 18, 2001.

Lindbloom, Roland E. "Jersey Honor Medals Listed," *New York Times*, January 5, 1946.

Lundstrom, John B. "Frank Jack Fletcher Got a Bum Rap," *Naval History Magazine*, Summer 1992.

Manson, Norma. "2 Aircrew Students Already Have Seen a Lot of War; One Got '10 or 15' Japs," *Youngstown Vindicator*, December 1944.

McMillan, Kelsey. "Aerial Gunner Training," Bomber Legends, thebombercommand.info.

"Mortally Wounded Airman Sticks to Guns, Downs Two," *Springfield* (MA) *Republican*, August 10, 1943.

"Nebraskans at War," Parts I and II, *Nebraska History: A Quarterly Magazine*, January–March 1944 and April–June 1944, Nebraska State Historical Society.

"Old Pilot, Young Bombardier Together Again at Gravesite," *Maine Sunday Telegram*, September 3, 1995.

"Orange Airman Awarded Congressional Medal," *Newark Evening News*, January 7, 1944.

"Parents See Air Hero Receive Medal," *Omaha World Herald*, January 7, 1944.

Rayner, P. A. "Airmen Fight for Lives in Shark Infested Waters," *New York Tele-graph*, February 3, 1943.

———. "Big Fires in New Raid Add to Rabaul Desolation," *New York Telegraph*, January 3, 1943.

———. "Nine Ships in Jap Convoy Hit," *New York World Telegraph*, April 3, 1943.

"Richmond Wife of Slain Aviator Receives Award," *Catholic Virginian*, February 1944.

Scher, Rhoda. "Death Took a Holiday," *The Oranges and Montclair*, August 1947.

"Sr. Commander Vaughan Veteran of 73 Missions," *Youngstown Vindicator*, November 1943.

Tremaine, Frank. "Admiral Halsey on Bougainville," United Press, November 16, 1943.

Turner, Cal. "Bartender Stirs Memories of WWII Mission," *Sunday Patriot-News*, August 4, 1985.

"Valor: Battle over Bougainville," *Air Force Magazine*, December 1985.

Veysey, Arthur. "Kenney Jolts the Japs," *Chicago Sunday Tribune*, September 24, 1944.

Wagner, Bill. "Sarnoski WWII Mementos Donated to Merli Center," *Scranton Times*, July 29, 2007.

Wiecks, Michael J. "The 1918 Influenza Epidemic in Cumberland County, Pennsylvania," *Cumberland County History*, Summer/Winter 2005.

Wilson, Edward O. "A Manual for Life," *New York Times Book Review*, November 9, 2014.

"Without 'Melodrama,'" *Newark Evening News*, January 5, 1944.

"World Battlefronts: For the Honor of God," *Time*, January 18, 1943.

Zeamer, Lt. Col. Jay, Jr. "There's Always a Way!" *American Magazine*, January 1945.

OTHER

Airforce.togetherweserved.com.

Air Information Bulletin Number 19, U.S. Air Force archives.

"B-17 Communication Equipment," airpages.ru.

"B-17E 'Lucy' Serial Number 41-2666," pacificwrecks.com.

"B-17 Flight Controls," warbirdinformationexchange.org.

Biographical Sketch of Jeremiah Zeamer (Zeamer Family Papers).

Bragg, Russell M. "First Bombing Mission," kensmen.com.

"Brigadier General Kenneth N. Walker," pacificwrecks.com.

Britton, J. T., Oral History, American Airpower Heritage Museum, Midland, TX, March 1, 1999.

"Capt. Lindsey on Skip Bombing," kensmen.com.

Cicala, Roger. "The Most Honored Photograph," petapixel.com.

Drea, Edward J. "New Guinea," U.S. Army Center of Military History.

Fletcher, Arthur A. "Penetrating the Philippine Blockade," kensmen.com.

43rd Bomb Group Official History.

Gammill, Ed. "From Boston to Sydney on the Queen Mary," kensmen.com.

"Japanese Submarines Prowl the U.S. Pacific Coastline in 1941," historynet .com.

"Jay Zeamer, Jr.," arlingtoncemetery.net.

Jay Zeamer Jr. papers (Zeamer Family Papers).

Jay Zeamer's Training and Wartime Experiences, as told to his brother, R. Jere Zeamer (Zeamer Family Papers).

Kostka, Del C. "Air Reconnaissance in the Second World War," Military History Online.

"Lt. Col. John T. Britton," togetherweserved.com.

"MacArthur Deserts 'The Battling Bastards of Bataan' and Escapes to Australia," pacificwar.org.au.

"Major Scott on Skip Bombing," kensmen.com.

Manuel, Lt. Col. Kent L. "General Kenney As a Strategic War Leader," research report submitted to the faculty of the Air War College, Maxwell AFB, AL, April 1996.

"The Mapping Mission," airforce.togetherweserved.com.

Marjorie Zeamer biography (Zeamer Family Papers).

"Mission over Buka," Jay Zeamer Jr. (Zeamer Family Papers).

"The Most Decorated Single Aircrew of World War II," theirfinesthour.blogspot .com, June 16, 2013.

"Old 666: Fantastic Voyage of the Cursed Bomber," Parts I and II, specialopera
tions.com.

"Pennsylvania at War 1941–1945," Pennsylvania Historical and Museum Commission, 1946.

"Pennsylvania's Second Year at War," Pennsylvania Historical and Museum
Commission, 1945.

Rembisz, Jim. "Wings of Valor II: Jay Zeamer and Joseph Sarnoski," homeof
heroes.com.

Report of the Borough of Carlisle, PA, 1922.

"Résumé of Skip Bombing," kensmen.com.

Schoger, H. G. "They Did Culver Proud," Culver Academies brochure.

Sketch of Early Life of Lt. Col. Jay Zeamer Jr., by Mrs. Jay Zeamer (mother)
(Zeamer Family Papers).

Sketch of Jay Zeamer Sr. (Zeamer Family Papers).

SS *Argentina* passenger manifest, January 23, 1942.

Stahl, George R. "A Monkey Rides My Shoulder." Unpublished reminiscences.

"Tugboat Annie," pacificwrecks.com.

"22nd Bombardment Group," historyofwar.org.

22nd Bomb Group Official History.

"22nd Bomb Group: The Red Raiders in Australia During WW2," ozatwar
.com.

WWII Air War. Washington, DC: National Archives and Records Administration. Six-DVD set.

YouTube interview with Jay Zeamer, 2007.

Zeamer, Jeremiah. "John Zeamer and His Descendants" from *Biographical Annals of Cumberland County, Pennsylvania*, J. H. Beers & Co., 1905.

INDEX

An *n* following a page number refers to the note section.

A6M3 fighter plane, 265
A-20 Havoc bombers, 138
Abenaki Indians, 12
Able, Johnnie, 191–92, 203, 212, 215, 230, 231, 250, 254, 255, 260, 269, 272, 274, 279, 282, 285, 286, 287, 289, 291, 301, 302
Admiralty Islands, 225, 248, 301
Advanced Flight School, 111, 243
African Americans, 128–29
Air Cadets, 243
Air Force (film), 193
Air Force News, 306
Air Force, U.S., 287, 302, 304
Air Force Reserves, 302
Air Power, 163*n*
air-sea rescues, 82*n*
Air Service, U.S., 36
    Engineering School of, 114
Akagi, 100
Albuquerque, N.M., 296
American Caesar (Manchester), 60, 66*n*, 145*n*
American Expeditionary Force, 27
American Pacific Fleet, 48, 189
amphibious landings, 92, 100, 102
Andrews, Frank, 113
Anschluss, 20
Argentina, SS, 61–63, 180

Arlington National Cemetery, 306
Army, U.S., 213
    African-American troops in, 128–29
    Center of Military History of, 253
    field manual of, 226
    2nd Raider Regiment of, 292
Army Air Corps, 23–25, 28, 32, 35–36, 47, 75, 115, 140, 188, 192, 302
    Advanced Flight School of, 24–25
    Aircraft Armorer course of, 32
    Bombsight Maintenance course of, 32
    Chemical Warfare course of, 32
    Flight School of, 23
    Primary Flying School of, 24
    Tactical School of, 114, 139
    see also Army Air Forces, U.S.
Army Air Forces, U.S. (USAAF), 4, 28–29, 44–45, 69, 84, 119, 128, 136*n*, 138, 146, 149, 182, 212, 215, 218, 225, 231, 243, 244, 297, 300
    beginning of, 36; *see also* Army Air Corps
    "Bomber Mafia" of, 146
    Caribbean Defense Command of, 112
    coveralls issued by, 106
    crews lost to accidents in, 65
    Japanese records vs. records from, 282*n*
    see also specific Bomb Groups

343

Army Air Services, U.S., 27, 114, 192, 234
Army Artillery Corps, U.S., 35
Army Corps of Engineers, 292
    ROTC program of, 19
Army Infantry Corps, U.S., 35
Army of the Potomac, 187
Army Reserves, 20–21, 303
Arnold, Henry H. "Hap," 36, 69, 116, 179,
    297–98, 301
Art of War (Sun Tzu), 186
Ashburn, Doyle, 11
assassination, 226
Associated Press, 203
Astro Tracker Dome, 256
atom bombs, 105n
Auschwitz, gas chambers at, 40
Austin, Bernard, 292n
Australia, 42, 53, 56, 60, 63, 64, 67–70, 76–80,
    83, 92–93, 98, 99, 102, 103, 106, 109,
    115–16, 119, 120, 121, 133, 138, 140, 142,
    168, 181, 190, 193, 203, 210, 221, 296
    hospitality in, 76–77
    immigration restrictions in, 128
    Japanese invasion of, 131, 133
    POWs from, 73–74, 129
Australian Imperial Forces (AIF), 77
Austria, 20
Axis powers, 66
Ayres, Lew, 224

B-17 Flying Fortresses, 28, 37, 38, 60–61, 67n,
    72, 74n, 75, 101, 110, 122, 127, 129, 144,
    147, 149, 150, 152, 162, 191, 201–2, 251,
    259, 265
    as able to "surf," 278
    attack on Rabaul by, 75
    ball turret of, 215, 216–17
    Boeing's construction of, 45–46
    Clark Airfield bombing and, 61
    communication equipment on, 208
    deadly fighting qualities of, 296
    interior of, 193–94
    Japanese respect for, 85
    lack of trained crews for, 221
    machine guns on, 207–8, 214
    maneuverability of, 151
    mortality rate for crews of, 216
    new series of, 296
    Norden bombsights on, 47–48
    nose as most vulnerable point of, 217–18,
     246
    piss pipes on, 217

reconnaissance flights of, 153–54
Zeamer's admiration for, 46–48, 111, 151,
    180
see also specific planes
B-18 Bolos, 38, 39, 48, 49, 57, 58, 61
    anti-submarine patrols of, 243
B-24 Liberators, 72, 111, 162, 221, 231, 232, 278
    speed of, 233
B-25 Mitchells, 138, 167, 197
    Gunn's modification of, 138
    in raids on Tokyo, 87
B-26 Marauders ("Widow Makers"), 36–37, 39,
    46–47, 50, 53, 57, 58, 78, 80, 85, 101, 108,
    109, 111, 142, 151, 223, 230, 278
    in Battle of Midway, 99–100
    in flight to Australia, 65
    landings with, 38–39
    in raids on Rabaul, 79, 82, 84, 85–86, 107
    takeoffs with, 37–38, 51, 106, 109
    in tropical storms, 84
Bagana, Mount, 1–2, 264
Baja peninsula, 53
Ballale, 227
ball turret gunner, 215, 216–17
Baltimore, Md., 32
Bangor, Maine, 33, 61, 63
Bataan, 67, 137
Bataan Death March, 60
Bate, Fred, 35
Bates, William, 21–22
Bates Method, 21–23
Battle Damage Assessment (BDA), 140
battle fatigue, 253
Battle of Britain, 35
Bayliss, Frank, 26
Bellows Field, 57–58
belly gunner, 215, 216–17
Benn, Bill, 140–44, 146, 147–48, 150, 161–62,
    164, 175, 176–77, 182, 220, 233, 262
    death of, 177, 185
Bethlehem Shipbuilding Corporation, 193
Bethlehem Steel Company, 193
Bismarck Archipelago, 58, 69, 70, 100, 120
Bismarck Sea, 70, 195, 202, 231, 232, 301
Bismarck Sea, Battle of, 197–99, 200, 243, 296
    Japanese losses in, 198–99
Black Jack bomber, 144, 148–49, 150–51, 178,
    219
Blanche Bay, 155
Bleasdale, Jack, 162
Blitz Buggy, 230
"Bloody Track," 101

Blues in the Nite, 219–20
Boeing Airplane Company, 28, 44–45
    B-17s constructed by, 45–46, 191
bombardiers, 28
Bomber Command, 106
Bomb Group Headquarters, 221
Bombsight Maintenance Course, 243
Booth, John Wilkes, 226
Boothbay Harbor, Maine, 12–13, 259, 300, 304, 306
Boston, Mass., 48, 49
Bougainville Island, 1–4, 159, 165, 169, 172, 173, 199, 227, 228, 237, 239, 255, 259, 279, 282n
    Australian coastwatchers in, 240, 251
    Japanese defense of, 238–39, 241, 252
    reconnaissance of, 237, 240–47, 248, 250–53, 257, 262, 264–65, 269–79, 287, 290, 291–92, 301
    reinforcements sent to, 238
    U.S. invasion and capture of, 292n, 293
    U.S. planning for invasion of, 236–37, 238–39, 251, 291–92
Boy Scouts of America, 14–15, 20, 24, 33, 108, 158, 299
Brandon, Henry, 222
Brett, George, 67–68, 69, 111–12, 113, 116, 136
Brisbane, 64, 65, 68, 76, 78, 92, 93, 115–16, 119, 121, 133, 143, 145, 220, 234, 240
Britton, John "J. T.," 242–43, 244, 246, 250, 256, 262, 269, 271, 275, 276, 282, 283, 285–86, 290, 301, 304
Britton, Josephine, 304
Brooklyn Dodgers, 157n
Brougher, William, 60
Browning, John, 213
Bryn Mawr University, 290
Buffalo News, 105
Buin, 227, 238, 239, 241, 262
Buka airstrip, 1
Buka Island, 1, 2, 238–39, 241, 251–52, 255–62, 267, 282n
    enemy fighters on, 260–61
    reconnaissance of, 252–53, 254, 255–62, 257, 263–64, 287, 291–92, 301
Buka Passage, 251, 254, 259, 260
Bull Run, First Battle of, 186
Bulova, Arde, 121
Buna, 101, 102, 103, 117, 119–20, 122, 139, 152, 156, 159, 160n, 167–68, 172, 195, 244, 245, 301
Burke, Arleigh, 292n

Burma, 235, 304
Bushido, 43, 85

Cairns, Australia, 132
California, 50, 52, 191, 303
California, University of, at Davis, 242
Cape Endiaidere, 285
Cape Gloucester, 196
Cape Torokina, 239
Carbondale, Pa., 29–30, 31, 193, 299, 303
Carlisle, Pa., 10–11, 30
Caroline Islands, 72
carpet bombing, 147
Catalina Flying Boats, 39, 68, 74, 80, 82n
Cat in the Hat, The (Dr. Seuss), 105
censorship, 57, 59
Charles, Thomas, 177, 182
Chennault, Claire, 235
Chicago, USS, 167
China, 40, 41, 49, 135, 235, 304
China-Burma-India Theater, 304
Choiseul, 236
Churchill, Winston, 168
Cicero, 300
Civil War, U.S., 186–87, 226
Clark Airfield, 60, 61
code breakers, 93, 99, 196, 201
Collier's, 49
Confederacy (aerial reconnaissance used on), 187
Congress, U.S., 66, 242–43
Congressional Medal of Honor Society, 301
Cooper, Merian C., 234–35, 297
Coral Sea, 75, 93, 94, 167, 232, 240
Coral Sea, Battle of the, 95–97, 99, 100, 102, 103, 116, 152
Corregidor, 59, 60, 67, 190
Cossacks, 235
Crowe, Jonathan, 105n
Culver, Henry Harrison, 17
Culver Military Academy, 15–16, 17–19, 211
Culver Rifles Honor Guard, 17–18, 24
Curtin, John, 78, 93

Darwin, Australia, 78, 128
Davenport, Walter, 50
Daytona Raceway, 26
Denver, University of, 215
Diamond Head, 57
Dillman, Forrest, 215, 217–18, 231, 256, 258, 261, 265, 275, 281, 282, 283, 290, 301, 303
Dinah, 264, 267
Distinguished Service Cross, 301

Divine, Colonel, 64, 108–10

Dobodura, 172, 197, 280–86, 289, 291

Doolittle, Jimmy, 87, 94, 98, 113, 115, 167, 227, 297

Dower, John, 42n

Draft Bill (1940), 242

Dr. Seuss (Theodore Geisel), 105–5

Duignan, Terence, 82n

Durand airstrip, 232

Dutch East Indies, 53, 232

Dwight Divine, 53

Dyminski, Hank, 189, 230, 242, 243

dysentery, 118, 204, 235

Eager Beavers, 203–4, 205, 207–9, 212–15, 217, 218, 221–23, 230–31, 307
  aircraft of, see Old 666
  Bougainville Island reconnaissance and, 241–47, 248, 250–54, 264–65, 285–86, 291–92
  Buka Island reconnaissance and, 252–53, 254, 255–62, 263–64, 285–86
  early reconnaissance flights of, 225, 248–50
  as most highly decorated combat crew, 301
  outlaw reputation of, 221, 224, 225–26
  in raid on Kavieng, 231

Earhart, Amelia, 68n

Education Department, Puerto Rico, 10

8th Air Force, 296, 134, 135, 140

8th Reconnaissance Squadron ("Eight Ballers"), 153, 154, 188, 191, 210, 240, 251, 296

11th Bomb Group, 175n

Eliot, T. S., 183

Empress Augusta Bay, 2, 239–40, 252, 261, 292

England, 79, 131, 168

Europe, 79–80, 134, 225
  U.S. primary focus on war in, 179

European Theater, 79, 117, 135, 146

5th Air Force, 134–36, 137, 139–40, 153, 163n, 243, 296
  Bomber Command of, 242
  dismal bombing record of, 141, 142–44

5th Bomber Group, Operations Command, 251

Fiji, 70, 98, 100, 142, 153

Finschhafen, 180, 182, 189

Finschhafen, Battle of, 301

First French Republic, 186

Fletcher, Frank Jack, 91–92, 94, 95, 240

Florida, 302

Flying Fortress (film), 193

Flying Tigers squadron, 235

Fort Dix, 23

Fortress Rabaul (Gamble), 67n

43rd Bomb Group, 28, 32, 36–37, 46–47, 48, 61, 110–11, 120, 122, 123–27, 130, 139, 146, 154, 176–77, 178, 180, 191, 193, 194, 200, 205, 223, 229–30, 231, 232, 241–42, 243, 248–49, 253
  on Argentina, 61–63
  flight crews relieved from, 221
  403rd Squadron of, 61–62, 181
  headquarters of, 237
  loss of planes and crew for, 176, 178
  90th Bomb Group's rivalry with, 232–33
  official Combat Diary of, 173, 197–98, 233–34
  Official History of, 296
  Operations Hut of, 224, 230, 241
  in raids on Rabaul, 173–74, 204, 205–7
  63rd Squadron of, 142–44, 148, 149, 161, 164, 179, 219, 233
  64th Squadron of, 162, 251
  65th Squadron of, 200, 201, 203, 204, 205, 211, 249
  skip-bombing tactic of, 139–40, 142, 143–44, 146, 147–48, 150–51, 161, 179, 220, 229, 233, 243, 249
  Zeamer's crew from, see Eager Beavers

Four Feathers, The (film), 235

Fourth Hague Peace Conference of 1907, 226

4th Marine Raider Battalion, 292

France, 115, 186, 187–88

Gamble, Bruce, 67n, 116, 296

Garbutt Field, 76, 78, 79, 87, 99, 103, 105, 108–9, 110n

Gasmata, 74, 82

Gavutu, 165

Gazelle Peninsula, 73

Geisel, Theodore (Dr. Seuss), 104–5

General Motors Tank Proving Grounds, 290

George Washington Parke Custis, USS, 187

Georgia National Guard, 234

German submarines, 62

Germany, Nazi, 20, 23, 33, 40, 41, 46, 66, 68–69, 77, 93, 116, 120, 135, 142, 168

Gilbert Islands, 166

Glenview, Ill., 24, 39

Goebbels, Joseph, 66n

Grant, USS, 56–57

Great Britain, 23, 40, 135
Great Depression, 14, 30, 45
Guadalcanal, 3, 92, 101, 102, 107, 121, 139, *141*,
    150, 166, 167, 168, 172, 173, 240, 241,
    261, 267*n*
  battle for, 238
  Japanese invasion and occupation of, 97–98,
    152, 188
  Japanese retreat from, 165, 167–68, 195
  U.S. counterinvasion of, 97–98, 159
Guam, 53
Gunn, Paul Irvin "Pappy," 137–38, 197

Halsey, William, 94, 166–67, 168, 169, 172–73,
    200, 227, 236, 237, 238, 239–40, 261,
    267*n*, 291, 292, 293
Hawaii, 42, 48, 53, 56–59, 60, 83, 94, 98, 99,
    109, 153
  anti-submarine patrols off islands of, 243
  reconnaissance of Japanese submarines in,
    57–58, 61
Hawthorne, Harry, 224, 241
Henderson Field, 102, 165, 188, 227
Hershey bars, 217
Hickam Airfield, 48, 57, 58, 64
high-altitude bombing, 161
Hirohito, Japanese Emperor, 40, 199
Hiroshima, Japan, atomic bombing of, 105*n*
Hiryu, 100
Historical Study No. 9, 128
Hitler, Adolf, 20, 33, 34, 40, 46, 66*n*, 168, 188
Honolulu, Hawaii, 48, 58, 306
Hornet, USS, 87
Horton Hears a Who! (Dr. Seuss), 105*n*
hot-air balloons, 186–87
Howland Island, 68*n*
Hughes, Howard, 84
Hughes Aircraft, 300
Huon Gulf, 68, 152
Huon Peninsula, 180
Hustad, Carl, 173
Huxley, Aldous, 22

Imperial Army, Japanese, 73, 85, 101, 152, 190,
    196
Imperial General Command, Japanese, 52*n*, 68,
    70, 74, 92, 168–69, 195
Imperial General Headquarters, Japanese, 41, 95,
    100, 131, 153, 165, 238
Imperial General Staff, 95
Imperial Marines, Japanese, 190–91
Imperial Naval Command, Japanese, 199

Imperial Navy, Japanese, 41, 74, 85, 86, 92–93,
    97, 109, 160, 163*n*, 195, 196, 231, 233, 261
  Air Service of, 48
  Combined Fleet of, 49, 72, 98, 100, 102, 189
Imperial Navy General Staff, Japanese, 98
Imperial South Seas Force, Japanese, 42, 56, 61,
    69, 70, 72
India, 135, 235
Indianapolis 500, 26
Indian Ocean, 61, 63
Indonesia, 168
Inoue, Shigeyoshi, 94, 95
International Correspondence School, 27
internment camps, 105*n*
intertropical front, 83
Ipswich, 306
Iran, 140
Islands of Destiny (Prados), 293

Jackson Field, 102, 128–29, 162, 201–2, 205,
    210, 212, 219, 224, 249, 250, 289
Japan, Japanese, 40–43, 46, 66, 78, 79, 86, 91,
    120–21, 147, 168, 305
  aircraft of, 84–85; *see also* Zeros
  Australian POWs of, 73–74, 129
  codes used by, 93, 99, 196
  in defense of Bougainville, 238–39, 241, 251,
    252
  defensive attacks of, from Rabaul, 82–83, 84,
    85–86, 155–56, 162
  Guadalcanal invaded and occupied by, 97–98,
    152, 188
  as ill-equipped for night combat, 83, 161
  invasion of Australia by, 131, 133
  losses of, 100, 102, 152, 159–60, 165, 167–68,
    198–99
  Midway assault planned by, 98–100
  New Guinea holdings of, 151, 180, 234
  Pearl Harbor attack of, 48–49, 50, 57, 59, 60,
    66, 91, 92, 93, 95, 100, 159, 167, 188, 190,
    192, 226, 228, 235
  Philippines invaded by, 59–61, 190
  Port Moresby air raids by, 128, 129–30, 132,
    164, 176
  Port Moresby assaults planned by, 92–95,
    100–102
  prisoners of war from, 268
  Rabaul occupied by, 68–74, 129, 139, 159,
    205–7
  reconnaissance flights of, 236
  in retreat from New Guinea, 122, 173
  Southern Strategy of, 153, 169, 200

Japan, Japanese (*cont.*)
  submarines of, 52–53, 57–58, 61
  territory held by, *125, 141, 294–95*
  territory surrendered by, 165, 167–68
  trade embargo on, 49
  U.S. stereotypes of, 86–87, 104–5
Java, 190
Java Sea, 222
Jeffers, Robinson, 256
JN-25, 93
Joerg, Norton, 14
Johnson, Lyndon Baines, 109*n*–10*n*
Johnson, Van, 297
Johnston, Ruby, 243–45, 246, 249, 250, 252,
    256, 258, 259, 262, 266, 267, 270, 271,
    273, 274, 275, 279, 282, 283–84, 287,
    289, 291, 301, 302, 304
Joint Chiefs of Staff, 36, 93, 168, 239
jungle rot, 118
Justinian I, Byzantine Emperor, 72

Kaga, 100
Kansas City Star, 105
Kavieng, New Ireland, 154, 225, 231
Kelley, Harvey, 11
Kelly, Colin, 174, 175*n*
Kendrick, George "Cowboy," 1, 4, 191, 192,
    208, 210, 214, 215, 225, 231, 246,
    250–51, 252, 254, 261, 262, 264, 265,
    271, 275, 276, 282, 283, 290, 301,
    302-3
Keneally, Thomas, 43
Kenney, George Churchill, 114–21, 127, 130,
    134–38, 139–42, 143–44, 145–46, 147,
    149–50, 152, 153, 160–61, 162–63, 164,
    169, 173, 175, 176–77, 178–79, 188, 196,
    199, 200, 201, 220, 231–33, 234–35, 237,
    240, 243, 288, 296, 297–98
Kila Kila fighter strip, 92, 117, 127, 130, 149
King, Ernest J., 66, 93, 99, 135, 168, 169, 172
King Kong (film), 123, 235, 297
Kiriwina Island, 82*n*
"Knights of the Sky," 26
Knox, Frank, 168, 227
Kokoda Track, 101, 102, 119, 120, 131, 152
kokutai, 41
Kondo, Nobutake, 160
Koolaus mountains, 48, 50
Korean War, 302, 303
Kosciuszko's Squadron, 235, 297
Krakatoa, 72
Krell, Walt, 38–39, 225

Lae, 68, 69, 82, 103, 108, 109, 129, 160, 167,
    178, 195, 196–97, 198, 199, 211, 235, 292,
    301
Lakunai airdrome, 73
Lamour, Dorothy, 123
Langley, Va., 114
Langley Field, 28, 33, 35, 37, 39, 40, 47, 48, 49,
    50, 63, 111, 180, 192, 194
Lardner, John, 78, 131
Lardner, Ring, 78
Latvia, 235
Lawson, Ted, 297
League of Nations, 70
Lee, Robert E., 187*n*
Levin, Meyer, 174–75
Lexington, USS, 94, 95
Lien, Harris, 244
Life, 199
Lincoln, Abraham, 186, 226
Lindsey, Paul, 222
Logan Airport, 19
"Lost Plane Procedure," 64
Lowry Field, Colo., 32
Lucy, see Old 666
Lufbery, Raoul, 26, 27, 286
Luke, Frank, 26, 297
Lunga Point, 267*n*
Luzon, 60, 61

M2 Browning, 213–14
MacArthur, Arthur, Jr., 66
MacArthur, Arthur, IV, 67*n*
MacArthur, Douglas, 59–60, 65–68, 69, 74*n*,
    76, 93, 105, 109, 110*n*, 111–12, 113–14,
    115–16, 118, 119, 121, 131, 134, 135–37,
    139–40, 145, 152, 160*n*, 163, 168, 169–70,
    172, 173, 177, 188, 190, 196, 199–200,
    231–32, 236, 237, 238, 292, 293
McCook, Neb., 215
McCullar, Ken, 144, 147–51, 156, 158, 179,
    233*n*, 262
  death of, 218, 219–20, 221
  in off-the-book raids on Rabaul, 178
  reputation of, 149–50
  Zeamer and, 177–78
Macfadden, Bernarr, 22
MacVane, John, 35
Madang, 159, 178, 196, 230, 236
Mainz, Siege of (1795), 186
malaria, 118, 242
Malaya, 77
Malaysia, 53

Manchester, William, 60, 66n, 145n
Manila, 59, 137, 138, 190
Manila Bay, 41, 59
Manus Island, 301
Mareeba Airbase, 182
Marines, U.S., 3, 102, 107, 152, 167, 168, 172,
    237, 238, 239, 240, 292
Marne, First Battle of the, 187
Marne, Second Battle of the, 11
Marshall, George, 36, 59, 66, 67n, 93, 111, 113,
    172
Marshall Islands, 166
Martin, Glenn, 38
Massachusetts Institute of Technology (M.I.T.),
    19–20, 23, 47, 114, 290, 300
Maxwell Field, 24–25, 39
Mechanicsburg, PA, 303
Melbourne, Australia, 65, 68, 69n, 133
Merchant Marines, 13, 63
Merchants Association of Orange, 299
Mexican Railway, 10
Mexico, 10, 52, 234
Michigan, 290
Midland, Tex., 304
Midway, 3, 98–100
Midway, Battle of, 99–100, 102, 109n, 159,
    188–89, 199, 293
Milne Bay, 102, 103, 172, 190, 197, 244, 245,
    302
Mindanao, 60, 67n, 74n
Mitchell, John, 227
Mitchell, William "Billy," 36, 89
Mitsubishi, 84
Mitsubishi G4M bombers, 73
Mojave Desert, 53
Montgolfier, Jacques-Étienne, 186
Montgolfier, Joseph-Michel, 186
Moore, Woody, 197–98
Morison, Samuel Eliot, 227
mosquitoes, 126
Moye, Albert, 80, 82
Muroc Dry Lake, 58
Murrow, Edward R., 35, 40
Mussolini, Benito, 66n
Myrtle Beach, S.C., 192, 302

Nakajima, Chikuhei, 41, 42
Nakamura, Mitsugi, 105n
Napoleon I, Emperor of France, 112
Nassau Bay, 292
National Cemetery, Visalia, Calif., 303
National Memorial Cemetery, Honolulu, 305

Naumann, Ernie, 251
Naval Intelligence, 152, 251
Naval Operations, U.S., 66, 135
Navy, U.S., 3, 19, 23, 27, 47, 52n, 66, 98, 137,
    172, 196
Navy Flight School, 21
Nazis, see Germany, Nazi
Nebraska, 303
Neosho, USS, 94n
Netherlands, 168
Newark, N.J., 11
Newark News, 299
New Britain, 69, 72, 74, 74n, 82, 107, 130, 154,
    162, 168, 169, 172–73, 177, 196, 225, 248,
    251
New Caledonia, 70, 98, 100, 153, 234
New Cumberland, Pa., 303
New Georgia, 159, 239, 241, 249, 267n, 292
New Guinea, 3, 68–69, 70, 74, 75, 82n, 92,
    96, 98, 100–102, 107, 109, 117, 119–21,
    122–23, 131, 135, 139, 151, 153, 163n,
    159, 167, 168–69, 172, 178, 180, 185, 194,
    195–96, 198–99, 217, 223, 231, 234, 236,
    237, 241, 244, 254, 277–78, 293, 296, 306
  Japanese retreat from, 122, 173
  northern coast of, 177, 188, 201, 232, 292
  see also Papua New Guinea
New Guinea Volunteer Rifles, 101
New Ireland, 82, 154, 225, 231
New Jersey, 50
New York, N.Y., 11, 61, 62
New York Times, The, 199, 283
New York Yankees, 157n
New Zealand, 65, 168, 236
Nimitz, Chester, 66–67, 92, 94, 97–98, 99, 101–2,
    166, 169, 172, 200, 226–27, 236, 239, 293
19th Bomb Group, 60
90th Bombardment Group, 162, 197, 205, 232
  combat record of, 233
  43rd's rivalry with, 232–33
Norden, Carl, 47
Norden bombsights, 47–48, 140, 143, 147
Normandie, 62, 181
North Africa, 77, 79–80, 168, 200, 243

Oahu, Hawaii, 48, 50, 57, 98
Ohio, 36–37, 38, 111
Old 666, 217–18
  A6M3 fighter attack on, 265–73
  bombing runs of, 230–31
  Bougainville reconnaissance and, 241–47, 248,
    250–54, 264–65, 285–86, 291–92

Old 666 (*cont.*)
  Buka Island reconnaissance and, 252–53, 254,
    255–62, 263–64, 285–86
  cannon shell damage to, 269–71
  crew of, *see* Eager Beavers
  cursed reputation of, 211
  in final landing at Dobodura, 285–88, 289,
    291–92
  first bombing mission of, 229
  flight test of, 224, 241
  in flight to Dobodura, 280–86
  gun mounted on nose of, 218
  Japanese After Action report on, 277
  longest continuous dogfight held by, 287
  machine guns installed in, 213–15
  as most heavily armed bomber, 218
  reassignment of, 296
  as reconnaissance plane, 210, 211, 225, 230
  restoration of, 212, 221–22
  in return to New Guinea, 277–78
  as salvaged from scrap heap, 210–13
  Zero attacks on, 273–76
Old Man, The, 230
Ooki, Yoshio, 263–64, 265, 267, 277
Open Culture (Crowe), 105*n*
Operation Cartwheel, 168, 169, *170,* 173, 199,
    239, 292, 301
Operation Cherry Blossom, *170,* 239
Operation Typhoon, 40
Operation Vengeance, 227
Operation Watchtower, 102
Orange, N.J., 9, 11, 12, 290, 299
Oregon Trail, 10
Oro Bay, 285
Overland Whippet, 18–19
Owen, Mickey, 157*n*
Owen Stanley Range, 80, 83, 101, 107, 122, 127,
    131, 149, 161, 177, 195, 217, 230, 234,
    249, 255–62, 280, 289

P-38 Lightning, 153
Pacific Ocean, currents in, 278
Pacific Theater, 3, 43, 53, *54–55,* 66, 78,
    109*n*–10*n*, 111, 136, 168, 176, 225, 232
  Allied war resources distributed in, 135
  Central, 169
  number of U.S. planes in, 116–17
  reconnaissance work in, 185–86, 188
  South, 166, 227
  Southwest, *71,* 72–73, 75, 80, 120, 134, 149,
    160, 163, 169, 178, 188
  see also specific areas and battles

Panama Canal Zone, 111
Pan American Airways, 235
Papua, Gulf of, 68, 249
Papua Bay, 224
Papua New Guinea, *see* New Guinea
Papuan peninsula, 80
Papuans, 69, 101, 122–23, 236, 245
parafrag bombing, 146
Patch, Alexander, 167
Pearl Harbor, Hawaii, 36, 41, 48, 57, 68, 93,
    105, 137, 166, 174, 226, 240, 305
  as supposedly impregnable naval base,
    49–50
  Japanese attack on, 48–49, 50, 57, 59, 60, 66,
    91, 92, 93, 95, 100, 159, 167, 188, 190,
    192, 226, 228, 235
Pease, Harl, 74*n*
Pennsylvania, 56
Pensacola, Fla., 137, 244
Pentagon, 297
Peppard, Harold, 22, 23
Pershing, John J. "Black Jack," 27
Petrarch, 220
Philippines, 3, 41, 50, 59–61, 65, 66, 67, 85,
    137–38, 169, 172, 190, 199, 222, 293
Piper Cub, 20
Pisgah, Mount, 15
PM, 104
Poland, 20, 46
Polifka, Karl "Pop," 153, 188, 191, 210
political cartoons, 104–5
Port Darwin, 60
Port Moresby, 68, 75, 80, 82, 92, 94, *96,* 98,
    111, 117, 121, 122–33, 143, 146, 148,
    153, 158, 162, 163–64, 177, 178, 180,
    188, 191, 192, 193, 195, 196, 197, 201,
    203, 205, 206, 217, 220, 235, 240, 243,
    245, 246, 249, 255–56, 268, 280, 286,
    290, 291, 301, 306
  beauty of, 123–24
  diseases at, 118, 126, 204
  importance of, 131, 133
  isolation of, 131
  Japanese advance on, 139
  Japanese air raids on, 128, 129–30, 132, 164,
    176, 223
  Japan's first planned assault on, 92–95, 100
  Japan's second planned assault on, 100–102
  lack of organization at, 118
  lack of radar installations in, 132
  maintenance personnel at, 212, 221
  Operations Hut at, 107, 149, 224, 230, 241

primary airstrips of, 127
replacements sent to, 221
scrap heap at, 210
wretched living conditions at, 117–19, 126,
128, 130, 204
Post Office, U.S., 140
Prados, John, 292, 293
Pratt & Whitney, 300
precision-bombing tactics, 147
press, publicity, 35–36, 40, 57, 102, 104–5, 115,
134, 136, 199
"pucker factor," 253
Puerto Rico, 10
Pugh, Herbert "Pudge," 192–93, 194, 203,
213, 231, 246, 251, 256, 258, 262, 265,
275, 276, 282, 283–84, 290, 291, 301,
303–4
Puller, Lewis "Chesty," 163
Punch, 105
Punchbowl, 305, 306
Putnam, David, 26
Pyle, Ernie, 43

Queen Mary, 181
Queensland, Australia, 162, 182
Quezon, Manuel, 59–60, 190
Quiet Man, The (film), 297

Rabaul, 3, 68–74, 81, 93, 95, 101, 109, 131, 142,
168, 169, 179, 185, 196, 199, 232, 236,
239, 248, 261
Australian POWs at, 129
Australian raids on, 80, 119
empty beer bottles dropped on, 173–74
Japanese defense of, 82–83, 84, 85–86,
155–56, 162
Japanese occupation of, 68–74, 129, 139, 152,
159, 165–66, 205–7
neutralization of, 292
reconnaissance of, 152, 154–55, 210, 211
skip bombing over, 147–48
U.S. invasion plan for, 172, 293
U.S. raids on, 75, 79, 80–82, 83–84, 85–86,
92, 106–7, 118, 119, 121, 147–48, 161–63,
164, 173–74, 178, 204, 205–7, 219, 222,
231, 296
Raft, George, 180
Ramey, Roger, 242, 254, 256
Randwick Racecourse, 181
"Rape of Nanking," 42
Raytheon, 300
reconnaisance aircraft, 153

reconnaissance missions, 2, 3, 52, 57–58, 61,
153–58, 185–89, 196, 202, 210, 211, 225,
237, 248–50
over Bougainville Island, 237, 240–47, 248,
250–53, 257, 262, 264–65, 269–79, 287,
290
over Buka Island, 252–53, 254, 255–62, 257,
263–64, 287
hot-air balloons and, 186–87
Japanese, 236
Reid River, 103
Richmond Army Air Force, 301
Rickenbacker, Eddie, 26–27, 186, 286, 297
Rising Sun, 3, 48, 56, 92, 95, 105, 210, 212,
228
Roberts, John, 211, 241–42
Roosevelt, Franklin, 40, 51, 103, 109n, 128, 135,
159, 163, 168
administration of, 49, 93
Roosevelt, Theodore, 307
Royal Air Force, British (RAF), 35, 142
Royal Australian Air Force (RAAF), 74, 76, 79,
80, 82n, 120, 128, 130–31, 238
Royal Australian Army, 69n, 101
Royal Australian Navy, 95, 97
Royal Pacific Hotel, 205–6, 207

Sacramento Air Depot, 53
Salamaua, 68, 69, 103, 129, 167, 196
Samoa, 70, 98, 100, 153
San Antonio Rose, 162, 163
San Francisco, Calif., 53
San Francisco Bay, 56
Sarnoski, Francis, 32
Sarnoski, Jennie, 181
Sarnoski, Joe, 4, 28–34, 40, 47, 48, 194, 200,
202, 203, 222, 229, 243, 245, 258,
262, 287, 297, 298, 299–300, 303–4,
307
on *Argentina,* 61–62
burial of, 291, 306
crew of, *see* Eager Beavers
death of, 283–84, 303
education of, 30
interests and talents of, 30–32
laissez-faire attitude of, 206–7
Medal of Honor awarded to, 301
musical talent of, 31
in Rabaul raids, 205–7
reconnaissance crew recruited by, 189–94
as roving bombing instructor, 181–82, 193
in transfer back to the states, 246

Sarnoski, Joe (*cont.*)
  in Wewak raid, 201, 202–3
  wounding of, 266, 267, 270, 274, 279
  Zeamer and, 33, 180–81, 182, 185, 200,
    205–6, 246–47
Sarnoski, John, 29–30, 32, 291, 299, 300,
  303
Sarnoski, Josephine, 29, 30, 32, 291, 299–300,
  301, 303
Sarnoski, Marie, 33, 180, 301
Sarnoski, Matilda, 31, 32–33, 34, 287
Sarnoski Rembisz, Agnes, 247, 303–4
Sarnoski, Victoria, 29, 207
Sarnoski, Walter, 30
Saturday Evening Post, 99
Schmidt, Eric, 140
scrofula infantum, 21
2nd Bomb Group, 28, 32
Seffern, Joe, 107–8, 110
Sepik River, 296
Seven Mile airdrome, 92, 118, 127, 128
  see also Jackson Field
Shokaku, 95
Signal Corps, U.S., 114
Simpson Harbour, 72–73, 74, 81, 82, 93, 120,
    142, 147, 152, 153, 154, 156, 161, 162,
    163n, 165, 173, 195, 196, 229, 244, 248,
    293–94
Sinatra, Frank, 140
Singapore, 59, 190
6th Photographic Reconnaissance Group, 296
  8th Squadron of, *see* 8th Photo Reconnaissance
  Squadron
"skeleton crew," *see* Eager Beavers
skip-bombing, 139–40, 142, 143–44, 146,
    147–48, 150–51, 161, 179, 220, 229, 233,
    243, 249
slaves, 73
Slot, The, 142, 150, 152, 166, 185
snap-roll attacks, 265
Solomon Islands, 58, 70, 92, 98, 100, 121, 139,
    141, 150, 159, 166, 168, 172, 173, 226,
    236, 237, 238, 292
Solomon Sea, 82, 83, 107, 232, 241
Soryu, 100
South, U.S., 187
Southampton, England, 61n
Soviet Union, 40, 168, 235
Spanish-American War, 59
Spanish Civil War, 120
Spence, USS, 292n
Spitfire, 153

Squirrel Island, 14
Stalin, Joseph, 168
Steelton, Pa., 193
Stimson, Henry, 36, 66
Stone, Charles "Rocky," 180, 182, 189, 203
Sudan, 235
Sudetenland, 20
Sun Tzu, 186
Sydney, Australia, 136, 137, 181

Tainan Wing, 109
Tanambogo, 165
Tavurvur, Mount, 73, 154, 155, 173
Temple University, 140
Tennessee, University of, 292
Texas, University of, 304
Thatcher, USS, 292n
"There is Only One Mistake: To Do Nothing"
  (article), 99
3rd Bomb Group, 138–39
3rd Marine Division, 292
13th Air Force, 251
Thirty Seconds Over Tokyo, (Doolittle), 297
Thirty Seconds Over Tokyo (film), 193, 297
Thompson, Russell, 14
Thues, Emile "Bud," 242
Time, 65, 139, 199
Toda, Sergeant, 174
Tojo, Hideki, 40
Tokyo, Japan, 87, 113
Tokyo Rose, 66n, 87
Tonolei Harbour, 165, 239
Torokina Point, 292
Townsville, Australia, 75, 77, 108, 123, 131, 182,
    204, 240
Tracy, Spencer, 297
Treasury Islands, 236
trimetrogon cameras, 210, 214, 225, 230, 241,
    246, 252, 260, 291
Trobriands, 82n
Truk, 73
tuberculosis, 21
Tugboat Annie, 244–45
Tulagi, 97, 165
Twain, Mark, 144
22nd Bomb Group (Red Raiders), 37, 39, 47, 48,
    50–51, 52–53, 57, 76, 77, 78, 87, 99–100,
    105, 107, 108–10, 111, 123, 128, 230, 247,
    258, 278
  Australia posting of, 64, 65, 68, 75
  in Hawaii, 57–59, 60
  loss of planes in, 178

Rabaul raids by, 69, 79, 80–82, 83–84, 85–86, 103, 106–7, 109, 118
reconnaissance flights by, 57–58
251st Imperial Air Squadron, 263

Union Army, Balloon Corps of, 186–87

Vaughan, William "Willy," 189–91, 192, 204, 214, 218, 231, 250, 274–75, 281, 282, 283–84, 287, 289, 291, 301–2, 304
Vella Lavella, 239
Vietnam War, 302
Villa, Pancho, 234
Visalia, Calif., 303
Vitiaz Strait, 197
V-J Day, 296, 305
von Clausewitz, Carl, 179
Vunakanau airdrome, 73, 86, 93

Waianae Mountains (Wai'anae, Waianaes), 48, 50
Waikiki Beach, 58
Wake Island, 91–92
Walker, Douglas, 163*n*
Walker, Kenneth Newton, 144, 145–47, 158, 160–64, 173*n*, 174, 195, 218, 233*n*, 278
Walter Reed Medical Center, 297, 298, 299
War College, 115
War Department, U.S., 59, 65, 67, 68, 102, 111, 135, 163, 290
War Shipping Administration, 62
War Without Mercy: Race and Power in the Pacific War (Dower), 42*n*
Washington, D.C., 297, 301
Washington, George, 187*n*
"Way of the Warrior," 43
Welles, Orson, 50
Wellesley University, 290
Western Union, 290
"We Swoop at Dawn" (poem), 247, 303
Wewak, 159, 178, 196, 201–2, 235–36
Willys-Overland motor company, 18
Winchell, Walter, 87
World War I, 10–11, 13, 22, 26–27, 36, 47, 56, 70, 114, 121, 137, 186, 187, 191, 213, 235, 286, 297
World War II, 20, 23, 33, 36, 40, 43, 46, 61, 76, 86
aircraft of, 84; *see also specific aircraft*
American planes lost during, 215–16
films made during, 193
Japanese-American internment camps in, 105*n*
nicknames given to planes during, 211–12

Rabaul air raids as longest battle of, 296
reconnaissance work in, 185–86, 188, *see also* reconnaissance
Roosevelt's declaration of war and, 51
skip-bombing tactic used in, 139–40, 142, 143–44, 146, 147–48, 150–51, 161, 179, 220, 229, 233, 243, 249
U.S. Airmen killed during, 291
U.S. Army's field manual in, 226
see also specific battles
Wright Airfield, 36–37
Wright brothers, 36
Wright Cyclones, 212

Yamamoto, Isoroku, 41, 49, 70–72, 98, 100, 160, 199, 238, 241
death of, 226–28, 231
Yamamoto, Suehiro, 277
Yamasaki, Commander, 174
Yorktown, USS, 94, 95
Youngstown, Ohio, 190, 302
Yunnan Province, 235

Zeamer, Anne, 12, 290
Zeamer, Barbara Ferner, 300, 307
Zeamer, Isabel, 12, 290
Zeamer, Jacquie, 300
Zeamer, Jay, Jr., 2–5, 11, 31, 33–40, 76, 77, 78, 80, 82–83, 84, 85–87, 99, 104, 114, 122, 123, 126, 128, 129, 131, 132, 133, 148, 149, 152, 174, 176, 179, 212, 229, 246, 285–88, 303
adventurous nature of, 9, 12–13
aeronautical engineering degrees of, 300
in Army Air Corps, 23–24
army training of, 24–25
attempted grocery run of, 204–5
Australia posting of, 64–66, 68, 75
B-17s admired by, 46–48, 111, 151, 180
battle fatigue of, 253
bomber assignment of, 27–28
Bougainville reconnaissance and, 241–47, 248, 250–53, 269–79
in Boy Scouts, 14–15, 24, 33, 108, 158, 299
Buka Island reconnaissance and, 252–53, 254, 255–62, 297–98
childhood of, 9–16
Cooper on, 297
as copilot, 36–37, 38–39, 50–51, 53, 79, 83, 107, 150, 151, 161, 230
crew of, *see* Eager Beavers

Zeamer, Jay, Jr. (*cont.*)
  at Culver, 17–19
  disobedience of, 202–3
  education of, 15–16, 17–18, 300
  enlistment of, 20–21
  exterminator role of, 43
  and failure to stick landings, 38–39
  first reconnaissance flights led by, 248–50
  in flight to Dobodura, 280–86
  flying expertise of, 38, 39
  funeral service of, 306–7
  in Hawaii, 57–59, 60, 61, 83, 305–6
  laissez-faire attitude of, 105–6, 178, 202–3,
    204–5
  love of water of, 12–14
  McCullar and, 177–78, 220–21
  marksmanship of, 17–18
  mechanical bent of, 11–13, 47, 204, 211
  Medal of Honor citation of, 282*n*, 297–98,
    299, 301
  in off-the-book raids on Rabaul, 178
  Old 666 salvaged by, 210–13
  Pearl Harbor attack and, 49
  physical appearance of, 223–24
  poor eyesight of, 21–22, 107
  promotions of, 58, 296–97
  in Rabaul raid, 69, 79, 82, 83–84, 85–86, 103,
    178, 204, 205–7
  Rabaul reconnaissance flight of, 154–58
  reconnaissance crew recruited by, 189–94

  reputation of, as B-17 combat pilot, 179–80, 201
  in return to New Guinea, 277–78
  Sarnoski and, 33, 180–81, 182, 185, 200,
    205–6, 246–47
  Silver Stars awarded to, 158, 203
  skin cancer of, 300
  in skip bombing missions, 150–51, 179
  slacker reputation of, 106, 107–8
  as substitute pilot, 179, 200
  as transferred to 43rd, 110–11
  unorthodox flying method of, 179
  on USS *Grant,* 56, 57
  in Wewak raid, 201, 202–3
  wounds of, 269–71, 276, 282, 286, 289–90,
    291, 298
  Zero downed by, 268, 269, 282
Zeamer, Jay, Sr., 9, 10, 11, 13, 21, 298
Zeamer, Jayne, 300
Zeamer, Jere, 12, 21, 50, 290
Zeamer, Jeremiah, 10, 56
Zeamer, John, 10
Zeamer, Marcia, 300
Zeamer, Marjorie, 9, 11, 13, 269, 290, 298
Zeamer, Sandra, 300
Zeamer, Susan, 300
Zeros, 82–83, 84, 85–87, 99, 109, 129, 151,
    155–58, 162, 179, 196, 197, 213, 216,
    217–18, 222, 224, 227, 229, 230–31, 251,
    265, 296
Zyklon-B, 40

ABOUT THE AUTHORS

BOB DRURY is the author/coauthor/editor of ten books, four in collaboration with Tom Clavin. His last solo book was *A Dog's Gift* and his adventure narrative *The Rescue Season* was adapted into a documentary by the History Channel. He has written for numerous publications, including *The New York Times*, *Vanity Fair*, *GQ*, *Men's Journal*, and *Men's Health*. He is the recipient of several national journalism awards, is a three-time National Magazine Award finalist, as well as a Pulitzer Prize–nominee.

TOM CLAVIN is the author or coauthor of eighteen books. For fifteen years he wrote for *The New York Times*, and he has contributed articles to many magazines, including *Golf*, *Men's Journal*, *Parade*, *Reader's Digest*, and *Smithsonian*. He lives in Sag Harbor, New York.